MARJORIE GRENE
SARTRE

NEW VIEWPOINTS
A Division of Franklin Watts, Inc.
New York, 1973

Library of Congress Cataloging in Publication Data

Grene, Marjorie (Glicksman) 1910—
    Sartre.

    Bibliography: p.
    1.   Sartre, Jean Paul, 1905—
B2430.S34G724   194   73-1311
ISBN 0-531-06358-5
ISBN 0-531-06487-5 (pbk.)

Cover design by Nicholas Krenitsky
Book design and original art by Rafael Hernandez

SARTRE

To my students
and especially to Kit,
who helped a lot

ACKNOWLEDGMENTS

It is a pleasure to acknowledge the assistance of two
UCD graduate students, Mrs. Kathleen McLaughlin and
Mrs. Susan Denning, in the preparation of this essay.
Mrs. McLaughlin helped me immeasurably in our dis-
cussions of philosophical problems in *Being and Nothingness* and the *Critique,* by reading and criticizing the
drafts of each chapter in turn, and with bibliographical
work. Mrs. Denning read the manuscript with great care
and accuracy and caught many of my errors. Professor
Philip Thody read the whole book and made a number of
interesting comments and criticisms; unfortunately, the
manuscript was already in the hands of the publishers
when I received his comments, so that I have not been

able to incorporate all of them. The series' former editor, Professor James Edie, made some excellent suggestions, and Professor David Olmsted, who also read the complete manuscript, gave me invaluable assistance in carrying them out. I am deeply indebted to them all.

I also wish to put on record my gratitude to the Philosophy Department's able administrative assistant, Mrs. Charlotte Honeywell, and her staff, who typed the manuscript in several drafts, and to the University of California, Davis, for research grants in the years 1970–1971 and 1971–1972 which enabled me to secure the assistance of Mrs. McLaughlin and Mrs. Denning.

I am grateful to the American Philosophical Association for permission to reprint my Presidential Address to the Pacific Division (1972), which was based on part of Chapter Five. Braziller and Company have kindly given me permission to quote from the Frechtman translation of *Les Mots,* and Literary Masterpieces, Inc., to quote from Hazel Barnes's translation of *L'Etre et le Néant.*

Cambridge, England
August 1971

My final chapter is concerned with the first two volumes of Sartre's work on Flaubert. Since I completed the manuscript, in August 1971, the third volume has appeared (Gallimard, 1972). A cursory reading suggests that it is pretty straight Sartrean "Marxism"; it therefore neither confirms nor (wholly) falsifies my final prognosis.

Boston
January 1973

CONTENTS

SARTRE

chapter one: the man of words

No philosopher, one suspects,
has ever produced so elegant, eloquent, and effective an introduction
to his own works as has Jean-Paul Sartre in
the autobiography of his childhood appropriately
named *Words* (*Les Mots*). Mercilessly and brilliantly,
he has pinned on his own collecting board the child that

was himself. It would ill befit an ordinary teacher and writer of philosophy to try to better his performance. Yet if Sartre were right about the relations of man to man, it would be only the outsider, the third man, who generates these relations: who generates, in this case, the relation of Sartre, famous writer of fifty-five, to Jean-Paul, small boy of five. Or, to reduce the terms to two, it is, according to Sartre's theory of literature, the reader who enters into a compact of freedom with the writer and so completes the work.

I want, then, in the spirit of either of these enterprises—as third man to the Sartre–Jean-Paul relation, or simply as reader—to take *Les Mots* as *entrée* to the examination of Sartre's vocation as a writer. But why examine this again, you may ask, when Sartre himself has given us so lucid and precise an account of the nature and origin of his calling? Because I want to show, if I can, that, in the light of that very account, Sartre is fundamentally a philosophical writer, who has sometimes embodied his arguments in literature, rather than a literary man who happens to philosophize. There are two reasons to argue at some length this rather obvious thesis. For one thing, *Les Mots* is not only a superb work of literature, which repays study in itself; it is, as I have already indicated, the best possible introduction to Sartre's philosophy, both its style and its doctrine. And for another, it is worth arguing that Sartre is first and professionally a philosopher, because as philosopher he is a self-acknowledged "existentalist," and existentialism has often been tagged (on occasion by myself among others) as more "literary" than "philosophical." Sartre himself, ten years ago in the *Critique,* publicly branded existentialism an "ideology," Marxism being, he swore, the only philosophy of our time, with existentialism its faithful ideological servant. More commonly, especially among its English-speaking expositors, existentialism has been labeled as a style of literature rather than a form of philosophy, not because it serves some higher school of thought, but because it is, allegedly, scarcely thought at all. It exclaims instead of arguing, so it is said; it rants instead of analyzing. Its themes, therefore, such critics aver, are best expressed in novel and drama, not in the sober guise of philosophical reflection. Thus if you want to know what Heidegger as existentialist has to say (even though he has never been one), read Tolstoy's *Ivan Ilyich.* If you want to know what Sartre as existential philosopher has to say, read his literary corpus, not his long-winded theoretical writings. If you want to know what the lot of them have to say, read Dostoyevsky, or Beckett, or heaven knows whom; but don't trouble with their supposed "philosophy." It is neither logic nor science, neither ordinary-language analysis nor pure, exact and exacting, phenomenology. So forget it!

Now, apart from the question of existentialism in general, whatever that may be, this is, for philosophically interested readers of the works of Jean-Paul Sartre, very bad advice. For the philosophical work of Sartre—*Being and Nothingness* in particular, but even, in part at least, that much reviled and admittedly prolix tome, *The Critique of Dialectical Reason*—repays close and repeated attention. One may disagree with it totally, but if one likes philosophy and is patient, one will find in it a surprising wealth of subtle and ingenious argument. What more can a philosophical reader ask? Truth, perhaps. But for us smaller fry, and indeed, even for the rare original thinker in philosophy, one way to truth is through the errors of one's great predecessors and contemporaries. Such is the case with Sartre. His work embodies, I believe, more incisively and more ingeniously than any other, the intellectual crisis of our time. It is worth wrestling with, both because we meet in it a philosophical intellect steeped, by training and by temperament, in the great European tradition, and because we can learn through it to grapple better with our own philosophical problems, which we have inherited from the same tradition.

But back to my thesis, which is to show, on the ground of Sartre's own "confession," that he is, and in what sense he is, a philosophical writer.

The epithet "man of words" that gives this chapter its title is adapted from the remark of Maurice Merleau-Ponty, Sartre's one-time friend, critic, and passionate admirer, that he was "too much of a writer." That remark has been amply substantiated by Sartre's own account of his vocation, its discovery and development. Picture the curly-haired three-year-old Jean-Paul in a sixth-floor Paris apartment, the adored child of his young widowed mother, the object of approval and admiration by the grandparents with whom they live:

> . . . there is no lack of applause. Whether the adults listen to my babbling or to *The Art of the Fugue,* they have the same arch smile of enjoyment and complicity. That shows what I am essentially: a cultural asset. Culture permeates me, and I give it off to the family by radiation, just as ponds, in the evening, give off the heat of the day.[1]

Sartre's grandfather, Charles Schweitzer, purveys French culture to the Germans, German culture to the French. Every year he re-edits his German reader. The whole family shares in the suspense of waiting for the proofs, and murmurs soothingly when, inevitably, he reviles his publisher. His study, filled with the French and

German classics, is a cultural shrine. There are grand-
mother's lending library books, too, and Jean-Paul's own
books that his mother reads to him ("I began my life," he
says, "as I shall probably end it, amidst books"), but it is
grandfather's study that sets the proper tone:

> In my grandfather's study there were books every-
> where. It was forbidden to dust them, except once a year,
> before the beginning of the October term. Though I did
> not yet know how to read, I already revered those stand-
> ing stones: upright or leaning over, close together like
> bricks on the bookshelves or spaced out nobly in lines of
> menhirs. I felt that our family's prosperity depended on
> them. They all looked alike. I disported myself in a tiny
> sanctuary, surrounded by ancient, heavy-set monuments
> which had seen me into the world, which would see me
> out of it, and whose permanence guaranteed me a future
> as calm as the past.[2]

Jean-Paul had to break into that closed, magic world. At
three he learned to read:

> I would climb up into my crib with Hector Malot's
> No Family, which I knew by heart, and, half reciting, half
> deciphering, I went through every page of it, one after the
> other. When the last page was turned, I knew how to read
> . . . I was wild with joy. They were mine, those dried
> voices in their little herbals, those voices which my
> grandfather brought back to life with his gaze . . . I was
> going to listen to them, to fill myself with ceremonious
> discourse, I would know everything![3]

It was, then, words that made him, and it was through
words that he, creator and magician, could in turn make
things: ". . . the Universe would rise in tiers at my
feet and all things would humbly beg for a name; to name
the thing was both to create and take it. Without this

fundamental illusion I would never have written." [4] However he has changed, that "illusion" has stayed with him. Nor iş it wholly an illusion, for it is his truth. It was through words that, for him, things acquired their reality, not, as for "practical" people, the other way around. Although, like most Parisian middle-class children, he spent summer vacations in the country, his reality was on the sixth floor, 1 rue de Goff, among the books:

> In vain would I seek within me the prickly memories and sweet unreason of a country childhood. I never worked the soil or hunted for nests. I did not gather herbs or throw stones at birds. But books were my birds and my nests, my household pets, my barn and my countryside.[5]

Even as ordinary an object as a table, he insisted later, got its reality from the name that evoked it.

And if words as read had "the thickness of things," so much the more power had they when, at six, he began to write. By the age of nine he had firmly established his calling as a writer. If, as he had thought, "to exist was to have an official title somewhere on the infinite Tables of the Word," then "to write was to engrave new beings upon them or—and this was my most persistent illusion—to catch living things in the trap of phrases: if I combined words ingeniously, the object would get tangled up in the signs, I would have a hold on it." [6]

He began, he says, in the Luxembourg, by charming himself with a bright simulacrum of a plane tree. "I did not observe it. Quite the contrary: I trusted to the void, I waited. A moment later, its true foliage would suddenly appear in the form of a simple adjective or, at times, of a whole proposition: I had enriched the universe with quivering greenery." [7]

Not that these words were written down, or even, as the child supposed they would be, remembered, but they gave him, he says "an inkling of my future role: I would impose names." [8] If words made him, he, by naming, made things. Not that he really made them, of course: that is the illusory part of it; but what he really made was—himself. If he has lost the illusion that there is real efficacy in words, if they have lost their "thickness," if he is convinced to the core of his being of his own view of the negativity of imagination, of the emptiness of his self-made world of words, he still writes, and will until he dies. Why? Well, why not? And besides, *that,* he confesses, is his character. Some time between 1911 and 1914, the die was cast.The child of words made himself their maker, made himself a writer.

What sort of writer? In terms of his own relation to words as he describes it, and in terms of his own contrast between poetry and prose, one would at first suppose: a poet. "The poetic attitude," he wrote in *What is Literature?,* "considers words as things and not as signs." [9] The ordinary speaker is "beyond words and near the object, whereas the poet is on this side of them." [10] For us ordinary speakers, meanings take us straight back toward the reality from which we had started, and which we are seeking to maneuver and control. Meanings for the poet, on the other hand, lack this practical vector; they cling to the words themselves. Meaning "is no longer the goal which is always out of reach and which human transcendence is always aiming at, but a property of each term, analogous to the expression of a face, to the little sad or gay meaning of sounds and colours. Having flowed into the word, having been absorbed by its sonority or visual aspect, having been thickened and defaced, it too is a thing, uncreated and eternal." [11]

Thus for the poet "language is a structure of the external world." [12] He considers words, not as signs to guide him to others and their activities, but "as a trap to catch a fleeting reality. . . ." [13] "In short," Sartre says, "language is for him the mirror of the world." [14] But so, for Jean-Paul, was his grandfather's library: "The library was the world caught in a mirror. It had the world's infinite thickness, its variety." [15] And when he came to write, it was the beings of his imagination that peopled his world. He lived outside ordinary things, through language, as poets do. For the poet, he was to write, "sees words inside out, as if he did not share the human condition, and as if he were first meeting the word as a barrier as he comes towards men." [16] That seems, to judge from his own account, the attitude through which he himself came to language and to literature.

Yet Sartre has never been a poet; he has never, since he began at six to compose romances, aspired to be one. Master of his native tongue as he can be when he likes, it is French prose of which he is master. True, there is poetry as economical in its style as *Les Mots,* the book now before us and as good an instance as any of Sartre's writing at its best. True, the poet can turn ordinary words, even ordinary sentences, into poetry. But in *Les Mots,* working the other way around, Sartre assimilates images which in another's hands might serve poetic ends, to the incisive economy of great prose. "Griselda's not dead," he writes at the conclusion, "Pardaillan still inhabits me. So does Strogoff. I'm answerable only to them, who are answerable only to God, and I don't believe in God. So try to figure it out." [17] The whole story in a nutshell, complete with worm inside. Or take as an example of the terseness and pregnancy with which he can write (not that he always or even often does so) the phrases in which he embodies the atmosphere of the smug middle-class environment of pre-World War I, reflected in the self-satisfaction of an idolized child: "My grandfather believes in Progress, so do I: Progress, that long, steep path which leads to me." [18] But alas, as a mere philosopher I feel myself helpless before a style, whether of poetry or prose. Read *Les Mots* and you will see: you will find set out before your eyes a rigid analytical frame in which a child and his environment are held fast to view—the man of words making out of his own words the picture of the incipient word-magician that was to be, and still is, himself.

Sartre, then, is a man of words, but of prose, not poetry. What sort of prose? we have next to ask. The passages I have quoted about poetry come from his essay *What is Literature?*, originally published as a series of articles in *Les Temps Modernes* after the war, when the journal was new and Sartre, as its founder and editor, was passionately engaged in formulating its mission and presenting it to the world. In the pages of *Les Temps Modernes* he contrasted the detachment of the poet, insulated from action by words and images, with the commitment—primarily the social commitment—of the prose writer. The poet, like the painter, Sartre believed, may dwell in his creation; so may his reader or viewer. Prose writing, he insisted, lacks that moment of passivity. It is first and last a compact between two freedoms, the writer's and the reader's. The prose writer wants by his writing to act on others, and to enjoin upon them action in their turn. Admittedly, the exact role of the writer varies from society to society. He may have—and had in the Middle Ages or in the French seventeenth century—the task of upholding the established order; he may have, and more appropriately has, the role of proto-revolutionary. It is he who holds up to critical light the inequities of his own society, even of his own class, and so, indirectly, calls for change.

Is Sartre, then, a prose writer in this sense? In his own account of the vocation which, from childhood, shaped his character we have seen how his relation to language, his life of imagination, cut off as it was from everyday reality, resemble the state, in his literary theory, of the poet. Yet, on the other hand, his picture of the young Jean-Paul romancing in the shadow of Charles Schweitzer's library is also the picture of the writer who seeks and needs a public. For one thing, the vocation imposed on him by his elders ("He will be a writer") was a social role. A conservative role, to be sure, as they saw it: he would be a teacher, like his grandfather, and supplement his salary by his pen, all safely inside and on behalf of the cultural establishment. More important: the child himself, if we believe Sartre's reconstruction, always thought of his productions as performances for an audience. He wanted, he says, to give men the reading matter they desired. In his mind's eye he saw his own great-nephew, round about 1980, poring over and admiring the message of his works. It was, it seems, one freedom calling to another yet unborn, a variant at least the prose writer as conceived in *What is Literature?*

And of course, much of Sartre's production does fit this formula, appealing, not indeed to posterity, but to his contemporaries, as, according to his own theory, the writer is supposed to do. His best short stories embody social themes: the civil war theme of loyalty and betrayal in "The Wall," the bad faith of the bourgeoisie and contrasting apparent good faith of madness in "The Room," anti-Semitism in "L'Enfance d'un Chef." In each case the writer puts before us a social commitment and a critique

of society to which, in reading him, we in turn are to com-
mit ourselves. His plays, too, clearly exemplify the character of the new theater as set forth in *What is Literature?*
Not individual characters, but ideas themselves, he tells
us there, now walk upon the stage. It is the ideological,
political arena that we enter when we watch a play. It is
political and social issues that the dramatist has personi-
fied and that the audience relives in watching. True, the
issues change as Sartrean theater and thought develop.
In *The Flies,* Orestes seeks *his* act; the characters of
Huis-Clos embody hell-as-the-others. These plays represent through action the Sartre of *Being and Nothingness,*
the doubter of humanity, as he puts it in *Les Mots,* who
proved man impossible but as doubter presumed to claim
exemption from his own proof. Later, when he turned
more explicitly to the external, material and social conditions, even (almost) determinants, of individual action, he
put upon the stage more explicitly political conceptions.
This is clear in *Les Mains Sales,* where party loyalty is at
issue, in *La Putain Respecteuse,* where American racism
is the theme, and so on. But the archetype of appeal from
freedom to freedom is still exemplified.

Yet there is something—indeed, there are several
things—wrong with this picture. For one, there is something too contrived about the theory of *What is Literature?*
itself. As with much of Sartre's theoretical writing, the
aperçus are many, yet the theme is too self-conscious, too
abstract. Merleau-Ponty remarked that while of course
the writer can write about writing, the painter cannot (at
least not quite so directly) paint about painting. But do
writers who are primarily imaginative writers, makers of
literature, not of argument, write so reflectively about
their works? Poets don't. When Emily Dickinson writes
poetry about writing poetry, it is the poem that speaks to

us, and the poet speaks from within it; it is not the reflection of the poet that speaks to us over and above the poem. Sartre might agree; but the prose writer, he insisted in the 1940's, is someone quite different—and so, in his recent essays on Flaubert he still seems to insist.

Is that correct? Is the novelist really so very different from the poet in his relation to his language on the one hand and to experience on the other? Granted, the lyric poet evokes, ideally, a *moment* of experience in which language and feeling resonate almost statically with one another, while the novelist ideally evokes a whole world into which one enters with him and in which one lives, sharing not only the here and now, but also the formerly and the not-yet of his characters and their concerns. Yet although the temporality is different, the aspect of indwelling within the work belongs to the reader, or hearer, in both cases. As we may feel with Yeats, for example, the poignancy of aging, so we live with Tolstoy in the Rostovs' ballroom, with Alexey in battle, with Natasha now nearly eloping, at last happily examining the newest baby's diapers. Tolstoy, no more than the lyric poet, urges us to action. We do contract with him; there is a compact of freedoms, but a compact to surrender, to see and to live, neither to accept a society nor to change it, but freely and in imagination *to be there.*

In short, the literary artist, whether poet or prose writer, does not come from outside his own vocation with a theme, exemplify it through his invention, and then ask us to wrestle with it. From within himself he is driven to reconstitute his experience imaginatively in language, and he asks us to do so with him. There can be a theater of ideas, indeed, as Sartre argues and has demonstrated by his own practice, but the novel of ideas, it seems to me, hardly ever succeeds as novel. Both Sartre and Beauvoir have suffered as novelists from having too clear and self-conscious themes which they proceed to impose upon their works and too clear and self-conscious ends for writing. It was not (to use the same example) the author of *What is Art?* who wrote *War and Peace* and *Anna,* but his younger predecessor. Sartre, on the contrary, comes to his literary task, as expounded in *What is Literature?,* from the outside, reflecting in terms of abstract principles on what literature ought to be and deciding to do it that way. Visually (except perhaps for *Nausea*), he is a philosopher who has determined on principle that plays or novels are the proper thing to write.

Besides, even it we take his own statement of the aim of literature at its face value, we find the vocation of the prose writer as he sets it out there in important ways unlike the calling that the young Sartre recalled in *Les Mots* had envisioned for himself. As I have already indicated, the one appeals to his contemporaries, the other to posterity. Further, while the one speaks from within a situation, the other is essentially apart from it.

As to the first point: the child romancer, imagining the destiny of his works, envisaged himself sometimes as discovered old and poor and belatedly acknowledged, but usually as dying in obscurity, leaving behind him a long row of volumes for the admiration of his "great-nephews." (Never grandsons; make what you like of that!) As Sartre rationalizes that singularly unchildlike childhood vision, he thought of himself as dead because he had no wish to live. To write, yes; to be admired, yes; but admired once the living writer, the maker of those immortal objects, was safely buried. That is far from the committed writer of *What is Literature?.* Not, of course, that the account of *Words* must be literally true; it is too contrived a piece of Sartrean existential analysis for the story to have been quite like that. Yet as an account of Sartre's vocation as a writer it has much more plausibility than does his theory of committed literature, of the writer as "permanent revolutionary." True, the author of *Being and Nothingness,* turning to political thought, must and can only become a revolutionary theorist: against the alleged values of his, or any so far extant, society, seeing human relations as he does in terms of alienation, oppression, conflict. But the kind of revolutionary he is and has become is not the natural outgrowth of a deep historical commitment; it is rather the necessary logical consequence of the way in which, in *Being and Nothingness,* and even in his early literary work (notably *Nausea*) he sees human freedom as the for-itself over against an alien-in-itself, radically in opposition to it, complete, yet completely other. This Sartrean freedom, total, yet so totally denial of what it is not and of what is not it, this freedom is the freedom of a Cartesian intellect. Beauvoir says of herself and Sartre when they were students: "We were encouraged by Cartesian rationalism, . . . we believed ourselves to consist of nothing but pure reason and pure will." [19] Descartes opened his *Meditations* (published when he was forty-five) "happily free of all cares and disturbed by no passions." His aim, it will be recalled, was to put aside all his former opinions, all his youthful prejudices, and to make a wholly new beginning in the cold clear light of an emancipated reason. This is the freedom of an adult intellectual, of an adult, indeed, who seems never to have been a child. And, *Les Mots* tells us, that is just what Sartre never was. True, he had eventually some ordinary years as a day boy at school. But that was not what counted most in making him the writer he is. What counted was the leap to the imagined *œuvre* as the objectification of the finished life. If the man has changed, as he insists he has, if he found, in the war and the resistance, in the injustices of postwar years, in Algeria and Vietnam, in Stalinism and Hungary, a social and political situation which he had to face; if he became, as he hoped, a writer for his day, nevertheless, his character—and his mind— are still that of the word-spinner cut off in time from the world around him, in a future which he can "totalize" precisely because it is separate in time from the day-to-day occupations that he has yet to live.

If, further, Sartre was cut off in time from his own "childhood" years, he was separated in space as well from his contemporaries. There he is, sitting with his mother on a bench in the Luxembourg, a puny wall-eyed child, detesting his own ugliness. (Why, he used to ask himself, must I always see that same face in the mirror every day?) Round about the affectionate pair other boys are playing together. Don't you want to play with them? asks Anne-Marie. No, says Jean-Paul. Shall I ask their mothers if you could play with them? Doubly no! The vision is devastating. But then there is his own world, 1 rue de Goff, up on the sixth floor, where he is himself, ruler and creator, where he reads his books and writes his romances:

> When my mother took me to the Luxembourg Gardens— that is, every day—I would lend my rags to the lowlands, but my glorious body did not leave its perch; I think it's still there. Every man has his natural place; its altitude is determined by neither pride nor value; childhood decides. Mine is a sixth floor in Paris with a view overlooking the roofs. For a long time I suffocated in the valleys; the plains overwhelmed me: I crawled along the planet Mars, the heaviness crushed me. I had only to climb a molehill for joy to come rushing back; I returned to my symbolic sixth floor; there I would once again breathe the rarefied air of belles-lettres.[20]

Of course, this description is not to be taken too literally. Sartre has his place also in Paris, not only on the sixth floor rue de Goff. The locales of *Being and Nothingness,* that café from which Pierre is absent, that apartment where Pierre hopes to dominate Therèse or Therèse Pierre, the Luxembourg itself: they are also Sartre. So is Rousseau, the Bastille, the Terror, so is the Fall of France, the Resistance, French Colonialism, the French Communist Party which he never joined: he is part and parcel of all these and they of him. But also Parisian is the very quality of his detachment: these roofs have an otherness, a belonging in otherness, that no other roofs could have. Compare, for instance, Sartre's relation to Paris with that of Joyce to Dublin. (Admittedly, Joyce belongs to the category, despised by Sartre, of "poet-novelist" or "novelist-poet," but the comparison is perhaps for that very reason so much the more apt.) Joyce, who was of course more literally an exile, never returned to his city after 1909. When asked why he never went back to the place that so haunted him, he answered: "Have I ever left it?" Sartre has lived all his life in Paris and one cannot imagine him elsewhere, yet his being *of* it is a looking down up*on* it, a detachment such as only a Weltstadt, perhaps only Paris, would permit. That is partly the difference between Dublin and Paris. Yet it is also the difference, I think, between an artist (poetic prose writer, or prose-writing poet, as you like), and a philosopher. The one, though in self-imposed exile, has never left his city; the other, at home, is always on the sixth floor, not quite down there at all.

That Sartre's relation to writing is reflective and philosophical is confirmed by an interview on "The Artist and his Language," in which he describes to his interlocutor his own attitude to words.[21] He does not live *in* language, he says. Nor has he interiorized it, so as to gesture with it, to use it simply; he *possesses* words. Egged on by his questioner, he explains this out of the peculiarity of his bourgeois childhood. "Property" is of course a bourgeois category. Words were his peculiar property because, he says, they were all the child Jean-Paul possessed. Living with his grandparents, without his own home, he became the proprietor of—the French language. The explanation is too pat; but the fact it seems to explain is important. For Sartre neither sets words between himself and things, to dwell in them poetically, as it were, nor does he simply use them as transparent signs, as his committed writer ought to do. They are his portable property; he manipulates them, he controls them. They serve neither to evoke images nor to point out paths of action. They are the wise man's counters; they convey concepts. Their primary use, in other words, is philosophical.

Not, of course, that Sartre is only a philosophical writer. Far from it. He himself remarks in the same interview: "I write so many languages," [22] the languages of literature, of the theater, of philosophy. But his own description here of philosophical style is precisely the description of the proprietor of words, who uses them as his own instruments in order from them to come to things. He distinguishes philosophical from scientific language by suggesting (not quite correctly, but that's beside the point) that scientific concepts have been stripped wholly of the ambiguity of natural language. Philosophical language, on the contrary, has a residue of ambiguity. The philosopher does not relish this unclarity of sense, however, as does the poet —who, indeed, lives by it. The philosopher tries to clarify and purify his concepts so that through them he can come to the reflective understanding of experience itself. That is the sixth-floor attitude, to the life. Armed with one's verbal tools, one comes down occasionally to look and measure, and even to share up to a point, then one goes back to one's perch aloft, sharpens and refines the tools themselves, the better to cope with one's little excursion below, and looks out over the roofs with a serene and distant understanding of the scurryings they conceal.

That is a caricature of philosophy if you like, though no more so than Lucretius' "well-fortified sanctuaries, built up by the teachings of the wise, whence you may look down from the height upon others and behold them all astray. . . ." But my point is twofold. First, whatever his undeniable powers as dramatist or prose stylist, Sartre's attitude to language is primarily reflective and philosophical rather than literary. And secondly, his attitude to language reveals him, not only as *a* philosopher, but as this philosopher. Both the manner and the matter of his philosophy are just what one would expect of the author, and subject, of *Les Mots,* and his story of the birth of his vocation sheds on his philosophy a most gratifying light. Much that was obscure becomes clear once one reads *Les Mots;* much that was clear but infuriating appears inevitable and coherent, even if not therefore true.

Philosophy, being sustained reflection on experience or some sector of experience, must be detached and must be abstract. But the detachment and the abstraction of Sartre's philosophical method are extreme. That seems a strange remark to make about an "existentialist." For "existentialism" is supposed somehow to deal with "concrete situations," to avoid the speculative system-building or the detached analytical ingenuities of other philosophical styles. Besides, apart from slogans like "man is a useless passion," which, Sartre himself admits, are literary intrusions into what should be a purely conceptual structure, what is most striking at first sight about his philosophical *magnum opus* is precisely his concrete descriptions: one misses Pierre at the café, one is discovered listening at the keyhole, one throws down one's rücksack too tired to hike further, and so on. Yet if we look more carefully we find that these phenomenological jewels are carefully placed in the setting of a highly abstract and ingenious argument. The major premise is: there is no human nature. The tools with which Sartre elicits the consequences of this starting point are the two concepts of his title: being and nothingness. I am, I make myself, as nihilation, as the denial of being; being is what I am not, by its very being it threatens me with non-being, yet not-being-it is precisely what I am. Even within consciousness the very "nature" of my being (which of course is precisely not a "nature") is to *want:* to be what I am not and to not be what I am. Out of the most abstract of dialectical contraries, being and nothing, positive and negative, inner and outer, self and other, Sartre has built his own philosophical edifice. It is as if one tried to construct the whole of Hegel's dialectic out of its first two steps, being and non-being. Anything else would compromise the self-contained isolation of the sixth-floor world.

Indeed, Sartre's early philosophical development seems to consist of a series of negative insights, or insights into negativity. Or if that is too sweeping a statement, there are at any rate two steps in his development which are clearly negational in character, and a third that is easily assimilated into the peculiar brand of "negative dialectic" that was to come.

Sartre spent a year in the French House in Berlin in 1934–1935. There he studied Husserl, and the lesson he derived from phenomenology was: that the ego is an illusion. This at least is the thesis that he developed in *The*

Transcendence of the Ego, published in 1936.[23] Like all good Frenchmen, he had set out from the Cartesian *cogito,* the "I think" which was for Descartes the starting point of all knowledge. This was meant to be a self-contained moment of consciousness. I am thinking about my thinking; subject and object are, in this indubitable moment, directly and indubitably at one. Husserl had shown, however, that all consciousness is *intentional;* it is *of*—an object (not a real object, that's beside the point—but of a target of my consciousness which alone makes it the consciousness it is). In itself, consciousness is an empty locus. Consciousness, for Sartre, however (being still Cartesian, even if drained of its content), is also momentary. I am no Cartesian substance; I have to make myself; but I make myself *ex nihilo* at every moment. Thus there is no stable ego, no self with a history. The real I is empty, the full I a mistake. For Sartre, then, the lesson of Husserl's intentionality is: that *nothing* has been inserted into the *cogito,* and dwells at the very heart of its being. Nothing is the engine that makes it run.

During these same years Sartre had been commissioned to write a survey of theories of imagination (also published in 1936), a survey which led him to develop his own conception of the imaginary. (The original part of the work, rejected by the first publisher, was published separately in 1939). [24] Here again, indeed, even more emphatically than in *The Transcendence of the Ego,* negativity is the operative concept. What is imagined is *not.* The life of imagination is the life of denial, of *de*-tachment par excellence. The work of consciousness, creation at every moment out of nothing, is also, in the thing created by the imagination of the artist, creation *of* nothing. Sartre has held faithfully to this view. Thus two of his most admired artists are, in the verbal arts, Genet and, in the visual, Giacometti. In Genet the "absence of connection with external reality," he writes

> is transfigured and becomes the sign of the demiurge's independence of his creation. . . . In the realm of the imaginary, absolute impotence changes sign and becomes omnipotence. Genet plays at inventing the world in order to stand before it in a state of supreme indifference.[25]

And Giacometti, he remarks, "became a sculptor because he was obsessed by vacuum." "Ironic, defiant, ceremonious and tender," Sartre writes,

> Giacometti sees empty space everywhere. Surely not everywhere, you will say, for some objects touch others. But this is exactly the point. Giacometti is certain of nothing, not even that. For weeks on end, he has been fascinated by the legs of a chair that did not touch the floor. Between things as between men, the bridges are broken, and emptiness seeps in everywhere, every creature concealing his own.[26]

In any medium, to imagine is to deny the real world, to make one's own non-space.

Yet all action is *in* the world; if the ego is empty, it is because my consciousness is out there, in things. To imagine is to make un-things which are nevertheless posited as negations *of*—the real. My being in itself is empty; it is wholly out there in the world, but as action: as wanting to make the world other than it is, in order, by that making, to make myself other. Thus my action, which is all I really am, is also negational: it is basically a posture of othering, of making what is —and thereby myself, who am nothing but my relation to that being out-there that I am not—of making what is into what it is not, or conversely of making what is not into what is. This conception of the finality of human being, which is fundamental to Sartrean philosophy, already lies at the basis of the third essay I want to refer to here: his *Sketch of a Theory of the Emotions,* published in 1939.

Emotion, Sartre argues there, is magical behavior, or more exactly, it is "an abrupt drop of consciousness into the magical." [27] I am always in the world, always acting to make myself over against the demands of the world. But the world has traps in it. It's like a pinball machine; you put in a coin, the balls start running here and there, but sometimes they run into blind alleys, fall into holes—anything but hit the jackpot. Ordinarily, of course, the metaphor of a game of chance is not *quite* accurate, for we treat the things in our world as manageable on the whole, we set ends and work toward them. Sometimes, however, the difficulties are too great; there is no rational action we can take. Sartre gives an example, or better a relatively trivial analogue:

> I extend my hand to take a bunch of grapes. I can't get it; it's beyond my reach. I shrug my shoulders. I let my hand drop, I mumble, "They're too green," and I move on. All these gestures, these words, this behavior are not seized upon for their own sake. We are dealing with a little comedy which I am playing *under* the bunch of grapes, through which I confer upon the grapes the characteristic of being "too green" which can serve as a substitute for the behavior which I am unable to keep up. At first, they presented themselves as "having to be picked." But this urgent quality very soon becomes unbearable because the potentiality cannot be realized. This unbearable tension becomes, in turn, a motive for foisting upon the grapes the new quality "too green," which will resolve the conflict and eliminate the tension. Only I cannot confer this quality on the grapes chemically. I cannot act

upon the bunch in the ordinary ways. So I seize upon this sourness of the too green grapes by acting disgusted. I magically confer upon the grapes the quality I desire.[28]

Here, he says, "the comedy is only half sincere." But if the situation is more serious, and the incantation seriously meant (though not, be it noted, grasped reflectively, with full consciousness), then emotion results. Take the example of fear:

> I see a wild animal coming toward me. My legs give way, my heart beats more feebly, I turn pale, I fall and faint. Nothing seems less adapted than this behavior which hands me over defenseless to the danger. And yet it is a behavior of *escape*. . . . Here the fainting is a refuge. . . . Lacking power to avoid the danger by the normal methods and the deterministic links, I denied it. I wanted to annihilate it. The urgency of the danger served as motive for an annihilating intention which demanded magical behavior. And, by virtue of this fact, I did annihilate it as far as was in my power. These are the limits of my magical action upon the world; I can eliminate it as an object of consciousness, but I can do so only by eliminating consciousness itself.[29]

Of course not every emotion is quite like this: there is active as well as passive fear—I may run away. I can grieve, too, either actively or passively. Basically, however, the structure is always the same. Either "consciousness is degraded and abruptly transforms the determined world in which we live into a magical world" or—as in horror— "the world itself sometimes reveals itself to consciousness as magical instead of determined, as was expected of it." [30]

Thus emotion appears as an escape-mechanism, a sharp alternative to the rational control of my environment. Its paradigm case is hysteria, or a child's tantrum: if you can't have the candy, scream! I *have* to act in the world, and if I can't act in a straightforward instrumental fashion, then I re-act: I cast a spell, I become a magician and the world becomes the kind of world that a magician needs. I make myself afraid and the world fearful; I make myself angry and the world infuriating.

This seems, at first sight, an all-or-none alternative of the same kind that we have found, in different contexts, in *The Transcendence of the Ego* and *The Imaginary*. Although the essay on the *Emotions* is intended to be phenomenology, or phenomenological psychology, its spirit is dialectical. Emotion is action as the refusal of action, the active anti-action of the sorcerer. But surely, one may object, the alternative of rationality *vs.* magic is not one recognized by the person who feels the emotion at the time he feels it, so how can this be correct phenomenology? Sartre in fact sees this very clearly. Emotion is a structure of consciousness, he argues, but not of self-consciousness. It is a structure of non-reflective, non-thetic consciousness which accompanies and underlies the central thrust of awareness. This is a theme elaborated in *Being and Nothingness,* perhaps the principal conceptual link that ties Sartre's abstract dialectic to the real flow of real experience, as, he says in *Les Mots,* the elevator at 1 rue de Goff tied his imaginative eyrie to the street below.

I shall return to the problem of non-thetic consciousness and its role in Sartre's philosophy of man when we come to *Being and Nothingness.* Both there and here, in these preliminary writings, however, it is the all-or-none spirit of Sartrean dialectic that prevails. I make myself each moment *ex nihilo;* in imagination what I make is also —nothing. Emotion is action as the denial of action. All my ways of being, as he was to put it in *Being and Noth-*

ingness, manifest freedom. Why? Because they are all ways of being my own nothingness. Action itself is always negating: making what-is-not be and making what-is-not-be. And emotion, the exorcising of the world, the negation of action, is still the action of negating. And so on.

Man of words, indeed! A juggler of words, perhaps, who means next to nothing by them? Faced with this sort of conceptual ping-pong, as it looks to be, one can sympathize with the student who described the subject-matter of contemporary continental philosophy as "perfectly perverse." But in philosophy even perversity, when perfected, can be, not only entertaining, but illuminating. It is astonishing what a complex and intricate structure Sartre has built out of his over-detached, almost nihilistic starting point. Assimilating for his own uses, yet with rare understanding, the philosophies of the past, he has produced in *Being and Nothingness* one of the treasure-houses of Western philosophy: a text one returns to again and again, not only for its catch phrases or for its strange truncated dialectic or for its occasional pieces of brilliant phenomenological description, but for the subtlety of its detailed arguments. It is surprising how complex and delicate this web of abstract words can be, and, indeed, how many real problems, out of its very detachment, it catches in its net. It is not only himself that the man of words, in *Words,* has caught (to change metaphors) in his pitiless mirror. In the conceptual mirror of man that he has set before us in his philosophical writing, although there is a basic distortion, an obsession with nothingness that strangely transforms the realities, there is also, even in the very set of the disproportions, much that is revealed.

Let *Words* have the last word. The man of the sixth

floor describes his career, both its constancy and its change:

> Today, April 22, 1963, I am correcting this manuscript on the tenth floor of a new building: through the open window I see a cemetery, Paris, the blue hills of Saint Cloud. That shows my obstinacy. Yet everything has changed. Had I wished as a child to deserve this lofty position, my fondness for pigeon-houses would have to be regarded as a result of ambition, of vanity, as a compensation for my shortness. But it's not that; it wasn't a matter of climbing up my sacred tree: I *was* there, I refused to come down from it. It was not a matter of setting myself above human beings: I wanted to live in the ether among the aerial simulacra of Things. Later, far from clinging to balloons, I made every effort to sink: I had to wear leaden soles. With luck, I occasionally happened, on naked sands, to brush against submarine species whose names I had to invent. At other times, nothing doing: an irresistible lightness kept me on the surface. In the end, my altimeter went out of order. I am at times a bottle imp, at others a deep-sea diver, often both together, which is as it should be in our trade. I live in the air out of habit, and I poke about down below without much hope.[31]

For those of us who live down below, the results are worth studying, on both levels.

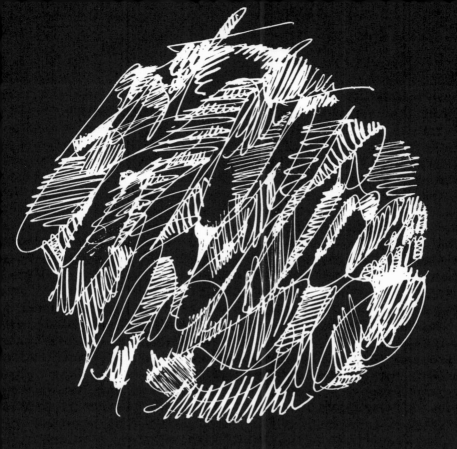

chapter two: sartre and his predecessors

I. descartes and the phenomenologists

introduction

Sartre, we have argued,
is in the first instance a philosophical, rather than imaginative, writer. He
works with concepts first and moves from
and through them to experience. The philosopher, however, does not snatch his concepts out of
thin air. In large part, he inherits them. He takes what men

have thought or are thinking and molds it into a new shape.
Even his innovations—concepts christened with new
names—usually have some affinity with the problems
of his predecessors, and, as he sees it, their erroneous
solutions. Ever since Plato, or even Parmenides, Western
philosophy has been firmly rooted in its own history. Sartre
is no exception. The derivations of his thought are clear,
and clearly acknowledged.

At the same time, one must admit that, from Plato onward, original philosophers, though philosophizing in one
way or another out of the history of philosophy, have often
been bad historians. What they want, after all, is not so
much to understand their predecessors as to use them.
They have their own problems, which, though generated
by the tradition, have been transformed by their own time
and character. Using the concepts and arguments of the
past for their own purposes, they fail to see and understand them as such, as the historian must try to do. In this
respect, Sartre *is* an exception. He does indeed use the
thinkers of the past (and present) for his own ends, but at
the same time he sees them with extraordinary clarity. In
his references, say, to Kant or Spinoza, he not only uses
their thought as a springboard for his own, but also exhibits a solid and scholarly penetration into their principles and views. His relation to Marx is less straightforward, as we shall see, but in general one finds in his
philosophical works an interweaving of themes in which
the original strands stand out for themselves with unusual
distinctness, while at the same time they are being
worked into a characteristically Sartrean pattern.

Compare Sartre in this respect with Heidegger.
Much more than Sartre, Heidegger considers himself a
philosopher in and of the history of Western thought.
Sartre does, indeed, take Descartes's *cogito* as a neces-

sary starting place; but to the tradition before that dramatic turning point he seems to be indifferent. Besides, he takes even the *cogito* as an eternal, not a historical, absolute. Heidegger's thought, on the contrary, is rooted in the first historical soil of Western thought—in the meanings of "truth" and "being" at the very beginning of our intellectual history. If he seeks "the destruction of metaphysics," he does so, not for any crass positivistic purpose, but out of reverence for history as such. For what he wants is to renew the beginning of Western thought itself. He wants to get back into the tradition so deeply that he can teach us how to live again its profound and fateful source. Yet from the point of view of historical scholarship, Heidegger is, in the main, a scandalous historian. His *Kant and the Problem of Metaphysics,* for example, illuminating though it can be, if used judiciously, for the study of the first *Critique,* is nine-tenths Heidegger. Much of his treatment of Greek philosophy, in the *Introduction to Metaphysics,* for example, is based on far-fetched etymologies embedded in the pompous profundities of the German Herr Professor at his worst. Though historically oriented, Heidegger is no "historian."

Admittedly, Heidegger himself would dismiss any demand for "scholarly accuracy" as superficial and irrelevant. It is a much deeper historicity, the very destiny of Being, that he is after. And woe betide us, not him, if we fail to follow him. So be it. My point is simply that Heidegger's "history," though at the heart of his method, is scarcely recognizable as history to the ordinary student of Western thought. Sartre, on the other hand, although he does not see his philosophical task as explicitly historical, appears to the philosophically schooled reader as, not only an original thinker, but, in a more humdrum way, a thoroughly competent professional philosopher with a sound historical schooling. For this reason, the relation of his own thought to the philosophers he most relies on comes through to the reader with unusual distinctness, and his own method appears, not indeed simply as eclectic, but as an idiosyncratic interweaving and re-making of familiar concepts and themes. It should help us, therefore, in approaching his philosophical work to look first at the use he makes of other thinkers both past and present.

Sartre's major predecessors—that is, the philosophers he most relies on in his own reflections—may be divided into two groups: Descartes and the phenomenologists on the one hand, and the dialecticians on the other. I am taking "phenomenology" here as the name of the school derived from Husserl and "dialectic" as designating the method of Hegel and his successors. True, one of Hegel's major works is also entitled "Phenomenology" (i.e., *The Phenomenology of Mind*), but it is from the modern "phenomenological method" that Sartre's practice derives, while it is the dialectical aspect of Hegel's philosophy that he adopts. Granted, the contrast I am making may, historically, be unfair to Hegel as phenomenologist; but in terms of influences on Sartre it is certainly plausible, and in terms of the major emphasis of Hegel's developed system it seems to me also not only permissible, but on the whole correct.

Descartes holds a peculiar position in this contrast. It is a residuum of Cartesian metaphysics which both limits the scope of Sartre's phenomenology and, in large measure, dictates the subject-matter as well as the style of his dialectic. Descartes is therefore Sartre's first, and, so to speak, constitutive forerunner. Yet the Cartesian *cogito* is also, as Husserl himself insisted, the necessary starting point of phenomenology; so in a way Descartes belongs with and among the phenomenological influences. But it is the *cogito,* with the idealism inherent in it (much as Sartre would deny such an allegation) that fatefully controls Sartre's dialectical reasoning as well as his phenomenology. The shadow of Descartes, therefore, presides over both sides of Sartrean method. More than the *cogito* alone, moreover, it is his Cartesian starting point in a number of its aspects—Cartesian freedom, Cartesian dualism, Cartesian temporality—that forms the framework of his thinking. In other words, the influence of Descartes is broader and deeper than simply the influence of the *cogito* as first principle and therefore of Descartes as phenomenologist or forerunner of phenomenology.

With this partial asymmetry in mind, however, I shall take Descartes along with Husserl and Heidegger as constituting one set of influences and the three great nineteenth-century dialectical philosophers, Hegel, Marx, and Kierkegaard, as forming another. Indeed, it can be seen in Sartre's early book *A Sketch for a Theory of the Emotions,* that the first three had already formed his thinking while the dialectical strand had just begun its work. The *Emotions* is a text in Cartesian phenomenology. Sartre there ranks himself quite by the way and automatically among those for whom the Cartesian *cogito* is an absolute, the necessary starting point of any sound philosophy. And in the introduction he sketches the contributions of Husserl and Heidegger, whose method he claims to be carrying forward in this essay.

Descartes

Sartre complains frequently about the bourgeoisie. He is, but hates being, a French petit bourgeois intellectual, and yet the class he despises has, he avows, nevertheless made him what he is. But much deeper and much harder to shake off in every French philosopher than the class he was born into is the influence of Descartes, the first and greatest French philosopher. Merleau-Ponty spent a lifetime fighting Descartes. Until very recently at least, Sartre never even wanted to fight him. Of course Sartre has long ago given up the Cartesian God. The old man receded into a Parisian sky one day when Jean-Paul was twelve or so, and he has never come back—except insofar as, for a committed atheist like Sartre, God has to be there to be denied. As a matter of fact in *Being and Nothingness* it is the traditional *definition* of God, *causa sui,* that man seeks to realize and cannot. But this is a Spinozistic rather than Cartesian formula, and it is probably Spinozistic being rather than Descartes's non-deceiving manipulator of all things that Sartre has in mind. In fact, it seems to me, the God of the *Meditations,* even for Descartes, was more a device to keep the divided world together than a genuine object of belief and worship, let alone a pervasive ontological foundation like the God of Spinoza. He is not hard to get rid of and Sartre has done the job thoroughly.

Cartesian substance, too, Sartre has eliminated, and by the same move to atheism. It is the *cogito,* this moment of my awareness which, though I doubt, even as doubter I must *be,* that is for him firm, unique, and the fulcrum of all philosophy. But that I as thinker am a substance, an independently existing thing worthy of immortality: that thesis can be supported only by my confidence that God created me at conception and will conserve me to sing psalms to Him in the hereafter. Departing, He has taken the substantial immaterial self away as well. But doesn't that leave the material world? Not as substantial. As every reader of the *Meditations* knows, the sixth meditation forms the weakest step in the series. That there are real external things I have succeeded in doubting at the very start so thoroughly that only God can reinstate them at the end—and even He can vouchsafe them only "practical," not perfect certainty. Usually, when my mind tells me "my leg hurts," it is in fact (if God's general rules are valid, and they must be if He is no deceiver), that piece of stuff out there whose aging veins are misbehaving. But there are, Descartes noted, amputees whose "leg" hurts. One can't be sure, as one is sure of mathematical truths, that the leg is *there.* So the whole of Cartesian cosmology, God and with Him the two finite substances, are easily dispensed with. Born into a late and secular century, conventionally Catholic in a Protestant household, Sartre can stop with the *Second Meditation* and let the rest go.

It is the first two *Meditations,* on the contrary, that establish the Cartesian method, that lay down as philosophical axiom the priority of pure consciousness and with this axiom a small but fateful cluster of metaphysical concepts which accompany it. All these Sartre has assimilated to his very bones.

First, the *cogito* itself: the pure consciousness of being conscious as the necessary beginning of philosophy. My senses sometimes deceive me; even about the most certain mathematical truths, given a deceiving demon to play tricks on me, I *could* be wrong. But my consciousness that I am now conscious of that consciousness—even if I were dreaming—could not be wrong. This self-contained now of self-consciousness is absolutely indubitable. It is the first and stable something, as Descartes put it, of which even the doubter of all traditional opinions and attitudes could have no doubt.

What is implied for philosophical method in this starting point? First, the primary tool of philosophy is intuition, not argument. The *cogito* is not an argument: in the

Meditations, there is no "therefore" between "I think" and "I am." I am, I think, Descartes declares, this is true every time I say it. What philosophy is after is the *aperçus* of consciousness into itself. True, as we shall see shortly, Husserl, claiming to follow Descartes's method, will transform the *cogito* into *cogitationes,* the thinking into thoughts, and Sartre will try (with important differences) to follow him in this. But what is common to all three, Descartes, Husserl, and Sartre, is the insistence that philosophical knowledge begins from a pure, evident, self-guaranteeing intuition and remains on (or recurrently returns to) the intuitive level so long as it is correctly executed. Indeed, for Sartre, not only philosophical knowledge (though that *par excellence*) but all knowledge is intuitive, as it was for Descartes. Argument is subordinate to insight and must be brought back to it.

Such insight, it should be remarked by the way, must be distinguished from the "understanding" (*Verstehen*) of the modern social scientist, sometimes associated with phenomenological method. We shall find in Sartre's *Critique* that "comprehension" (*Verstehen*) is a second-order instrument, secondary to the reflective awareness of the individual's nature and destiny. Only after a series of complex dialectical maneuvres can we achieve the "comprehension" of social functions and structures and of men as agents in society. The primary intuitions, the insights we have to cultivate first, are not sociological comprehension, but the self-awareness of a pure reflective consciousness.

For the ideal of philosophical knowledge, with Sartre, as with Descartes and Husserl, is absolute certainty: "apodeicticity," that is, *necessary* truth. This is not of course physical necessity, which is always hypothetical, contingent upon postulates and upon given circumstances. Physical laws always say, if such and such were given, then so and so would happen. Nor is it logical necessity, which says, if A, then not non-A, and so says nothing real. The necessary truth of the phenomenologist from Descartes through Husserl to Sartre must be luminousness itself: the self-evident. That was the basic methodological insight of the *cogito* which all pure phenomenologists have still to follow: they seek the self-guaranteeing, the pure light of reason illuminating itself by its own rays and leaving out of account all the universe outside that beam. The metaphor betrays itself: for light always falls on *something,* not itself—we will return to that point with Husserl—yet the ideal remains—only the self-evident is worthy of acceptance as philosophical truth.

Empirically, however, we can easily see that the insights we have into social action, into the ordinary situations of others' lives and of our own—for as living embodied beings we have always been, since our prenatal existence, dependent on others, influencing them and being influenced by them—we can see that these everyday insights fall short in their ordinary operation of such apodeicticity. Day by day, in our bodily situations, we are fallible. Even logicians and mathematicians, let alone ordinary mortals, make mistakes. Three centuries after Descartes's *Fourth Meditation* we still fail to confine our wills within the bounds of our understandings. We still judge probabilistically, we gamble and go wrong. How can I escape, as philosopher, this seemingly universal fallibility and achieve self-evident truth? Only—again Sartre agrees with Descartes in the seventeenth century and Husserl in the twentieth—by a disciplined reflection which detaches the reflecting consciousness from its factual enmeshment in the contingent givens of the factual world. That world, Sartre believes, is indeed all I have, and I am always out there in it. But I philosophize by detaching myself from it, setting myself, as consciousness conscious of itself, over against it. Only in this way can the necessary purity of philosophical thought be initiated or maintained.

It may be objected that I am unfair to Sartre in putting him so unequivocally inside the tradition that seeks for philosophy unadulterated apodeictic truth. He himself has called Husserl's search for necessary truth, his attempt to construct a range of apodeictic philosophical sciences, madness—though the madness of genius. Yet in the *Critique* Sartre himself is still seeking "apodeicticity," and even if he never finds it (though in the *Critique* he thought he had), it remains his ideal. If it is an empty ideal, so much the more strenuous is his search for it, so much the more emphatic his insistence on the intellectual development that could alone implement its fulfillment.

The peculiar detachment of the Cartesian philosopher is evident in Sartre's case if we compare, briefly, his style of philosophical reflection with that of two other twentieth-century writers. Take, for example, C. I. Lewis, a philosopher very far from Sartre in method and interests. Lewis, too, recognized explicitly that the method of philosophy is "reflection." But the reflective method for him is that of a practical man in a world of practical concerns, both ethical and intellectual—for the intellectual interests even of the pure scientist are for Lewis ultimately linked to practice. Here we are, in this humdrum, murky world, trying to find out, from within, what it is all about. The achievements of science, the moral dilemmas of our fellow men, are all grist to our philosophic mill; but we never lose the awareness of being one of our fellows ourselves. From within society and its demands, we withdraw a little, to look around us and ask on what principles our actions, both more and less immediately practical, might be based. But we have never radically doubted—could never doubt—the evidence of our bodily senses, from which, after all, all our "external" information flows. The empirical and the conceptual, though on reflection we find them to be logically independent, are not sharply separated in fact and we attempt no method to achieve their radical separation. It is in empirical situations, both developments in physics and the givens of ethical life, that we try to separate abstractly these conceptual strands. Embodiment, fallibility, contingency, and immersion *in* the real world are all essential to this kind of pragmatic reflection from the start. Pure consciousness, the tool and the medium of phenomenology, is here neither the starting point of philosophical reflection nor its desideratum.

Much closer to Sartrean philosophizing, and indeed deeply motivated by the need to come to grips with it, is the thought of Merleau-Ponty. But the same contrast obtains. For Merleau-Ponty, perception, which expresses my embodied being with and in the world, is what comes first. Perception, as he constantly argues, is primary, in its epistemological status and its ontological import. Reference to the *cogito,* the moment of pure reflection in which I as pure consciousness am purely aware of being conscious, comes late in the text of his *Phenomenology,* and remains, in its purity, an object of thought, not an achievement, let alone a starting point. Here I am, he says, thinking about Descartes's *cogito.* But when I think about myself thinking about the *cogito*— or about anything else—what I find is no pure consciousness at all but a situated, historical, embodied stretch of thinking, feeling, listening, seeing in all the ambiguity of my being-in-the-world. And Descartes's own *cogito* must in fact have been like that: Descartes, after all, was a mathematician with certain interests and aspirations—in particular, the aspiration of finding a secure and permanent foundation on which to build, first, mathematical physics and then, flowing from it, a universal science. His dream of finding a new and infallible method of reflection was guided by his own mathematical genius and by the confidence of the new scientists of his day that a revolutionary method of knowledge could and must be found to keep the new discoveries on a secure and systematic path. Only in that historical situation was there a Cartesian *cogito.* But in that situation it was not in fact the *cogito* it seemed to be. It was the claim of a historical, thinking-and-feeling human being—a claim which, in its full implications, has proved, as so many of our claims prove, to be illusory.

Now Sartre, of course, if he has abandoned the metaphysical superstructure of the *Meditations,* God and finite substance, is also far from the intellectual interests of the historical Descartes. His conception of the method of physics (which is not Descartes's conception of it) does, as we shall see in connection with the *Critique,* have a certain influence on his own method. But it is far from central, and at the stage of his development when he wrote *Being and Nothingness* it is hardly operative at all. What interests him is not what in fact interested Descartes, the discovery of a new method on which to found the sciences, or what was to interest Husserl, the discovery of a new method on which to found the philosophical sciences and, through this foundation, to justify the positive sciences also. What interests Sartre is the *cogito* itself as the moment of pure determined self-awareness. It is this, in and of itself, this moment which for a more pragmatic or more empirically oriented thinker does not exist, even as an ideal—it is precisely this moment which for him is the unique and necessary starting point of philosophical thought.

But, it will be objected, the starting point of *Being and Nothingness* is not really the Cartesian *cogito,* totally aware of its own self-awareness, not the reflective *cogito* which is the first sure step to a unified science, but the pre-reflective *cogito,* a consciousness (of) self which is in fact self-forgetting. The example Sartre gives in *Being and Nothingness* is, counting my cigarettes: there are twelve. Thetically, that is, in terms of the center of my attention, it's the cigarettes I'm thinking of, not myself as counting them. But if you ask me what I'm doing, I say automatically, "Counting my cigarettes." So I *was* aware, though "non-thetically," of my own consciousness as well as, "thetically," or explicitly, of its object. This move to the non-thetic, non-focal consciousness (of) self had been made, in fact, already in the *Transcendence of the Ego* and *The Emotions.* Is not this a fundamental, non-Cartesian, even anti-Cartesian move? I shall of course return to the pre-reflective *cogito* and its place in Sartre's philosophy when I come to analyze the argument of *Being and Nothingness.* But against this objection one can say here: first, Sartre does expressly take the *cogito* itself (even though he is going to transform it) as an absolute beginning. And secondly, the Sartrean *cogito,* even though it will have lost the explicitly reflective character of the original, still carries with it many of the implications of the Cartesian first principle. Sartre not only retains, as I have been arguing, the ideal of intuitive, detached, pure self-evident knowledge (to be attained, presumably, in *Being and Nothingness,* when he turns in Chapter III of Book Two, from the pre-reflective to the reflective level). He retains also, as I have suggested, the corollaries of the *cogito:* Cartesian freedom, Cartesian dualism, and the Cartesian concept of time. In this, indeed, he goes much further than does Husserl in his loyalty to the essential Cartesian strategy of the *Meditations.* Before I go on to consider Sartre's relation to Husserl, therefore, let me look briefly at these three, Cartesian co-ordinates, so to speak, of his thought.

First, freedom. God, Descartes had said, gives laws in the universe as a king gives laws in his kingdom. For Sartre, there is no God, every man is king, and king just as Descartes's God was king. Man is wholly free. In his introduction to a collection of Cartesian texts, Sartre expressly celebrates this Cartesian concept,[1] and *Being and Nothingness* may itself be considered a long paean to Cartesian freedom. We are indeed *condemned* to be free: our destiny of freedom is a burden, for the comforting substantiality of the Cartesian self is no longer ours to attain. When we try to fill our freedom in, so to speak, to give ourselves stability and content, we betray ourselves: we borrow from elsewhere, from the past, from social convention and myth, we fall into bad faith. And yet we remain free: consciousness surging up over against the world, bringing negation into the world, making ourselves at every moment. No look of the Other, no torture, no past commitment can negate that fundamental fact: at every instant *I* and only *I* decide. Sartre says that he has changed. His Orestes now shocks him. He knows how determined by his society, his class man is. Yet even in the *Critique* he insists that every man is sovereign. There is, he claims, no *foundation* of sovereignty, as political theorists have tried to argue. Why not? Because, though through very devious dialectical channels, the derivation of the sovereignty of "the Sovereign" is from the sovereignty of man as such, which is total and, though always alienated, still inalienable. If you genuinely start with the *cogito,* that is how it has to be. This pure moment of consciousness, self-dependent and self-sustaining, is the first foundation of thought and of being, of knowledge and of reality.

But is it? If you really start with the *cogito,* you start by *cutting out all else.* The *cogito,* the moment of freedom, of self-choice, of the project through which I surge up as my self, has to be over against all that is not this moment, all that is not my self. To accept the *cogito* is to accept dualism, not, indeed, a dualism of substances, but a dualism of consciousness against what is rejected: the out-there, the extended and external, the other-than-myself-here-now-aware-or-myself-here-now. Within this basic, radical dichotomy of self and other, of act and object, as we have already seen and will see yet again, all Sartre's thinking—however socio-political, however dialectical it may become—is sternly and uncompromisingly confined. Both the to-and-fro dialectic of *Being and Nothingness* and the more tortuous but still largely negational dialectic of the *Critique* take their direction and their character from this Cartesian starting point: the opposition of consciousness as "for-itself" and the "in-itself," the "mere" being, to which it is opposed. The man of the *cogito,* of detached self-consciousness, over against his objects, the man of the sixth floor, remains. He is still Orestes, making himself by his own act, for, but also against, his city. He is still Roquentin—however thick the forest of chestnut roots (even, as he calls it in the *Critique,* the human forest), they are still nauseating. They threaten him, because as himself he has to be their Other, their denial, and they are his denial because he has to be, if he is to be at all, pure consciousness, self-making and self-maintaining over against all else.

Can he so make and so maintain himself? Of course

not. Hence, as we shall see, the dialectical in-and-out that is to follow. But he can seem to—for a moment. The *cogito,* of course, is momentary. I am, I think, *whenever* I am aware of thinking. Beyond thought, I need God to recreate me. Time itself is a string of beads, of which I have one only at any time. As we shall see in *Being and Nothingness,* the Cartesian instant haunts Sartre's argument. Though he denies it, he wants it. Good faith could exist, Orestes could really make himself, only if he could find that instant. Like the apodeicticity of Cartesian knowledge, the instant remains as the ideal. And so it must for any pure phenomenological method whatever, even, I would venture to suggest, with Husserl, despite the subtleties of his description of temporal consciousness. For what is intuited as evident must be presented—and what is presented must be present *in* the present. The past is no more, the future is not yet, it is the unique moment of present truth at which phenomenological description aims.

Again, on these three concepts—freedom, mind-body dualism, and the atomic concept of time—it is instructive to contrast Sartre and Merleau-Ponty. Merleau-Ponty rejects all three of these Cartesian notions. In the first instance, he abandons dualism, seeking to found our being-in-the-world squarely in the thoroughgoing ambiguity of a psychophysical existence. But the ambivalence of our existence as embodied beings lends indirection and qualification also to our freedom. "We never see our freedom face to face." The fact that I live in and out of this body and this bodily situation means that my choices rise up *within* a given set of contingent circumstances, *within* what Sartre would call "facticity," not over against it. Similarly, time for Merleau-Ponty is not a string of moments, but truly historical from the start. He attempts, with some modification, to follow the lead of

Husserl's *Inner Time Consciousness;* he is certainly not in pursuit of a Cartesian present moment.

Husserl

So far I have been speaking of Sartre's Cartesianism, which is the starting point of his phenomenological method; it also provides the boundaries as well as the first principle for his philosophical reflections and achievements from his first to his most recent publication: from the *Transcendence of the Ego* through the *Critique* to his work on Flaubert. In *Emotions,* however, and in *Being and Nothingness* as well, he makes it plain that he has derived a great deal also from the twentieth-century phenomenologists Husserl and Heidegger. Having already touched on Sartre's debt to Husserl in connection with *Transcendence of the Ego* and *The Imaginary,* let us now look a little more systematically at the connection between Sartre and Husserl, mediating the connections by comparing Descartes and Husserl.

Descartes's first *Meditation* puts into operation what has come to be known as the principle of methodological doubt. To approach a new and certain beginning of knowledge, he prepares the way by taking as false, for the time being, all opinions which he had previously accepted on dubitable grounds. Husserl, without denying, even *pro tem,* the beliefs of ordinary life, follows an analogous method insofar as he holds such beliefs in abeyance. He "brackets" the whole of "reality" as accepted by the natural standpoint. He performs an *epoché*—that is, a holding in suspense of everyday beliefs. He thus puts to one side, also, the philosophical problem of the reality of the external world, eliminating the transcendent, in the sense of what lies beyond consciousness, altogether from his inquiry. In this, indeed, he is more radical than Descartes, who will try to reinstate this other-than-conscious-ness, both God and matter, in the third and sixth *Meditations* respectively.

Secondly, beyond and before and immune to doubt, we find the *cogito*. This move, at least in the *Cartesian Meditations,* Husserl accepts, like Descartes, as the only proper beginning for a sound, necessary, and "scientific," philosophy. Yet Husserl accepts Descartes's principle in a spirit that is not Cartesian. His starting point is different from Descartes's in two significant aspects. First, the *cogito* for Descartes is uniquely self-guaranteeing because it is self-reflective. I am thinking now about my thinking now. The idea and its object collapse into one another in perfect unity. What Husserl constantly speaks of in his *Meditations,* however, is not the *cogito,* but *cogitationes,* not the "I think," but thoughts. What characterizes consciousness for him is *intentionality,* the fact that thought is always directed toward a target. It is never purely and simply self-identical as the Cartesian *cogito* is. Descartes had found as his firm and secure starting point a unique moment of thinking cut off from anything beyond its own identity with itself. Although Husserl, too, wants to bracket, to hold off from consciousness all that is not purely conscious, it is not just this unique self-identical moment he wants to examine. It is *any* phenomenon of consciousness in its unique intuited structure that interests him. Looking at consciousness in this way, he finds, not a pure and collapsed self-reference in which thinking and thought are one, but a vastly complex structure of thinking and its target—a structure which can be opened out, he hopes, into a wide range of phenomenological sciences. This move promises not only much knowledge, but secondly, the avoidance of much error. Descartes thought to move from the *cogito* to transcendent objects and thus he re-embarked, despite his inspired beginning, on the speculative metaphysic that has led so many philosophers astray. But the new phenomenological method, Husserl believes, with its self-conscious reduction, is not accessible to the mistaken path that Descartes takes as he proceeds from the *cogito, via* God, to reconstruct the world. All the discoveries of phenomenology, Husserl insists, are to remain definitively within the sphere of consciousness. There is to be no advance to dogmatic metaphysics, to the assertion of trans-conscious realties as such. There is plenty of work for philosophy to do within the sphere of immanence, in examining the *cogitationes* both in their active and their passive aspects, seeing them in their essential structures, and inquiring into their constitution by consciousness itself.

How does Sartre stand in relation to all this? Although he does not start from an explicit position on either methodological doubt or its cousin the *epoché,* he seems to accept something like it, at least insofar as he begins in *Being and Nothingness* within consciousness, with the "pure phenomenon," which could only have been reached by some such method. Yet he has not seriously executed the Husserlian reduction. He has not put himself faithfully on the level of consciousness so as to remain there. I shall return to this point shortly.

But the chief peculiarity of Sartre's phenomenology, and of his dialectic too, stems from the way in which he takes the *cogito.* For he both accepts Husserl's revision of the *cogito* to *cogitatio* and refuses to accept it. Thought *is* of an object, he has argued in the *Transcendence of the Ego,* so the thinking as such is empty. Yet he cannot resign the *cogito* itself. If it is always *of* something other than my thinking that, in the first instance, I am thinking; nevertheless, non-thetically, in a peripheral or submerged fashion, so to speak, I am also, conscious (of) myself as doing so. (Remember the cigarettes already referred to!) Now I could of course think thetically about my thinking and even about my thinking about my thinking by turning to a higher, reflective level. In this case the object of my thinking would be a previous thought or previous thinking. The same move could be made by Husserl, or Descartes if he thought about it, but such reflective regression does not alter the fundamental structure of thought as intentional—or, for Sartre, of the *cogito* as pre-reflective. In fact, for him the regressive reflection would be viciously infinite, could one not cut it short with his *cogito* as a non-reflective absolute. And it is on this structure, the pre-reflective *cogito*, that the argument of *Being and Nothingness* rests.

Moreover, Sartre not only retains the *cogito,* if in altered form; he takes the object of the *cogitatio,* not as the immanent target of thinking, but as outside it. He reintroduces—has never really abandoned—the Cartesian extended thing. He has, indeed, as we have seen, abandoned its substantiality, but its sheer exteriority, its otherness-than-consciousness remains. In fact, consciousness, emptied by the insight into intentionality, turns out to be nothing but the *other of that otherness:* the in-here as a negation of the out-there. The move to intentionality in Sartre, therefore, is not a move within consciousness to open up its immanent complexities; it is a leap which both empties consciousness and places its object transcendently out in the world. Thus Sartre seems to have taken from Husserl just one insight: thought is always of an object. At the start he has retained a pre-reflective *cogito* as surrogate for the Cartesian and has taken the intentional object as transcendent rather than reduced, thus generating out of a phenomenological base the dialectic of Nothingness and Being from which no God, whether benevolent or deceiving, will rescue him.

Yet Sartre is a phenomenologist. If he accepts a minimum of Husserlian doctrine, he is—or at least has been on occasion—a superb practitioner of the descriptive method in philosophy. Without anticipating in detail the argument of *Being and Nothingness,* let me try to illustrate if I can what this method, stripped of Husserl's technicalities, amounts to, and how Sartre uses it.

The slogan of phenomenology is "back to the things themselves." But "things," of course, after the *epoché,* are not transcendent things: phenomenologists are not asking whether what there is is "really" mind or body or something different from either. They are trying to look without philosophical or scientific prejudice at the content of experience as experience, both on the side of the experiencing, in memory as against perception or imagination, for example, and of what is experienced, as physical object, person, animal, art work, space, time, and so on. The principal function of "bracketing" from this point of view is to turn the philosopher's attention from distracting—often even insoluble—speculative problems to the domain of consciousness, where he can seek to inspect impartially and accurately what he does unquestionably have: the whole field of his own consciousness as he is conscious of it. He can seek to describe fully and soberly the content of his experience and the manner of experiencing it. It is out of this medium of consciousness, after all, that all the pronouncements of the so-called positive sciences have to be elicited. Without the consciousness of mathematicians, in its peculiar style and with its appropriate conceptual objects, there would be no mathematics; without the consciousness of physicists, no physics; without the consciousness of social scientists, no social science. It is a given style of experience, with its peculiar targets and its peculiar ways of taking them, that constitutes a given kind of positive science. The same goes for segments of the field of consciousness before and beyond science: aesthetic experience, religious experience, the experience of everyday life in all its manifold aspects. Phenomenology as pure description is the *sine qua non* of all philosophical criticism or justification.

"Pure description," however, has been cultivated in the main by literature and psychology. If we are to take phenomenological description as it is intended—as philosophy, not literature or empirical science—we must consider briefly how it is distinguished from both of these —admitting that it is also, of course, connected with both.

Phenomenologists may use examples from literature, and the literature of consciousness lends itself peculiarly to this use. Phenomenologists like, for example, to quote Valéry's *M. Teste.* Sartre in particular borrows numerous descriptions from Proust. And of course, being an imaginative as well as a philosophical writer, he can either produce a story with a philosophical lesson or place a phenomenological description within a literary text. In *Nausea,* for example, he is doing both: writing a philosophical argument in fictional form, and using descriptions that might well find their place in a more conventional philosophical text—for instance, the description of listening to a hit tune on the gramophone—in the context of the novel. Similarly, in *L'Enfance d'un Chef,* the description of the child's consciousness in relation to his mother could easily be transposed into a phenomenological account of intersubjective experience as such. Yet there is a difference, even though it may be difficult to specify it exactly.

For one thing, it is a question of the proportion between imagination and intellect. The phenomenologist uses his imagination systematically, and abstractly, in "eidetic variation." That is, he *imagines* the present experience, both its content as experienced and the manner of experiencing it, shifted slightly one way and another. And he does this in order to cultivate a vision that is primarily *intellectual,* the vision of essences as such. True, the novelist, too, however precisely he may describe the feel of a given conscious moment, produces a work that is also in some sense "eidetic." If "Marcel's" (or "I's"?) consciousness or Bloom's consciousness were *only* "Marcel's" or Bloom's, no one could read *Remembrance of Things Past* or *Ulysses*. There must be enough generality to permit imaginative participation by the reader. But in literature, however "universal," it is the *imaginative* participation that is primary.

Further, it is *participation* that the novelist has to seek, whereas with the phenomenologist what is sought is *re-enactment.* It is not Husserl's "primordial world" that I enter into in reading his *Cartesian Meditations;* if I read Husserl seriously, it is my own consciousness that, in following him, inspects itself. I am with Bloom on the way to Glasnevin or with the great-aunts acknowledging the gift of wine. In inspecting, with Husserl, the nature of the *cogitatio,* I am with—myself. To put it philosophically, the tool of the literary reader is Humean sympathy, while the tool of the philosophical reader is Cartesian self-awareness. Even when Husserl comes to the problem of intersubjectivity—or when other phenomenologists like Scheler or Stein describe the phenomenon of "empathy"—it is *my* awareness of others as mine that is being investigated. Thus, for literature and phenomenology, both aim and process differ.

Is phenomenology, then, the same as introspective

psychology? Husserl is emphatic in rejecting such an identification. And in the *Emotions* Sartre, too, though he is by no means obsessed with method as was Husserl, emphasizes the distinction between phenomenology and phenomenological psychology. It is the latter, he says, that he is partly practising there, but with the aim of a phenomenology, not a psychology, of the emotions in mind. Psychology, even when introspective, is an empirical science. It asks the subject to report exactly his conscious state under certain contingent experimental conditions. Admittedly, the phenomenologist may sometimes seem to be doing the same thing. In his lectures on "First Philosophy," for example, Husserl keeps referring to the fact that if I eat santonin everything appears yellow. A simple empirical generalization, it seems, or, in a given instance, abstracting from the empirical conditions, a simple introspection: everything looks yellow. And the phenomenologist may indeed simply bracket the question of existence and describe in detail his consciousness at this very moment. But that would be in itself of little interest to any philosopher. What really interests him is the essential structure of, say, visual perception on the one hand (as distinguished from memory or imagination), and the color yellow on the other, as distinct from red or from a "bright" sound. Such insights he seeks, not by a simple description of this very experience here-now, as experienced here-now, but rather by the method already mentioned, that of "eidetic variation." In other words, he systematically imagines alterations in his present experience. If he does this carefully and well—and of course always within the "reduced" field of consciousness, with all extraneous "factual" questions held in abeyance—he will come to exercise the chief occupation of phenomenological research: the inspection of essences. It is in this method of eidetic variation that his skill chiefly resides, and it is a vast and systematically related range of essences, all within the field of consciousness itself, that he claims to grasp.

Note: these phenomenological essences are not Platonic forms, subsisting in some remote transcendent place; they are necessarily as they in fact appear *within experience itself.* The phenomenologist does not seek to explain the existence of material objects, for example, as Plato did by calling them "participants in some higher reality." Indeed, he refrains from asking *whether* they exist at all. He takes the experience of a material object, which he, like every one, has, and asks what kind of experience this is. Now, short of the sophistications of the physicist, material objects are of course experienced chiefly through perception; so he is asking on the one hand what perception is and on the other what perceptible objects are. Varying his actual (but reduced) experiences slightly and systematically in his imagination, he finds, for example, that perceiving essentially contains anticipations of gradual and coherently interrelated variations in the aspect of the perceived object from "different points of view." He also finds that for perceiving, unlike memory or imagination, these variations are never finished: there is always an aspect *to be perceived,* there is an open horizon of perceptibility inherent in the very nature of perception itself. Abstaining from speculation even in the rudimentary sense in which he accepts "on faith" that there is a world and he is in it—though of course noting the inherence of that primordial faith in his ordinary consciousness—he simply but precisely and exhaustively describes the essential structures of the experience itself as such.

To banish metaphysics, to stick to experience itself, was of course the aim of empiricism. But phenomenology is neither empirical in its method nor empiricist in its intent. Husserl himself, however, acknowledges the kinship: the great empiricists, he believes, were trying to describe the givens of consciousness, but they were too deeply committed to the speculations of the "new corpuscular philosophy" and too naïve about the relation of philosophical to experimental method to succeed in carrying out their program. Only in the twentieth century has philosophy acquired the necessary methodological self-consciousness to carry through what Locke or Hume had attempted—that is, the systematic investigation of the pure field of consciousness by consciousness itself with the aim of discovering the full range of its essential structures. It is description in this systematic and philosophical spirit that the phenomenologist undertakes.

It should be remarked parenthetically that eidetic description is, for Husserl, still only a way-station, though a vast and fruitful one, in the development of phenomenology as a whole. Ultimately, for him phenomenology seeks not only to describe the structures of consciousness, but to *found* them. Phenomenology, ultimately, is *transcendental* phenomenology, in which I see not only the manifold "objects" of experience and the manifold ways of experiencing them, but my own *constitution* of both these out of myself as "transcendental ego." Thus it seems that the "I" *almost* makes the world. This apparently idealist issue of phenomenology Sartre never accepted, and it need not concern us, at least not directly, in dealing with the influence of phenomenology on his philosophy. Insofar as Sartre pursues phenomenological method, it is the descriptive techniques of this tradition, not its transcendentalism, that he is following.

Let me illustrate this here by taking just one example, not the famous "look" in which I am caught at the keyhole, but a description which precedes it in Sartre's development of the experience of the Other. There is, he says, clearly a direct and immediate relation to the Other which occurs in my ordinary life. I can point to it, but to understand it I must examine more carefully its ordinary appearance. Very well. "I am in a public park," says Sartre:

> . . . Not far away there is a lawn and along the edge of that lawn there are benches. A man passes by those benches. I see this man; I apprehend him as an object and at the same time as a man.[2]

What does this mean? Sartre asks. What do I mean, when I affirm that this object is a man? This is plainly a philosophical question. What concerns Sartre, however, or any phenomenologist, is not the use of the word "man" or the sentence "There is a man," but the structure of the experience itself as such. Try eidetic variation: think of him as inanimate, as a puppet. In that case:

> . . . I should apply to him the categories which I ordinarily use to group temporal-spatial "things." That is, I should apprehend him as being "beside" the benches, two yards and twenty inches from the lawn, as exercising a certain pressure on the ground, etc. His relation with other objects would be of the purely additive type; this means that I could have him disappear without the relations of the other objects around him being perceptibly *changed*. In short, no new relation would appear *through him* between those things in my universe: grouped and synthesized *from my point of view* into instrumental complexes, they would *from his* disintegrate into multiplicities of indifferent relations.[3]

By contrast with this imagined variant—that is, seeing him as an object—to perceive him as a man is to grasp "things" and the world in a different organization: ". . . Perceiving him as a *man* . . . is not to apprehend an additive relation between the chair and him; it is to register an organization *without distance* of the things in my universe around that privileged object." [4] The original external relation of things to things remains, indeed, "the lawn remains two yards and twenty inches from him," but it is now coupled with another, a distanceless relation: the lawn is "also as a *lawn* bound to him in a relation which at once both transcends distance and contains it." Thus:

> Instead of the two terms of the distance being indifferent, interchangeable, and in a reciprocal relation, the distance *is unfolded starting from* the man whom I see and *extending up to* the lawn as the synthetic upsurge of a univocal relation. We are dealing with a relation which is without parts, given at one stroke, inside of which there unfolds a spatiality which is not my spatiality; for instead of a grouping *toward me* of the objects, there is now an orientation *which flees from me*.[5]

This is only the beginning of Sartre's analysis. He will assimilate this description and others to the ontological thrust of his basic categories. But at crucial points in its development, it is often on these descriptions of experienced structures that his argument rests. Even the tendentious epithet "hemorrhage" applied to the Other's appearance in my world has its foundation in that description in which suddenly my centeredness in my own thoughts and perceptions runs off, loses its centrality, as I am taken into his perspective and so lose hold of my own. My own everyday life world, which lets the whole of my surrounding field revolve around me as center, suddenly loses its ordinary structure. It flows away, immediately and unpleasantly, like uncontrollable bleeding. Ordinarily I control my world, just as ordinarily my body contains and bounds my blood. I don't usually notice this; indeed, I live in and by not noticing. But suddenly the center shifts: I run off into a mere peripheral item organized around another center, and by that very running off I see myself as usually the center of my own world of action—as in a hemorrhage, I feel by shocking contrast the "normal" containment of my circulating blood which has suddenly gone out of bounds. It is flowing off and I am flowing with it.

Admittedly, as my speculation on "the Other as hemorrhage" indicates, such phenomenological foundations are in Sartre's case quickly elaborated in a style controlled by his overriding dialectical interests. And, indeed, many of the sections of *Being and Nothingness* entitled "Phenomenology of—" are more dialectical than descriptive. Take one further instance. In the section on the past in the "Phenomenology of the Temporal Dimension" Sartre chooses as an example the statement: "Paul in 1920 was a student at the Polytechnic." [6] What is it, in terms of the structure of consciousness, to experience what is intended by such a statement, to be aware that something *was*? There is a phenomenological core to the inquiry, but the answer is given—and argued for—in a style as speculative as St. Augustine's. For Sartre does not just describe, he argues in terms of concepts like being and non-being, facticity, contingency, and of course the for-itself and in-itself dichotomy. He comes to grips with others' theories (in fact he starts from a reference to "theories of memory"), with James and Claparède, with Descartes, Bergson, and Heraclitus. Thus even what Sartre calls phenomenology, in his own philosophising, has been taken up into a highly speculative enterprise. The strictness of Husserl's descriptive method is not his style. Yet the phenomenological foundation is there. Sartre has adopted from phenomenology, not only the methodological thesis that philosophy must begin from and remain within the field of pure consciousness, not only the thesis of the intentionality of consciousness —the principle that every consciousness is *of* an object —but also the use of accurate description of moments or aspects of consciousness, combined with eidetic variation, as a philosophical tool.

Heidegger

So far, so good. But Sartre acknowledges indebtedness to two contemporary phenomenologists: Husserl and Heidegger. The two influences are hard to combine, and the way in which Sartre in fact combines them shows this to be the case. Heidegger was also Husserl's student, and *Being and Time* is still recognizably a phenomenological work, but with the very great difference that it has wholly renounced any Cartesian starting point. Methodological doubt, the *cogito,* consciousness as the medium of philosophy—all this Heidegger has systematically bypassed. Consciousness is not a category he needs or uses; the starting point is being-there—Dasein, the individual human being—in and with the world. Husserl found, in a philosophy of immanence, a clever way to evade the question of "the reality of the external world." Heidegger, starting with my being *in* the world, among things ready-to hand for my use, was shocked that the question was ever asked. I am *there* from the start.

Rejecting the Cartesian starting point of phenomenology, moreover, he has cast aside all the more emphatically the metaphysical remnants of the Cartesian universe that we have found Sartre retaining. Both on Cartesian dualism and Cartesian temporality, and even freedom (though more obscurely), his position is plainly and radically different from Sartre's.

Since he is working with *Dasein,* or human being, not with consciousness, Heidegger has in fact gone beyond—or behind—the kind of philosophising for which the mind-body problem arises. He does not, like Merleau-Ponty, try to wrestle with the problem of embodiment from a post-Cartesian point of view; he has simply made a detour around it. Now as far as body goes, this may be a serious omission. The relation of man to his body would seem to many philosophers as well as psychologists an essential problem for any account of human existence as such. It would seem to demand a place among what Heidegger calls the "Existentialen," the fundamental categories of my being as such. Be that as it may. The point here is simply that Heidegger is working within a single basic category, being-in-the-world; he is concerned neither with body as body nor with mind as mind. Sartre, on the contrary, while remaining a Cartesian, cannot start from being-in-the-world as a neutral third. He is a *cogito* man; he must start from consciousness. Yet he does make heavy use of the basic Heideggerian concept. How can he do so? He does it, I think, by combining being-in-the-world with Husserl's intentionality, and identifying consciousness of—an object, with my being in—a world. But to do that, to read being-in-the-world in the spirit of the *Meditations,* Descartes's and Husserl's, rather than of *Being and Time,* is precisely to break the world apart. Instead of a unified world-in-which-I-am, we have the for-itself (*poursoi*) against the in-itself (*en-soi*). The "inness" of the "in," though captured sometimes along the way in some of Sartre's best descriptions, is always pushed aside again by the "over-against" of the detached consciousness confronting its Other.

Heideggerian *Dasein,* secondly, is essentially historical and belongs in its lived world precisely because it is historical. Heidegger's concept of temporality is, again, radically anti-Cartesian. Time for Heidegger, that is, "lived" or "existential" time, is the stretch of a personal history which thrusts itself into the future as what it is resolved to be, doing so out of its past—the past, at the same time, of the world into which it has been thrown—yet always drawn aside from this primary aim by its attraction to the present. *Dasein,* even inauthentic, everyday *Dasein, is* because it "temporalizes," living its past toward its future, despite its present, or, if it attains authentic existence, resolved to make its past truly inwardly historical in its assimilation of the authentic present to its destiny. Sartre, on the other hand, is in search of a Cartesian instant which, could he find it, would be, if temporal at all, withdrawn from the stretch of time.

And yet, as we shall see in more detail later, there is much that Sartre has taken over from Heidegger's account. Man has to make himself: he is his future as his possibility. Sartre's "project" is a translation of Heidegger's "resolve," which is directed to what is yet to come. But though making himself he is not his own foundation: he has to make himself out of his past, out of what contingency provides him with—these bodily endowments, this family, these neighbors, this society. All this is past, a translation, again: Sartre's concept of "facticity," of radical contingency, is, at first sight at least, but a Gallic rendering of Heidegger's "throwness," or *Geworfenheit,* which expresses the sedimentation of the past.

Yet even where Sartre speaks in temporal terms, the relation between the three temporal modalities is fundamentally different in the two philosophers. For Heidegger, the primary tense is future: it is his self-transcendence, his being-ahead of himself that primarily defines man. The synonym of transcendence is existentiality: for self-transcendence is fundamentally what existence *is*. So for Sartre, one may say, is the project: if there is for him any one most basic philosophical axiom, it is that man must make himself; he has to be in aspiration what he is not in fact, and that means, to *not* be what he is in his own projection of himself. But even for the project, the ideal is instantaneous self-creation, choice NOW. And in the light of this ideal, temporalization is the *loss* of the instant. It is flight. So he describes it, again and again. The moment of the pre-reflective *cogito,* the moment of pure reflection, difficult, if not impossible, of attainment: these moments of conscious being are what I forever flee. I escape from self-making into a past to which I gave a false substantiality: it is my history, my ego, as a thing. I escape into the future, into an imagined—and therefore nihilating—vision of what I am not. Sartre does indeed borrow much from Heidegger on temporality. But from all his excursions into Daseins-analysis he is pulled back, every time, by the lure of the instant. Except for dread, which is momentary— which is perhaps the only true instant I might, with luck, achieve—he sees the span of time, in Heidegger's terms the original structure of time, in the last analysis as a falling off, an escape from what ideally ought to be into what (alas) is. From the thought of the Cartesian pure self-conscious moment he darts out as far as it will let him in the direction of Heideggerian being-in-the-world, only to be pulled back, time and again, to the center that holds him fast. He is, to use a favorite word of his own, haunted by the instant. The primacy of time as stretching and stretched eludes him.

In the case of freedom the situation is more difficult to disentangle. For one thing, Sartre's concept of freedom is Cartesian through and through. Cartesian freedom is not just there as ideal, hovering over his thought, so to speak; freedom for him is Cartesian freedom, substantively, to its very core. And for another thing, freedom explicitly appears, in *Being and Time,* only in the description of authentic existence, as "Freedom to Death." But this concept of Being to Death is one that Sartre emphatically rejects. (My death *is* something to others rather than to me.) It is the description of being-in-the-world at the everyday level that Sartre seems chiefly to follow, and this is not, explicitly at least, an analysis in terms of freedom as such. Nor does Sartre's use of "freedom" resemble its development in Heidegger's "On *the Essence of Ground"* where it is a central concept. On the contrary, Heidegger has there begun to make more explicit the rooting of human being in Being, in this case through an identification of freedom and "ground," a relation which, though already present in *Sein und Zeit,* has come more and more to dominate much of his later work. Such a conception of being Sartre would certainly reject.

Nevertheless, the portrait of the for-itself, free yet caught by facticity, making itself yet always out there in the world, plainly derives much from Heidegger's analysis of human being. If the bone structure of Sartrean freedom is Cartesian, much of the physiognomy bears a Heideggerian stamp. First, as I have already pointed out, Sartre's concept of man's self-making is conceived in terms that run closely parallel to Heidegger's. Not that the "project" *really* is Heidegger's "resolve." The being-in-the-world of *Being and Nothingness* is a very different condition from that of *Being and Time.* As we have already seen, even the "in" is different. So is the world: primarily, it is the inertial, the pure exteriority of classical physics. The "things ready to hand" which are the "nearest things to me" in Heidegger's version have, in Sartre's case, to be derived by a complicated argument revealing first my body, then the Other, and finally the human world as a set of techniques which I can use. Again, Descartes's *thinking mind* and *extended matter,* if de-substantialized, remain to haunt, and dichotomize, the world. But many of the single concepts, though woven into a characteristically Sartrean pattern, are, as we have seen, certainly derivative from *Being and Time.*

Sartre follows Heidegger, moreover, in distinguishing an inauthentic from an authentic style of existence—in distinguishing, in other words, our fundamental freedom from the enslavement to which we (freely) bind ourselves in our ordinary lives. The insistence that at one and the same time we have as free beings to make ourselves, and invariably fail to do so, is one of the principal themes of what is usually called existentialism, and its outstanding recent expositors have been precisely Heidegger and Sartre. Of course here, too, there are differences. For example, in Heidegger's account, "forfeiture," my loss in the "they," is inescapable. Even the rare authentic individual cannot escape it. Sartre's bad faith, on the other hand, would, one gathers, be left behind by the true self-creator, could such a one arise. And authenticity itself has a different goal: it is being to death in the one case, and in the other the pure choice of myself. Dread, the dizzying sense of nothingness, has the same function for both philosophers: it is the unique experience which may raise to true freedom him who faces it. But, again, its object is different: for Heidegger, my own finitude, my annihilation in death; for Sartre, the non-being, the emptiness of the "self" I have to make.

How then can we sum up the relation of Sartre to Heidegger? Best, perhaps, in terms of Sartre's relation to

Descartes and Husserl as well. Fundamentally Cartesian in sympathy and starting-point, Sartre has taken the turn to intentionality, from *cogito* to *cogitiatio,* and within the medium of consciousness, wholly alien to Heidegger's own thought, has interjected a number of central Heideggerian themes. They are still recognizable, yet, transposed into consciousness, also altered, if not in their appearance, then in their ontological import.

Such an interweaving of disparate themes could be achieved, however, only with philosophical tools alien to phenomenology itself. They have to be treated dialectically. And indeed it is the dialectical strand in Sartre's thinking, derived from a different tradition, that carries his argument even in *Being and Nothingness* and has since come more and more to dominate his thought. It is to that other line of influence that we must turn before we can see how the two principal inheritances are worked together in *Being and Nothingness* itself and later (though with a very different balance of ingredients) in the *Critique.*

chapter three: sartre and his predecessors

II. the dialecticians

dialectic

Being and Nothingness
bears the subtitle *An Essay on
Phenomenological Ontology*. Phenomenology as such, however, at least in Husserl's sense, stringently abstains from ontological
inquiry. The "things themselves" it seeks to describe
are "things" as consciously experienced; their "being" be-

yond or before the *epoché* is not in question. To become ontology—an inquiry into being—philosophical reflection must move beyond description; the philosopher must question what he sees about its being. To put such a question would be inappropriate to a method of pure description. Admittedly, Heidegger began as a phenomenologist, yet his philosophizing is directed, first and last, to "the question of being"; indeed, he asks about human being only because this is the only being for whom its being is in question. But what Heidegger starts from, as we have seen, is not the "data" of pure consciousness; it is being-in-the-world that is the medium of his inquiry. And being-in-the-world already entails an "understanding of being" which gives the ontologist matter to look at in what might still appear a quasi-phenomenological fashion. If one starts, like Sartre, with the *cogito,* however, no such recourse is available. To move from the *cogito* to the question of being, one must move from description to some other style of philosophical inquiry.

The means Sartre has chosen for this movement is dialectical. Indeed, in the *Critique,* as its title implies, the dialectical method has come to dominate his thought. The whole argument of that book is in fact a defense of "dialectical reason" and an attack on its contrary, "analytical reason," as the possible tool of social and political understanding. But even in *Being and Nothingness* it is the admixture of dialectic with description—or, better, the weaving of description into a dialectical argument—that characterizes the peculiar mode of Sartrian phenomenology. I have already given an example of this process in the case of Sartre's "phenomenological" study of the past. Now let us see if we can establish at least approximately what "dialectic" consists in, first in general—at least in post-Kantian philosophy—and then in the particular case of Sartre in so far as his method is related to that of his predecessors, especially to Hegel, the founder and greatest practitioner of this method of modern philosophy, and through him to his two great critics (and followers), Kierkegaard and Marx.

Hegelian dialectic, like phenomenology, though it came a century earlier, was meant to liberate philosophy. Phenomenology was intended to take us back to the things themselves, to a broader vision of the content and activities of conscious life than conventional methods or the prejudices of traditional metaphysics and epistemology had permitted. Nineteenth-century dialectic had also undertaken a liberating return—not in the first instance to things, but to thought. Where phenomenology was to seek intellectual vision, dialectic had attempted to enter into the life of thought itself in its inmost and living development. Kierkegaard complained of Hegelian dialectic that the System was never finished. At its best, it was not meant to be. It was Thought itself as alive, as moving, not as completed, even in the profoundest insight. Dialectic is a process, not a state; it is a movement of concepts. Yet it is not the movement of proof. Dialectic is not, in the logician's sense, logic. A logical argument is always equivalent to the statements "A is A" or "Not both A and non-A." If it contains more than this tautology, it is invalid. For in strict logic one can elicit from the premises of an argument only what is already contained in them. But dialectic is the *development* of concepts: they grow under the philosopher's touch; at the end of his reflection they are not what they seemed to be at first—and yet they are also more than they seemed to be.

That may sound like nonsense. Surely, it may be objected, a concept must be precisely defined. What follows from it, follows, and what doesn't, doesn't. If one fails to admit such rules of logic, not only does one talk nonsense, one cannot talk at all. Of course, in fact "one's mind wanders"; one starts out thinking about one thing and is "reminded" of another. I look at the pampas grass in my garden and am reminded of the pampas grass staff carried by the leader of the "vizards" at an Irish Halloween. But this is a purely contingent and external conjunction. Experience, atomic in its elements, produces by the "gentle force of association" (or, in modern terms, "conditioning") the conjunction of disparate contents. One can hardly call this a "concept" "developing". Pampas grass is pampas grass, wherever I happen to have seen it or to whatever use it happens to be put. Now it must indeed be admitted that ordinary logic is uniquely binding; to abandon it altogether would mean to abandon discourse of any reasonable kind. And it must also be admitted that experience often ranges externally and associatively over logically stable and disparate units. But are the units we conjoin in thinking really atomistic in their nature, and is the movement of joining them exclusively associative in its procedure? It seems that to get somewhere, at least somewhere new and interesting, thought must move in a fashion somehow different from this.

Here I am, for example, thinking about dialectic. I have to write a chapter about its influence on Sartre. Every time I start a chapter, there is blank paper and myself, and I can't imagine what led me to think I could fill it in with anything that makes sense. I had an outline in mind for the whole book, but each time I begin on a part of it there seems to be next to nothing there. When I think of Hegelian dialectic, in particular, I think first (by association if you like) of formulae like "substance must become subject," which, I must confess, means to me nothing or worse than nothing: it means a lot of word-juggling and pretended system-building. But then I think of the concept of a growth of thought, and I wonder if this process of writing isn't, on a small scale, an instance of dialectic in that sense. When I tried, for example, in the preceding chapter, to explain the difference between a phenomenological and a literary description of consciousness, I found, in talking about the relative weight of the imaginative and intellectual components, that there was also a difference between participation in the one case and re-enactment in the other. I hadn't known that before; my concept of phenomenological description had developed. And here I am, it seems, hoping to go through the same process with "dialectic." So my thinking seems to instantiate the Hegelian conception: the concept I am thinking about develops as I think about it in ways I hadn't dreamed of. Before this the Hegelian method had always seemed to me almost a pure fraud; now I find that there is something it's about—namely, the very process I am going through in trying to understand it. Perhaps, then, the best model for Hegelian dialectic is heuristic: thought in search of what it does not yet know. Formal, logical proof is a device to encase thought *found:* when we know what we have and want to find it an elegant dress. Even in mathematics there is that duality. The great German mathematician Gauss is said to have remarked that he first discovered a theorem and then tried to prove it. And the most famous account of discovery, of the search for the unknown, is by the mathematician Henri Poincaré. But if there is a growth of thought even in the most formal science, how much more must this be so for philosophical reflection. One lets a concept germinate; it flowers, not as some seed catalogue had promised, but surprisingly. It is this notion of a self-unfolding, a self-development of thought that forms the core—at least to non-Hegelians, the intelligible core—of the dialectical method. Instead of starting at the outset with precisely defined concepts, one starts with a concept and watches it develop, engages oneself in its development, so that the concept itself is richer at the close of one's inquiry than it appeared at the beginning. Dialectical argument in philosophy, then, is (minimally) argument in which the concepts themselves are transformed as the argument proceeds.

Let me give an example of this from the history of philosophy. Immanuel Kant was a philosopher who certainly did not consider himself a dialectical thinker. For Kant, "dialectic" means fallacious argument; the Dialectic of Pure Reason for him is a set of invalid speculative arguments which Reason inevitably but unsuccessfully develops. Yet as the British Hegelian Edward Caird demonstrated, Kant's *Critique of Pure Reason* is itself a dialectical work in the sense I have just suggested. This is clearly so, for example, in Kant's treatment of "space" and "time." These two concepts first occur, in the Aesthetic, as the twin forms of all appearance: all outer sense is spatial, while all sense, outer and inner, is temporal. In the Analytic, however, this symmetry is broken. In his analysis of the activity of mind in organizing (or having organized) experience, Kant gives time first place as that from which the argument proceeds. Taking subjective temporal experience as the minimal starting point, he shows that it is the categorial rule-giving of the mind, ultimately held together by the fact that I *could* unite all my experience by an "I think," which has always already transformed such a pure subjective flow of "experience" into the experience of objects: of an organized nature in objective space and time. Thus time as subjective is the minimal starting point, and the objective space-time of nature the issue of the argument. Temporality and spatiality themselves have developed from the parallelism of the Aesthetic to their roles as principium and issue respectively of the Analytic. And of course time itself develops in the Analytic also: from the purely inner-sense time of the Subjective Deduction through the homogeneous temporal patterns of the Schematism to the objective time that is produced as correlate of space in the Objective Deduction and the Principles. Any argument whose concepts thus develop as it proceeds is dialectical in the sense we have been considering here.

Nevertheless, this is a minimal concept of dialectic as Hegelians intend it. For if Kant's method is one of "isolation," this means that the whole panorama was there from the beginning. Experience is structured as the whole *Critique* finds it to be. If our understanding develops as we follow its argument, the structure of experience was always already there, eternally, as it is and as we are coming to see it. Hegelian dialectic is much more radical than this. For Hegel insists that, if thought develops, its object too develops, and by the very same process. Or if it doesn't, it's an inferior object, fit only for the maneuvers of ordinary logic, not for philosophy. In real conceptual thought, Hegel insists, the "firm ground" that ordinary (logical) reasoning possesses in the ordinary logical subject at rest "begins to sway," and this swaying movement itself "becomes the object of thought." [1] Thus the very development of thought, Hegel alleges, is at the same time the development of its object—or better, perhaps, the development of thought is thought's own object.

But is this so? Can one identify thinking and what it is the thinking of, and say that the development of thought is also the development of what the thought is thought of? The concept of the atom, for example, has developed almost out of recognition since its inception in Ancient

Greece with Leucippus and Democritus. But whatever the foundation in nature, which, through atomism, man has been seeking to understand, *that* surely is still the same. Even if nature itself is basically process, its development is not to be identified with the development of our own conception of it. However theory-laden scientific concepts, laws, and principles may be, and however deeply theories are influenced by the *Zeitgeist* of a given discipline in a given period, what such concepts, laws, and principles aim at is an understanding of something that transcends the act of understanding, of something that lies beyond the theory's understanding of it. Scientific knowledge has often been equated with prediction and truth with verifiability. That would perhaps be a truncated Hegelian concept, for if the truth of a matter is what we will be able to verify about it, then the object (what is known) does develop with the subject—in this case, the experimental scientist. But that is precisely what science does not do. It seeks to find out how things work, not how scientists work. Even a pragmatic concept of truth, when carefully formulated, like C. S. Peirce's, makes it plain that what knowledge (at least natural knowledge) is after is not prediction for prediction's sake, but the indefinite range of unforeseeable future consequences which are the mark of the real. Our thoughts *about* a natural phenomenon may develop indefinitely, but the phenomenon itself always outruns our thinking about it; the two are never identical, the development of the thinking is never identical with the development, in nature, of what it is the thinking about.

Now up to a point—or beyond a certain point, perhaps—I think Hegel would have had to admit this. Whatever his merits in other fields, that is why he is such a superficial philosopher of nature. But what if we are thinking about experience itself rather than about its external objects? Then, surely, our very experience is transformed by our thinking about it. Experience reflected on can never again be naïve; it has been transformed by my thought about it. It is the experience it was—it is presented in memory, or at least leaves its "traces" in my life history, even if not remembered. But it has also irrevocably vanished; I can never, having reflected, have that non-reflective immediate experience again. Yet at the same time, since it has acquired a new dimension through my reflection, my experience has also been enriched. That is in fact the chief movement of Hegelian dialectic, embodied in the ambiguity of the German *"aufheben":* a given reality is cancelled, yet preserved and elevated to a higher level of reflection. And for the individual's experience there seems, at least with respect to the relation of naïve to reflective experience, to be something in it.

The range of Hegelian dialectic, however, far outruns individual consciousness. It is humanity, not the schoolmaster of Jena or even the Berlin professor, whose "development" Hegel claims to be re-creating. In his *Logic,* the systematic crown of the Dialectic, he even claims to be re-creating "the thoughts of God before creation." Is this an empty boast, or is there really a content in Hegel's work to match this claim? It is sometimes said that the merit of Hegel is in fact the rich empirical content of his writing. Because of the very generality of his fundamental concepts he can fill them in with a mosaic of what would now count as sociology or psychology much more illuminating than the narrow philosophy of the Enlightenment could provide. And the movement of the dialectic, exhibiting the manifold phases of a given kind of experience, may prove applicable when one turns from it to the real world to find instances of the structures one has been expounding. Sometimes, on the other hand, it is history that Hegel is said to illuminate most profoundly: the development of "the Western mind" from Greece through Rome and Christianity, to the French Revolution. Now admittedly all this may indeed be mined out of Hegel's work. Yet his own claim, and that of his chief philosophical followers, has nevertheless been more dogmatic. It is not only the empirical or historical, but the eternal unfolding of Being itself as absolute mind, that he constantly insists on as the ontological foundation of his method. One ought not to save him for common sense by ignoring entirely his own claim.

In any case, it is Sartre's debt to the dialecticians, not "dialectic" as such, that interests us here. And what Sartre takes over from Hegel is not the empirical content of his work, though he sometimes treats of some of it, nor his insight into history; what Sartre adopts from Hegel goes much deeper than any particular bits of information or ways of classifying them. Admittedly, the Hegelian influence comes relatively late in Sartre's career, but it goes deep. Sartre is Hegelian, and has become increasingly so, first in his style of philosophizing, in the way he uses concepts. Further, the central concepts he uses both in *Being and Nothingness* and in the *Critique,* also belong, if not to Hegel, then certainly to the German idealist tradition. And finally, however emphatically he may claim to reject systematizing speculation in general and idealist systems in particular, there is also something in Hegel's ontology itself that Sartre retains. Let us see if we can sort out these three aspects of his debt, focusing chiefly on *Being and Nothingness,* but with an occasional glance at the *Critique* for confirmation or contrast.

Sartre and Hegel

First, his method. The structure of Sartre's argument, in both his major philosophical works, *Being and Nothingness* and the *Critique,* is dialectical in the minimal sense described above. He opens up avenues along which he can let his basic concepts move—in a movement which is also to alter them, so that they become, at the end of the argument, different and richer than they were at the beginning. He does not (at least in *Being and Nothingness*) set up premises from which to draw correct logical conclusions; instead he sets up starting points from which to move to surprising, even contradictory, positions, which nevertheless combine with what precedes to take him along to still further surprising combinations. Granted, again, even the most inspired dialectician cannot abandon ordinary logic; if he did, he could not argue anything in any style. But "ordinary logic," for the dialectician, is an uninteresting, dead skeleton of thought. It is thought's growth that interests him.

Compare, for example, Sartre's ontological argument, proving the existence of Being in itself, with the traditional one, proving the existence of God. The most perfect being, St. Anselm said, must exist. For suppose you think of a most perfect being which does not exist. Non-existence is an imperfection, a lack; so this is not the most perfect being: you can think of a more perfect being —the one who does exist. The argument is, on the face of it, a *reductio ad absurdum.* A non-existent most perfect being is a non-perfect most perfect being; therefore the very concept "most perfect being" already entails the existence of the entity of which it is the concept. Now of course it has often been argued—either against Anselm or even for him (in the first instance by Anselm himself in his reply to Gaunilon)—that this is no "argument," but the elucidation by one of the faithful of his faith. If I did not believe in God as the real, existent, most perfect being, I could not work the argument. But that (*contra* Kant) is just what makes it a *good* argument, not a bad one. I, the believer, am eliciting, in logical style, the implications of the proposition: there is God. The non-believer cannot follow my argument, not because it does not follow from my assertion, but because he has not made the assertion. Indeed, he asserts its contradictory; so how could he possibly draw the same conclusion? The argument may be a *petitio principii,* but it is so only in the sense in which all sound arguments contain in their premises what will follow in the conclusion.

Now look at Sartre's ontological argument (or a very free paraphrase of it). His starting point is consciousness, here-now, as the consciousness it is. But consciousness *is* not simply; it is *"for-itself,"* that is, aware of itself. There is a doubleness, a reflexivity, about consciousness. The lawn in the park is just there, the man passing by it is there too, but by knowing he is there he has both doubled its being there and separated himself from it: he *could* be elsewhere. And yet it is not really himself the man passing by is (thetically) aware of. What he is aware of is that, strolling through the park, he is on his way home. Consciousness, Sartre has learned from Husserl, is never simply of itself, but of something which it is not. Thus the very reality of the man passing by, as the reality of a consciousness, is for-itself *as* directed toward what is not for-itself—toward the simple reality, the "being in-itself," of the lawn, the park, the apartment over beyond the park that he is walking *toward.* The for-itself in its very nature as for-itself points to the in-itself. Thus if we understand the for-itself, if we really think about *its* nature, we are directed from it to the in-itself, to its essential target. But the for-itself does not *contain* the in-itself, as a premise contains its conclusion, as God (who, if He is, is in—and for—Himself) contains His own existence. No: we move, we are moved, from the for-itself *to* the in-itself, whose otherness, whose negation, the for-itself is. The man is not the lawn; as a conscious being he is the being who makes the lawn, who makes the park, the-stretch-to-be-traveled between himself and home. It may *be* as the pleasant green sward that he can stroll across before he has to trudge the less pleasantly resilient pavement; it may *be* as the short-cut he can take to hurry belatedly to an important rendezvous. In either case, indeed in any case, it is what he takes it for; and yet however he takes it, however he possesses it, he takes it as what is not himself—at leisure or in haste, contentedly or nervously—but the space he has to cross to get where he is going, and he is the consciousness he is as its other, as the need to transcend it, to get to the other side. Thus the for-itself refers us away from itself to the in-itself as its necessary other, the not-for-itself to which, in its being as for-itself, it is necessarily directed.

Now, admittedly, in this to-and-fro movement from consciousness to its contrary, from for-itself to in-itself, as Sartre calls it, we already have, in little, the whole argument of *Being and Nothingness*. In this sense one could say that Sartre, like any philosopher, is only going to elicit from his premises what is already contained in them. And even in the *Critique,* as we shall see, though he has dropped the concepts "for-itself" and "in-itself" as basic categories, he is laboring deviously and painfully to elicit a social theory from the same premises from which he had been arguing in the earlier work. But the premises themselves, I think it is fair to say, are clearly dialectical. For it is the contradiction between consciousness and nature, between for-itself and in-itself, that makes the whole thing work. The logical use of contradiction, as in Anselm's argument, is to eliminate an impossible—because a self-contradictory—position, and so, indirectly, to support the position one wishes to defend. But in dialectical argument it is "contradiction"—or at least contrariety—that makes a new position possible: thought takes a position, finds it "contradicting" itself, takes a new position modifying, and thus in a sense "denying," the first, a position which, opening onto a new "denial," leads to a new position, and so on. Only by seeing the second position as "contradicting" the first and by assimilating it as a new position are we enabled to move at all. In this sense, illogical though it may sound, dialectical argument uses contradiction, not indirectly, through the *reductio,* but directly, as the very engine of its movement. It is not just any statement of what there is, any set of primitive propositions, from which Sartre is seeking to deduce first his theory of the individual and later of society. It is the living relation of intentionality to its object, the relation of consciousness to what it is consciousness of, which is not what it is and is what it is not: it is this relation, vexing and in appearance contradictory, yet capable of application to every field of conscious life, that Sartre is exploring and developing— if in different modes, as well as with different content—in both his major works.

In *Being and Nothingness,* as we have seen, phenomenological descriptions—Pierre not in the café, the girl "innocently" letting a would-be lover hold her hand, the exhausted hiker throwing down his rücksack—are the perches, so to speak, from which the flight of the argument takes wing. The description is opened out so that a movement of concepts develops from it. Pierre's absence haunts the café: it is not just this collection of faces and table and waiters and chit-chat, it *is*—where Pierre is not. In the scene itself the looseness from what is, the otherness than being, that marks the human condition becomes apparent to us. One may wonder, perhaps, what would have happened if Pierre had been there. Would we have had a plenum of being and so have missed the move to otherness which makes the argument go? No, of course not. Pierre would have failed me somehow. He would have denied the favor I had come to beg of him; or he would have aged since our last meeting twenty years ago. Somehow Pierre-not-being-my-idea-of-Pierre would have haunted our meeting, even had we met. But the descriptions Sartre uses are nevertheless characteristically those that will most effectively make the ferment of contradiction work. And similarly, his arguments work by finding contradiction as their outcome. Thus out of the move to being as what consciousness is directed to, he raises the question of the question—and the question, it appears, is that to which one may obtain a negative reply. I seek, and may not find. Surely sometimes I seek and find. But such a quietus of consciousness is not what would help dialectic, and especially Sartrean dialectic, on its course. The to-and-fro of position and negation is what makes the argument move, from start to finish.

So far I have been trying to characterize Sartre's method as dialectical; but inevitably the concepts he is working with have also already been exhibiting their characteristically Hegelian stamp. The overall movement of Hegelian dialectic is from mere being, in-itself, through consciousness, for-itself, to what Hegel considers the ultimate ground of all reality—the Concept as Being-in-and-for-itself. Sartre, good Cartesian as he is, begins with consciousness, the for-itself, but is directed by Husserl to its target, which, in Hegelian fashion, he describes as sheer being, as the in-itself. The for-itself-in-itself is then what his for-itself is in search of. Being in the mode of what is other than being, it longs to be simply, or rather to be what it is—that is, to be for-itself and so not to be simply, and yet to be for-itself as being is, as being pure and simple. The major Hegelian concepts, therefore, take on a new movement and lead us to a different, and much less self-satisfied, finale. But they are the very same Hegelian counters, though used in a different context and with a different intent.

Indeed, the very concepts "Being" and "Nothingness," as Sartre uses them, are Hegelian. Compare, for example, in its very broadest outlines, the ontology of Sartre's *Being and Nothingness* with that of Heidegger in *Being and Time*. Both works are concerned with Being; both works make a great deal of Nothing or of a sense of Nothingness—of what Sartre calls nihilation—as somehow essential to human life. And both works are phenomenological: they seek to describe the essential structures of human existence as being-in-the-world. For Heidegger, however, Being is the framework of the investigation from the very start, temporality is discovered as its essence, nothing as the end—in death—to which its temporality must ultimately relate. In one phase of the work after another, he is recurrently boring into some part of a total structure which is always already there from the start. Sartre, on the other hand, uses Nothingness to open up Being: it is Nihilation that makes the for-itself the being it is—namely, the being that has to be what it is not and not be what it is. Instead of digging down into *Dasein,* as Heidegger does to uncover the temporality on which it has always already rested, a temporality which had been half seen in the inadequate understanding of Being characteristic of the human manner of being in the world,

Sartre takes a pair of contraries, Being and Nothingness or Being and non-Being, and lets them work on one another to show us the kind of being we have to be. Being and time are not dialectical opposites; far from it. Time, for Heidegger, is the inmost sense of being; "nothing" serves, through dread, as agency to reveal that truth. "Being" and "Nothingness," on the other hand, are the dialectical contraries par excellence: the first pair of the whole Hegelian system, out of which all else is made to grow. It is temporality, indeed, that comes between, in this case, as my consciousness flees its own nothingness, trying vainly to find a solider being in the pseudo-substantiality of my past or the deceptive promise of my future. Thus though Sartre calls his work "phenomenological ontology," that description applies more clearly to Heidegger's magnum opus, while in Sartre's case even the phenomenological aspect is in large part a means of access to an argument that is Hegelian, not only in method, but also in the conceptual apparatus with which it works.

In the *Critique,* moreover, Hegelian concepts as well as Hegelian method have become even more strikingly dominant. The phenomenological and even the long historical descriptions are ruthlessly assimilated into a series of moves with concepts like necessity, intelligibility, alienation: concepts that have characterized modern dialectical philosophy from Hegel to the present. We shall see more of these concepts when we examine the arguments of both books. But the point here is simply this: even the "Being" of Heidegger's and Sartre's titles differs profoundly, precisely through the Hegelian character of the latter. Heidegger's "Being" is typically his own—though allegedly Parmenidean, Nietzschean, or what you will, it is decidedly not Hegelian. It is not the opening counter in the series of dialectical moves, but the all-enclosing medium, the Being through which all beings are. Sartre's "Being" *is* Hegelian: the other-than Non-Being in relation to which the Being of human being in its very non-being, in its alienation from being, is to be exposed.

If Sartre's chief concepts are Hegelian, moreover, so, in a sense, is the ontology that he builds with them. Of course he is not, like Hegel, an "absolute idealist," or so he vigorously insists. Yet there are remnants in his thought even of this: both of the "absoluteness" of Hegelian thought and of its idealism, the former in both *Being and Nothingness* and the *Critique,* the latter chiefly in the argument of the later work.

First, as to Hegelian "absolutism," or the hope of an all-inclusive issue of philosophy in identity with an all-inclusive reality: this issue Sartre admittedly despairs of, yet, as a desideratum, it dominates his thought. In *Being and Nothingness* man wants to become God, and fails. In the *Critique* Sartre tries to lay the groundwork for understanding history, and that would mean, he makes plain, to understand it as a *whole:* as totalization. By why, if I seek anything—and of course, as human, I do—must I seek *absolute* Being? Why, to understand history, must I understand it *all?* Only the spirit of Hegel—and the Spirit of Hegel, the Absolute Mind which all reality imperfectly reveals—could give the answer. That spirit—of needing totality, even while admitting our inability to achieve it— plainly broods over Sartre's work.

But what about Hegel's idealism? This, surely, Sartre has relentlessly abandoned. In terms of *Being and Nothingness,* the for-itself is always out there—in the world, with the in-itself, as its negation to be sure, but with no content other than that negation. In that sense—as what is there to not be—it is the in-itself that makes the for-itself be what it is not. Even if, as we shall see, my body is known as all consciousness, it works the other way too; my consciousness, as to its content, is all body. And in terms of the *Critique:* well, Sartre is allegedly a Marxist. The dialectic is material; there is no reality except the existent, practical, biological organism, and the non-living inert matter in which it finds, and through which it tries to fulfill, its material needs.

Yet there is an idealistic aspect to both arguments, more emphatically (if paradoxically) in the explicitly "Marxist" one. Body comes in late in *Being and Nothingness,* not as lived, but as known, as the explicit object of knowledge. It is consciousness that is both starting place and framework of the whole; consciousness in its quintessential being as choice, as agency, is firmly opposed to its other: passivity, exteriority, or body. Even the emotions, as we have noted in Sartre's early treatise on that subject, and as is still the case in the account of *Being and Nothingness,* are not "bodily passions" invading consciousness, but modes of choice, magical devices of consciousness for acting on the world. Consciousness is no longer substance, as for Descartes, acting, and sometimes being acted on by, that other substance, body, to which it is so strangely and closely allied. Consciousness is pure act, always act, it never stops acting: we are "condemned to be free." And so Hegel is vindicated. Substance has become subject with a vengeance.

In the *Critique,* moreover, the whole point of the argument is to prove that there *is* a dialectic which can be understood in history: and that means not just a movement of class-antagonisms over and above the people who suffer from this movement. It means a movement in which the "practical organisms" engaged in action and in suffering understand, out of and in their own actions, the movements of which they form part. What Sartre claims to object to in Marxism is that it leaves out of its dialectic the individual existent, the freely self-chosen project of the for-itself. But what he really seems to be objecting to as the argument proceeds is the alleged failure of Marxism to make dialectical necessity "intelligible"—and that seems to mean, for him, a failure to identify dialectical processes with the self-understanding of the agents who shape them and are shaped by them. A process that is truly dialectical must be intelligible. But what does it mean to be intelligible? To be intelligible must mean to be of the nature of reason; it must be the understanding of itself by itself. Substance, again, becomes subject: only the reflective coalescence of the material happening with its conscious, its ideal meaning, makes it what it really is. However grounded in matter, in need, in scarcity, in the facts of economic and political life, this is still idealism. In its ontological import, as well as in important aspects of its method and in the provenance and meaning of its central concepts, Sartre's philosophy owes to the Hegelian at least as much as it does to the phenomenological tradition.

Sartre and Kierkegaard

With this very sketchy account of his relation to Hegel, however, we have not finished with Sartre's debt to the Hegelians. We must take account of his debt to Kierkegaard and Marx, Hegel's two greatest nineteenth-century critics. For Sartre's dialectic uniquely combines themes from all three.

The kinship of Sartre's philosophy with Kierkegaard's is obvious, and has been much discussed. Kierkegaard was the first "existentialist"; Sartre is the greatest latter-day "existentialist." True, the label was thrust on Sartre, but he has accepted and even adopted it. Kierkegaard, finding in Hegel's dialectic an empty play with ideas, had insisted that what matters is the dialectic, not of essence, but of existence—and by this he meant human, indeed, subjective, existence. Taking dialectic not only in its methodological, but also in its ontological aspect, he urged his reader to plunge into the real development, not of some "Absolute," but of his living, suffering self. And a century later Sartre remarks: ". . . we ought to oppose to Hegel Kierkegaard, who represents the claims of the individual as such." [2] The emphasis on dread (*angoisse*), moreover, as liberating mood, stems, historically, through Heidegger from Kierkegaard. True, in each of the three cases the situation that arouses dread is different. For Kierkegaard, dread is of my nothingness before my infinite Maker; for Heidegger, dread is of my coming nothingness in death; for Sartre, it is of my total responsibility for my own choice of myself, which, as nihilism, rests on—nothing. Yet dread in each case is somehow dread of nothing and it is dread in each case that can uniquely awaken the individual to his own true resolve.

All that is by now commonplace. Yet to speak of a major "influence" here seems questionable. That the first dialectic of the individual is Kierkegaard's is not to be denied, and Sartre acknowledges this priority. But all the influences that have been dealt with so far—Descartes's, Husserl's, Heidegger's, and Hegel's—form essential and inextricable strands of Sartre's thought. He has assimilated their thinking, or aspects of it, as deeply as he had assimilated in imagination the daring of his childhood heroes. His kinship with Kierkegaard, however, seems to me in the last analysis rather a parallelism than an influence. The individual in search of himself, finding himself, in that search, before an abyss of nothingness: that is, after all, the characteristic of our time. Its source could be said to be Nietzsche as much as Kierkegaard, or Dostoyevsky as well as a host of lesser literary figures. Or, as Raymond Aron does, one could refer it to Pascal, substituting the absence of God for God. Admittedly, Sartre not only refers to Kierkegaard in this connection, but also acknowledges the influence, if not of Kierkegaard directly, at least of Jean Wahl's existentialism. And at the beginning of his *Questions de Méthode* he treats briefly of Kierkegaard's existentialism in contrast to that of others, such as Jaspers. Yet one cannot imagine Sartre really steeped in the reading of Kierkegaard as one is sure that he has steeped himself in the writings of his other sources. The two thinkers differ too extremely both in interest and in philosophical style.

Kierkegaard considered himself primarily—as Louis Mackay has ably argued—"a kind of poet," one who uses philosophy for poetic ends.[3] Sartre, we have seen, is certainly not a poet, and, at least as we are considering him here, he is not even primarily an imaginative prose writer. He is a philosopher who has sometimes cast his arguments in fictional or dramatic form. True, both men have produced a corpus of literary-philosophical works which form in each case a coherent whole. But to understand what Sartre has to say as philosopher we can use the tools of philosophy: the conventional knowledge of the history of thought, imaginative re-enactment of philosophical description, conceptual participation in the course of dialectical argument. To understand what Kierkegaard has to say, except in a few sections of his most "philosophical" writings, in particular the *Philosophical Bits* and *Unscientific Postscript,* we have to read him as we would a poet: lingering in his moods, revelling in his language, his wit and humor, his irony.

Moreover, Kierkegaard is a religious poet, while

Sartre's philosophy is programmatically atheistic. Kierkegaardian dread stems from the individual's dizzying awareness of his distance from the Maker to whom he owes his very Being. The Sartrean individual is utterly alone, wholly responsible, making himself as the negation of a barren field of being, in itself wholly devoid of meaning, or even, in its inertia, of power. When the Sartrean for-itself is threatened, moreover, it is primarily by the Other, who rises up as an alternative center of existence. Kierkegaard, it seems, never really noticed the human Other, even as Hell. It is Abraham confronting God that moves us in *Fear and Trembling;* Isaac is a stick. It is the seducer who matters in the aesthetic stage of *Either-Or;* Cordelia is a null. It is Judge William, the ideal married man, who is supposed to matter in the ethical life, though he is stuffy and unreal enough; his wife can scarcely be said to exist at all. My inner consciousness, miserable sinner that I am—and God; these are the entities celebrated in Kierkegaard's poetry. It is the poetry of worship and of prayer, of an ingrown, breast-beating worship and prayer, alien or exaggerated even to many Christians, let alone to a thinker so far removed from religiosity as Sartre. Even as a negative limit of the for-itself's development, as suggested earlier, God, for Sartre, is the cause of itself, the for-itself-in-itself, Spinoza's one infinite, wholly complete, and wholly actual substance. For Kierkegaard, He is Father, Maker, and Master, stern Judge, and Merciful Pardoner of Sins. It is not His self-sufficiency which matters, but His overwhelming power and overflowing goodness. *"Causa sui"* would be from a Kierkegaardian point of view an empty phrase. So it is for Sartre, too, in the sense that it refers to no real entity; I cannot point to any Being that is or could be its denotatum. But as the ideal of what I seek and can *not* find it is significant, and crucially so, whereas God the Father for Sartre is simply an old gentleman whose acquaintance he made, briefly and superficially, in childhood, and with whom, he confesses, he might, given other circumstances, have got on well enough, but who in fact bowed out of his social circle long ago. Indeed, he not only doesn't know him any more; he has demonstrated that He can not exist—or rather that *causa sui,* his philosophical alias, is non-existent. The living God of Kierkegaard or Pascal is, for him, not even a worthy target for disproof.

Even as dialecticians the two writers differ, at least in the overall direction of their respective dialectics. Granted, they are both Hegelian, and as such their philosophical interests and arguments are similar, often strikingly so. Thus Sartre's use of modal concepts in *Being and Nothingness,* for example, is reminiscent of Kierkegaard on possibility and necessity in the *Bits.* In general, indeed, modal concepts seem to be dear to the hearts of dialectical philosophers. Sartre's account of the immediate structures of the for-itself, again, strikingly resembles Kierkegaard's account of the self in *The Sickness to Death.* Thus Kierkegaard, in a passage which is both a parody of Hegelian method and its apotheosis: "The self is a relation which relates itself to its own self, or it is that in the relation . . . that the relation relates itself to its own self; the self is not the relation but . . . [the fact] that the relation relates to its own self." [4] Sartre similarly detaches the self from substantial status, and makes it, though more negatively, relational: "The for-itself is the being which determines itself to exist in as much as it can not coincide with itself." [5] For both philosophers, moreover, this self-related being, the being which *is* the stretch of its own relation to itself, is grounded in a being other than itself. Kierkegaard writes: "Such a relation which relates itself to its own self (that is to say, a self) must either have constituted itself or have been constituted by another. . . . . Such a derived, constituted relation is the human self, a relation which relates itself to its own self, and in relating itself to its own self relates itself to another." [6] And Sartre: "The for-itself in its being is failure because it is the foundation only of itself as nothingness. In truth this failure is its very being, but it has meaning only if the for-itself apprehends itself as failure in the presence of the being which it has failed to be; that is, of the being which would be the foundation of its being and no longer merely the foundation of its nothingness—or, to put it another way, which would be its foundation as coincidence with itself. . . . Human reality is its own surpassing toward what it lacks; it surpasses itself towards the particular being which it would be if it were what it is. Human reality is not something which exists first in order afterwards to lack this or that; it exists first as lack and in immediate synthetic connection with what it lacks." [7] In the one case, to be sure, the transcendent Being to which we are referred is the Hebraeo-Christian God, and in the other, inert exterior Being-in-itself; yet both the movement of their thought and the insight it carries are closely parallel.

In short, the concepts both philosophers are working with have the kind of generality which characterizes Hegelian philosophizing, and their use is the kind of quick to-and-fro that, again, marks dialectical argument. One wants to say: word-juggling. How else can one characterize Kierkegaard's, "The disrelationship of despair is not a simple disrelationship but a disrelationship in a relation which relates itself to its own self"; [8] or Sartre's, "In order for being to be lacking or lacked, it is necessary that a being make itself its own lack; only a being which lacks can surpass being toward the lacked." [9] Yet there is not only brilliance in the juggling, in its speed and skill; through it one sometimes gains insight that the more moderate methods of analysis fail to achieve. It is irritating that this is so; there is surely something about the method too facile to be true, the concepts it uses are surely too entirely general to convey anything about concrete reality. Yet they do sometimes convey something: in this case, of the self-and-other relatedness of human being, a thesis fundamental to any adequate philosophy of man. In Kierkegaard's case, moreover, there is immense variety of psychological insight in his typology of despair; and there are similar observations of special cases here and there in *Being and Nothingness*. To make such comparisons here, however, would be tedious and irrelevant. I want simply to emphasize that both these philosophers are in fact practitioners of Hegelian dialectic at its best.

Yet they are dialecticians with a difference, both in their interests and in the devices they use to implement them. Kierkegaard, once more, is a religious poet: his aim is to bring himself—or his reader, could he find him—to tremble before God, to live *in* that terrible yet glorious confrontation. Sartre is an ontologist: however much he claims to stress the individual, it is the *Being* of the individual, his having to be what he is not and not be what he is, that he wants to exhibit and make intelligible. Kierkegaard seeks *indirect* communication: hence his host of pseudonyms. What he has to say is really the unsayable, one either lives it after him or fails to hear it. For Sartre, on the contrary, "all is significance." In its very nihilation, in its contradictions, human reality brings meaning to the world, makes even the in-itself intelligible. Reason must triumph. Even passion, we have seen, must be interpreted as action, because it must be rational: it must be some way, even if an absurd one, of making sense. If man "tries to become God and fails," at least he tries, and he must be able to give reasons for his efforts. Given these different aims, finally, their means of attaining them differ accordingly. However abstract Kierkegaard's manipulation of concepts in passages like those quoted, his aim is always existential: it is self-inspection and self-transformation that he is after. True, Sartre, in *Being and Nothingness* at least, taking off from phenomenology, often uses examples more concretely within his arguments, yet he seeks a much more general and conceptual issue. Kierkegaard engages his fictitious characters, scenes or stories, as well as his dialectical arguments, in the one aim of self-development of the religious life. Sartre devotes both description and dialectic to the cause of ontology: of seeking to understand the being of myself and the being other than myself that is the in-itself. "What we desire to appropriate in an object," he writes, "is being and is the world." [10] This is a Hegelian aim, as it has been the aim of all systematizing thinkers; it is the aim against which Kierkegaard rebels. Sartre, whatever concepts he has borrowed from Kierkegaard, and whatever methods he shares with him, far from abandoning the goal of the System, has made it his very own.

Sartre and Marxism

There remains the question of Sartre's relation to Marxism. This is a question I shall deal with more thoroughly when we come to the *Critique,* but let me put it briefly here in order to complete my account of Sartre's dialectical predecessors.

If Kierkegaard turned the dialectic to the individual's inner existence, Marx turned it, not only "right side up," but outward: to the material conditions of life, to labor and its exploitation by capital. How can one thinker coherently make both these moves at once—both inward to my consciousness and outward to the class struggle? Yet that is just what Sartre claims to have done. Indeed, he seems to have come to Hegel through Marx; it was dialectical materialism that led him to dialectic—but to existential dialectic, of all things. The three dialectics assumed their roles in his thought contemporaneously; if the Marxist one—in its peculiar Sartrean form—takes the stage more conspicuously in the *Critique,* it had been patiently waiting in the wings for its cue.

Sartre himself has told the story in the opening pages of the *Critique,* or rather of *Questions de Méthode,* the treatise on method written in the 1950's for a Polish journal, which forms its introduction. His formal education, he says there, though officially "idealist," had included no initiation into dialectical thought. The famous lectures of Kojève on reading Hegel took place between 1933 and 1939, when Sartre was already teaching philosophy in a *lycée.* In 1925, on the contrary, he writes, "the horror of dialectic was such that even Hegel was unknown to us." [11] Marx and Marxism, he says, were only referred to from the outside: Marx must be read "to be refuted." Even the communist students dared not refer to such topics in their official lives; they would have failed their examinations. Sartre did read *Capital* and *The German Ideology* in this period, but though he "understood it luminously," he confesses, he nevertheless understood it not at all. "To understand is to change, to advance on one's own; that reading did not change me." [12] Marxism came to him, not as political or social theory, but as a "reality": "the heavy presence, on my horizon, of the working masses, an enormous and sombre body that *lived* Marxism, that *practiced* it and that exercised from a distance an irresistible attraction on the petit bourgeois intellectuals." [13] This has been its primary role for Sartre all along: it is a reality that lures him, that moves him—he longs to serve it, to *be* it; but it is not *his* reality. At the time, he says, its philosophy did not seem to him and his contemporaries to have any privileged position. "We said to ourselves; 'Here are the conceptions of a German intellectual who lived in London in the middle of the last century.'" [14] And despite his later insistence that Marxism, or rather the position of Marx himself (as he interprets it) is the *only* philosophy of the twentieth century, this external relation to Marx has never been overcome. His very adulation of Marxism in the *Critique* and other postwar writings rings not quite true. "Marxism" as he conceives it seems still to be his Other, the Other to which he must surrender, yet on his own terms.

And these terms are still, as they were at the outset, existential. The reaction of his contemporaries to their idealist training, Sartre recalls, was to embrace against the smooth system of their teachers a darker and theoretically (though only theoretically) more violent mood. They revelled in Unamuno's "tragic sense of life." They celebrated Wahl's *Toward the Concrete,* seeking, however, to take "concreteness"—life in its full richness, in its individuality—as starting point, not conclusion. This was the turn to existence—to the sense of individual crisis, even of individual despair—which Sartre, like so many contemporary writers, did indeed "advance to on his own," and from which, Marxism or no Marxism, he has never retreated. This position, with its stress on the inner quality of experience, its sense of human isolation, of the "darkly felt split between things as they are and things as they ought to be," all this he could indeed assimilate, whether as Cartesian individualist, as phenomenologist concerned to describe the data of consciousness in all their purity, or as the man who had been that lonely child recalled in *Les Mots.* (No, maman, don't ask the other boys to play with me; but perhaps I can imagine how miserable, deep down inside, each of them too must be!) Philosophically and politically, Sartre recalls, the position he and his friends took at this period was a kind of pluralism: a position essentially of the right, which refused to "totalize," refused to subsume the crisis of the present under its proper dialectical, and Marxist, rubric. It was the war and the occupation, he says, which taught them better. Or, if one follows Simone de Beauvoir's account, it was first the Spanish Civil War (where after all the officially Marxist state was on the side of justice) that brought political events emphatically to the attention of these young academicians. Between Franco and Hitler they came to see (so they allege) that pluralism is fascist. They were rescued by the tragic events of the 1930's and 1940's. They fled from the bourgeois right to the banner of revolutionary socialism, which, though without ever embracing any party of the left, they still proudly fly.

Is this a true story? Yes and no. First, parenthetically, let us put to one side the equation of pluralism with fascism. If fascism has a theory at all, it is a "totalizing," not a "pluralistic" one. Liberal democracy, the official theory of the bourgeoisie, is a far cry either from the clericalism of the Falangists or the blood-and-soil mysticism of the Nazis. By the weakness and folly of its adherents it did indeed permit their rise; but that does not make it philosophically their equivalent. To insist as uncompromisingly as Sartre does on the dichotomy of fascism = pluralism versus Marxism = "totalization" is to indulge once more in the same kind of dualistic either-or that makes him so fundamentally unpolitical, indeed, so unhistorical a thinker. Nor am I contradicting myself here. Sartre is an excellent historian—of philosophy. But it is precisely the imprecisions, the half-lights, the muddles of *real* history that he fails to see.

Yet his account is convincing in so far as it concerns, not the history of our time, but his own development. It illuminates the intimate relation of the existential to the "Marxist" aspect of his thought, and enables us to understand how both the general intent of his philosophy and some of his central concepts could take on a quasi-Marxist slant. First, the existentialist's "tragic sense of life" became for him the conceptual instrument through which he sought to recognize, alongside the politicians of the left and the masses they claimed to represent, the real oppression and injustice of the real world. He sees the step to existentialism now as the revolt of a petty bourgeois intellectual against the dominant class to which, nevertheless, he still belonged. He and his friends expressed their rebellion, at the time, in what he later found to be inadequately practical terms: they talked of "essences" and "ideas"; even the violence of their revolt was purely conceptual. However, in Sartre's case at least, it seems to me, the reason for the intellectual cast of his rebellion was not, in the last analysis, the fact that he was still a bourgeois, expressing his dissatisfaction with the establishment of the day by denying its monistic (idealist) solution in favor of a looser, pluralistic position. His rebellion was intellectual because it was an intellectual's, indeed, a philosopher's, rebellion, not that of a practical man.

Though he still seeks to found the whole panorama of history on *praxis* or the action of the individual, his own *praxis,* as *Les Mots* makes very clear, is verbal and conceptual. It has none of the spirit of calculation that all politics, even revolutionary politics, demands. He insists on "man in situation," but theoretically; the messiness of the practical situation eludes him. He has indeed been a committed writer, not admittedly in the sense of commitment to a party, but in the sense that he has publicly and emphatically espoused, over and over, the cause of the exploited or the oppressed, and the cause of revolutionaries who seek to overthrow exploitation or oppression. He does indeed support those who man the barricades. But it is not his métier to tear up the paving stones himself. This is the posture of the *theoretical* revolutionary, the man who simply and loudly says "no" to what there is, but it can also be the posture of the existentialist, certainly in the Sartrean form of existentialism: an existentialism, without transcendent values, without God, in which the lonely individual sees over against his own project, his own aspirations, the nauseating insufficiency of what in fact *is* to his own ideals.

There is, it seems to me, something in common with Marxism in this existentialist attitude, both in its general intellectual strategy and in some particular concepts that Sartrean existentialism and at least some forms of Marxism share.

In general, the in-itself/for-itself dichotomy lends itself, in a very abstract fashion, to a "Marxist" position in social and political philosophy. If one seeks to go beyond the purely subjective dialectic of the inner man, the alternative is—totalization. Over against myself as agent is the in-itself as meaningless, indefinitely extending exteriority, as threat to myself as for-itself, and this "in-itself" includes the dehumanized "humanity" of social institutions. True, I can take the world as a complex of techniques for my action; but I can also take it, alternatively, as a vast snare to objectify me, to deny my humanity. Indeed, society as institutionalized *is* the inhuman. It is expropriation, act become inertial. I swing back and forth, therefore, between my aspiration to an impossible good faith, to pure act, in here, and the threat, the wickedness of all that is out there. I am by no means asserting that this is Marxism; but it does share with Marxism its utopian component. Either all is well or nothing. And since it is never the case that all is well, one must take up a position of revolutionary nihilism: don't fool yourself, all there is is rotten. If Sartre is to take a political stand, that is the only one his existentialism, his search for the purely active act, could possibly allow him.

Certain concepts, moreover, which play a crucial role in the argument of *Being and Nothingness,* are already, if not Marxist, at least surrogates for their Marxist analogues. An obvious candidate is "alienation." If Marxist alienation was a function of capitalism, of the laborer's possession by the machine, for Sartre alienation, in the sense of the flight from the instant of pure activity, is the human condition as such. The two conceptions have in common, if nothing else, the Rousseauist thesis that man, born free, is everywhere in chains, and chains of his own making. Freedom is the true humanity, but men are fated to lose it through their own agency. Dialectical materialism sees this loss in economic history and the exploitation of the working class by capital. In *Being and Nothingness* Sartre sees it in the individual's own self-deception. But the formal alternative is the same: free action is humanity, and it is lost by human agency.

A second parallel, finally, is the concept of class struggle. Though he approaches it in *Being and Nothingness* by a course very different from any Marxist argument, and though he has to prove with immense circuitousness in the *Critique* that there can be "struggle," Sartre sees the togetherness of human beings as arising primarily from conflict. In *Being and Nothingness,* there is no "we-subject" except indirectly. A and B and C all hate the D's, for example, who want to objectify and thus exterminate them. They are united as a we-subject by common hatred of the us-object whose *raison d'être* is to make such an object of them. Thus the understanding of social history becomes essentially the understanding of the class struggle. And out of such hatred, the envisagement of political action is the envisagement of revolution, of overthrowing the exploitation that is the Other's use of me, or, indirectly at least, of us. Again, if Sartre's individualism lends itself to any political philosophy, it will be some sort of theory in which exploitation and the revolt against exploitation are at the heart of the interpretation of social structures.

In these limited senses then, Sartre's "Marxism" and his existentialism, however far apart these two traditions may appear, form equally integral aspects of his philosophy even before the expansion of the "Marxist" theme. Yet if we look back at the influence of the three dialecticians, it is Hegel who wins hands down. Both the dialectic of the for-itself and the dialectic of social *praxis* Sartre develops, ultimately, with a virtuosity, an ontological persistence, that seem to be inspired, through contact with existentialism and Marxist literature, in the last analysis by Hegel himself. If his dialectic is narrower than Hegel's in empirical content or poorer in concrete historical insight, what limits it is not so much Kierkegaardian introspection, let alone Marxian concern with the realities of economic life; what limits the scope of his dialectic, as it limits his phenomenology, is the presiding genius (perhaps the evil genius) of French philosophy: the spirit of Descartes. In both his major works of philosophy of date, Sartre is, or has become, a Hegelian dialectician whose speculation is nevertheless confined within the bounds of Cartesian dualism and of a truncated Cartesian rationality. That this is so—and in what respect—will become apparent as we follow the argument of *Being and Nothingness* in its main movement, and look more carefully at some of the problems that loom up before us in its course.

chapter four: being and nothingness

the argument

from the phenomenon to being

It is fashionable nowadays
to identify philosophy with something called "conceptual analysis."
Conceptual analysis is certainly a tool of philosophy; but what is it used *for?* The answer to
that question seems to divide philosophers into two di-
vergent camps. First, there are those who reflect upon, and

within, experience in order to seek a clearer understanding of experience itself, of the ordinary world, whether of everyday life or of some specialized discipline. But then there are also, recurrently, those who philosophize in order to seek, beyond and behind everyday experience, some special insight into the really real. As things appear to us, they are forever changing. Is there not some permanent reality behind them which they somehow express and which, if we follow the right method, we can come to understand? Philosophers, it seems, habitually return to this question, yet never come to a final answer—an answer that once and for all will put the search to rest. Kant found an ingenious solution, which, as it turned out, merely exacerbated the problem. There are really real entities, "noumena," he claimed, behind the phenomena, but, though we keep trying to grasp their nature, it is *our* nature never to succeed, and, as far as claims to knowledge go, we should stop trying. We can know things only as they appear, not as they are "in themselves." Kant's was a most unstable "solution." There, over the fence, are the things in themselves, but we must be content to nibble away at our phenomenal meadow, with the greener grass of reality exasperatingly out of bounds. The two greatest movements of European philosophy since Kant, Hegelian dialectic and Husserlian phenomenology, were both concerned to eliminate the Kantian dichotomy. The question of how Hegel in fact meant to do this—by bringing everything (in the *Phenomenology of Mind*) within the scope of experience, or by swelling out the human, experiencing person (in the *Logic* and elsewhere) into a kind of suprahistorical super-superego— that difficult question, fortunately, need not concern us here. It is in the phenomenology of the twentieth century that Sartre had found the cure for the ailment Kant had bequeathed to us. Husserl has abolished the noumenon. If thought is always of—an object, that object is not the hither side of some hidden "X"; it is simply, as object of thought, what it appears as, and no more. But that is plenty. For the phenomenologist's "phenomena" are not the mythical "impressions" of Hume or the sense data of the positivist's dream. They have the full richness of experience itself; stripped of speculation, without conventional superstructures, they can be studied accurately and systematically, so that a structured range of objects and modes of experiencing them are displayed, all luminously appearing as they are—since it is appearances that they are. It was with confidence in this enterprise that Sartre had written his sketch on the emotions and had discovered how affective consciousness, normally non-thetic, can serve on occasion as magical surrogate for the rational control of objects. The position he reached there remained as starting point of *Being and Nothingness*. Not only is non-thetic or "pre-reflective" consciousness the first principle of that work and the subject matter of its first major theme; the theory of the emotions is also retained, recurring, as we shall see, in the last, most frankly "ontological" phase of the argument. Or, to make a more general point, Sartre firmly maintains his affirmation of Husserl's success in doing away once and for all with the shadow of Kant's thing-in-itself. It is from that achievement and its implications that his argument begins. Sartre draws a clear distinction between the Kantian phenomenon, which relates to the noumenon as appearance to being, and Husserl's theory of the phenomenon, which holds that there is nothing behind the appearance: the phenomenon, supported by nothing other than itself, refers only to itself and to the total series of appearances. If we start honestly within consciousness, within experience as experienced and experiencing, there is no question of any hidden reality. "Consciousness has nothing substantial; it is pure appearance in the sense that it exists only to the degree to which it appears." [1] And even when we move, *via* the ontological proof, from consciousness to being, it is not noumenal being that is in question, but the transphenomenal being of phenomena—the being of this table, of this package of tobacco, of this lamp, the being of the world implied by consciousness. Thus, the phenomenon, freed of its inacessible noumenal alternate, is before us in its complete being as the pure appearance that it is.

Yet the resolution of the Kantian dichotomy turns out to be itself unstable, or so Sartre argues in the Introduction to *Being and Nothingness*. Concurring in modern philosophy's rejection of the noumenon, his Introduction nevertheless proceeds to demonstrate the instability of phenomenology and to transcend it in the direction of an ontological inquiry. The argument is condensed and obscure, but worth disentangling, since it lays the foundation for the structure of the work itself. I shall therefore examine it in some detail before going on to trace in much more general outline the course of the argument that follows.

In Section One, Sartre begins, as we have seen, by accepting modern thought's banishment of the Kantian noumenon. Much of what he says in this section applies, incidentally, as much to "phenomenal*ism*" as to phenomenology. It is the rejection of speculative metaphysic, even in its most vestigial form, that he is referring to, a rejection common to many schools of thought. Thus he speaks here of Poincaré and Duhem as well as of Husserl. But since he describes his own enterprise as "phenomenological ontology," it seems reasonable to read this opening argument also as that of a philosopher starting from what he believes to be Husserl's method and modifying it in his own way. In any case, what matters here, first, is simply the rejection of the noumenon, a step on which phenomenalism, with its modest empiricism, and phenomenology, with its more ambitious aims, agree.

Beginning, then, with this fundamental thesis of modern philosophy, Sartre proceeds to make a number of opening moves which set the stage for what follows. First, he examines, and apparently validates, the claim that modern thought by "reducing the existent to the series of appearances" has overcome a number of "dualisms." First, it has transformed the contrast of internal and external: there is no inaccessible "inside" to objects "behind" their apparent surfaces. Instead there is simply the appearance contrasted with a series of appearances equally apparent. It has also abolished the contrast between appearance and reality: the phenomenon is the existent, there is no lurking "really real" of which it is the appearance. For if the phenomenon is relative to some one, yet it is nevertheless absolutely itself; it is at least relative-absolute. Nor, thirdly, does the duality of potency and act survive; behind the act there is no power or disposition "in view of which" the act is possible. What about essence and existence? Here, too, there has been a change. We have the appearance of the existent, or the existent as it appears, still contrasted with its essence, but the latter, being simply "the manifest law of the series of appearances," is equally apparent. It is not an essence off in some other world, as "essence" once was thought to be.

Through all these alterations, Sartre proceeds to argue, we have not so much abolished all dualities as we have converted them into a single new contrast, that of finite and infinite. The existent, we have already seen, manifests itself in a series of appearances. Each such appearance is finite, but the series must be infinite. Why? The series must be infinite, first, Sartre insists, simply because each appearance appears to a subject. For even if an object should manifest itself through only one aspect or "profile" (*Abschattung*), even if I always perceived only that one aspect, only this side of G. E. Moore's inkwell, for instance, I always have the possibility of perceiving it from other points of view. That is what "perceiving" means. From the side of the appearance itself, secondly, we can also draw the inference that the series of appearances cannot be finite, for this would mean, Sartre argues, "that the first appearances do not have the possibility of *reappearing,* which is absurd, or that they can all be given at once, which is still more absurd." [2] What, then, has the theory of the phenomenon accomplished? What it has done in fact is to replace *reality* (belonging to things) with *objectivity* (belonging to phenomena), and, Sartre points out, it has justified this change by an appeal to infinity. Again, this statement would be equally characteristic of Husserl's account of perception as the series of profiles of an object systematically interrelated by receding into an infinitely expanded horizon, and of a phenomenalist formula like John Stuart Mill's "permanent possibility of sensation," since a finite series could not be "permanently" possible. Sartre proceeds to gloss this thesis in characteristically Cartesian fashion.

What is "reality"? "The reality of that cup is that it *is* there and that it is *not me.*" [3] Now in modern terms we interpret this to mean "that the series of its appearances is bound by a principle which does not depend on my whim." [4] This statement in turn is interpreted both from the *subject* and the *object* side. First, the appearance in itself would be simply a "subjective phenomenon," this appearance to me here now. To achieve a principle of organizing appearances, therefore, the subject must transcend this appearance in the direction of the series: "he must *seize Red* through his impression of red," [5] where by "Red" is meant precisely the principle of the series. Or, similarly, he must seize the electric current through the electrolysis—that is, through its manifestations. But all this, though achieved through the subject's transcendence of the appearance, in fact establishes the objectivity of the object. So we can equally well argue, from the object side, that "on principle an object posits the series of its appearances as infinite." [6] So the appearance, too, not only the subject to which it appears, itself demands that it be "surpassed to infinity." Without that surpassing it could not be apprehended as "an appearance of what appears," as appearance of an object, albeit a phenomenal object.

The new opposition, therefore, replaces all the traditional dualities. So Sartre declares. But he now proceeds to reinstate them all within this single principle— to reinstate them, indeed, as more radically opposite than they had been before. First, external/internal: the object, of which each appearance is one aspect, is totally *in* this aspect (since there is no "real" thing behind it), yet at the same time totally *outside* it (since the series itself, which is infinite, and the principle of which makes the object objective, never as such appears in any one aspect). Similarly for potency and act: if the appearance is what it is, and potency is banished, a new "potency" returns—the potency "to be developed in a series of real or possible appearances." [7] Finally, essence and existence are again, and more radically, divorced. For Plato, for example, who represents for most of us the most extreme "two-world" philosophy, forms do indeed exist apart from the phenomena, yet the phenomena share in that higher being. Indeed, they have such existence as they have in view of that very sharing. Now, however, we have abolished participation, since the essence is that which is manifested by an infinite series of manifestations. But then it is never manifested, even imperfectly, in any one. Thus we have, within the theory of the phenomenon, not only a single dualism, but an aggravation of all the old ones. In every case, in fact, an original polarity has been transcended or replaced, only to give way to a sharper opposition, if not an outright contradiction. This conclusion, concealed within the compression of the initial argument, Sartre will draw out to its full paradoxical consequences in the seven hundred pages to come.

The process is prefigured in the remaining sections of the Introduction. Section Two cuts apart "the phenomenon of being" and "the being of the phenomenon," and presents in little the theme to be elicited from the next section. We find that even the pure appearance can be questioned about its being, and, indeed, must be so: the two are not identical, nor does the phenomenon as such, even the phenomenal object as such, of itself reveal its being. True, there is no "being" *behind* the phenomenon. As phenomenon, as existence, and even, in the principle of its appearances, as essence, it is coextensive with its being. Yet it is also different from its being, since, transphenomenally, we can ask—indeed, cannot avoid asking—what its being is. The phenomenon reveals itself; that it is, is the condition of its revelation. Yet if, in turn, we take *that* phenomenon: that it is, *the phenomenon of being,* as a revelation, we want in turn to ask about the being *on the basis of which* it is revealed. Thus, the phenomenon, even the purest phenomenon, transcends itself in the direction of ontology.

Two points should be noted about this brief section, one parenthetically, the other as a fundamental premise of the whole argument. First, when Sartre considers the possibility of a direct revelation of being as phenomenon, he finds being disclosed to us by an immediate access which is affective rather than intellectual (typically, Sartre cites "boredom" and "nausea"), and ontology becomes the description of being as it presents itself directly to us. We may put aside here the question why Sartre prefers "boredom" or "nausea" rather than, say "wonder" or "ecstasy." But essential to the very structure of the argument is a remark tucked into the final paragraph of the section, which both anticipates the thesis that "all knowledge is intuitive" and indicates the way in which Sartre's ontology is to transcend knowledge. This move, beyond or behind knowledge to some other relation to being on which it rests, is fundamental to the structure of the argument to come. Yet Sartre seems to introduce it almost unawares. We have to establish first of all, he writes, "the exact relation which unites the phenomenon of being to the being of the phenomenon." [8] To do this, he continues, we should "consider that the whole of the preceding remarks has been directly inspired by the revealing intuition of the phenomenon of being." [9] In other words, we have tried to take being not as the mere *condition* of appearance, but as itself "an appearance which can be determined in concepts"—as other appearances can be determined if we either list their properties or move toward their "meaning," that is, their essence as the principle of the series of appearances ("Red" through red . . . etc.). But this attempt has shown us that in the case of being we cannot make such a reduction: the phenomenon of being exceeds our grasp either through properties or meaning; it still points to being as *trans-*

phenomenal. So, Sartre says—and this is the fateful step—"we have understood . . . *that knowledge cannot by itself give an account of being."* [10] In other words, knowledge is the direct presentation of phenomena; it is intuition, "the act of a clear and attentive mind," in its si-mon-pure self-contained direction toward what it sees. The reach beyond appearances to being, therefore, is a reach beyond knowledge. The phenomenon of being not only leads beyond the phenomenon to its being, "requir-ing a foundation which is transphenomenal": [11] in leading us that way, it also leads us beyond knowledge itself to some fundamentally non-cognitive attitude. Sartre con-cludes:

> What is implied by the preceding considerations is that the being of the phenomenon, although coextensive with the phenomenon, can not be subject to the phenomenal condition—which is to exist only in so far as it reveals itself—and that consequently it surpasses the knowledge which we have of it and provides the basis for such knowledge. [12]

It is in the next section, on "The Pre-Reflective Co-gito and the Being of the Percipere," that we decisively make this move from the secure inspection of the phe-nomenon *as known* to a precognitive foundation for knowledge. At the same time it should be noted that the two theses established in the previous section, the trans-phenomenality of being and its precognitive import, will be confirmed in radically divided areas. It is conscious-ness that will reveal to us a precognitive dimension, and it is being as such, being-in-itself as radically other than consciousness, that will take us beyond the phenomenon to ontology. The phenomenon has twin transphenomenal roots, but they are far from identical twins. The phenomenon appears to—consciousness, and that consciousness, as knowing consciousness, is founded in the precognitive moment of the not-yet-reflective *cogito:* I am counting my cigarettes, non-thetically aware of myself as counting. The phenomenon which appears, on the other hand, *is,* and as being *it* demands the transphenomenal, demands a being other than consciousness as the condition of its appearance. Thus consciousness is tied to itself behind and before knowledge in the pre-reflective *cogito,* and at the same time catapulted into the obscurity of sheer being, being which is coextensive with appearance, yet at the same time its ontological obverse.

Sartre opens this next stage of his preliminary argument by proposing to consider once more the possibility of resting in the phenomenon, of accepting the Berkeleyan identity *"esse est percipi,"* "To be is to be perceived." It will not work, he holds, for two reasons, one in the nature of the *percipere,* of perceiving, one in the nature of the *percipi,* the perceived.

The examination of the former makes more explicit the view of knowledge hinted at in the previous section and establishes its first and primary consequence. Knowing, Sartre holds, is the explicit, intentional confrontation of the act of knowing with what it knows. But is knowing itself known? If it were, we would be started on an infinite regress, from the idea to the idea of the idea and so on indefinitely—a regress which, once started, would never stop. I would know my knowing and in turn my knowing of my knowing and my knowing of my knowing of my knowing and . . . Only an initial resting place, a rooting of knowledge in something other than knowledge, could cut off this intolerable regression before it starts. I have already mentioned, in discussing Sartre's Cartesianism, the transformation of the *cogito* from reflective to pre-reflective, which he effects in order to cut short this regressive process; but I must recapitulate briefly here in order to put the Sartrean "absolute" where it belongs, at the head of his argument.

We start from the phenomenon as apprehended, that is, as known. What knows, however, is consciousness: "The law of being in the knowing subject is *to-be-conscious*." [13] *This* being—"to-be-conscious"—will turn out on the one hand to be entirely phenomenal: consciousness *is,* utterly lucid, it is pure appearance, its existence is its appearance. But on the other hand, it is also transphenomenal, for it is the being *of* the knowing subject. Yet it is not being *simpliciter,* for it is the being of consciousness. And consciousness, of course, is inescapably intentional. It is always consciousness *of*—. Not that all intentionality is cognitive; there are also, for instance, Sartre admits, "affective states of consciousness"; they, too, are *of*—, but in some other way. But here it is the pure phenomenon—that is, the object of knowledge—from which we have started; so it is knowing consciousness, which is always consciousness of—its object, that we are interrogating, and it is the precognitive foundation of knowing consciousness that we are about to discover.

Sartre's argument here is brief, definitive, and, I believe, invalid, slipping in an unwarranted minor premise which, though unstated, suffices to impose on all that is to follow, both in this work and later, the bias, sometimes slight, sometimes extreme, but always distorting, that characterizes his philosophy.

"The necessary and sufficient condition for a knowing consciousness to be knowledge *of* its object," he asserts," is that it be *consciousness of itself* as being that knowledge." [14] That it is a sufficient condition is clear enough, for "my being conscious of being conscious of that table" does indeed suffice for my being conscious of it—not for its existence in itself, but for its existence for me, insofar as I *am* conscious of it. But why is this "self-consciousness" a necessary condition? This is where Sartre's argument is obscure and, indeed, as I see it, fatally misleading. This is where he ought to have renounced his Cartesian heritage, but failed to do so.

Being conscious of itself as being the knowledge of its object is a necessary condition of a knowing consciousness's being consciousness of its object, Sartre argues, because "if my consciousness were not consciousness of being consciousness of the table, it would then be consciousness of that table without consciousness of being so. In other words, it would be a consciousness ignorant of itself, an unconscious—which is absurd." [15] Granted, the concept of an unconscious consciousness is indeed a contradictory and thus an absurd one. But why must a consciousness conscious of something other than itself, as, following Husserl, Sartre agrees all consciousness is, be, because ignorant of itself, not conscious at all? Consciousness is defined as other-directed; that doesn't make it unconscious. On the contrary, it is just its vectorial character, its consciousness of what is not itself, and therefore, one might suppose, its lack of consciousness of itself, its "ignorance" of itself if you will, that *makes* it conscious. Husserl may be mistaken—or, better, Husserl as interpreted by Sartre may be mistaken—in holding all cognitive consciousness to be thetic, positing its object explicitly and centrally. It may be—and I believe it is—the case that there is always a non-thetic foundation, a foundation of what Michael Polanyi calls subsidiary awareness, at the root of even the most plainly intuitive, positional (or, in Polanyi's language, focal) awareness of an object. But why must that non-thetic residue be introduced, as Sartre introduces it, as consciousness (of) *self?* On the contrary, the non-thetic ground of consciousness is, in most of our dealing with the world, a set of clues on which we rely, from which we move, in order to make out, through them, the outlines, the meaning, of our focal object in the world, not of ourselves. The subsidiary is indeed interiorized, it is *mine,* but it is not *me,* or no more so than is the focal object I comprehend through it and with its aid. It is the crutch I lean on to advance out there into and with the world. To attend *from* it, and by means of it, *to* the world is indeed the necessary condition of knowledge—but that is by no means the same thing as to turn from the world to awareness, even subsidiary awareness, of myself. Nor is forgetting myself in my concentration on what, *via* the non-thetic, I seek to posit, to be identified with unconsciousness. Quite the contrary: the outward thrust of subsidiary awareness is the very transcendence of self that makes intentionality possible.

Why does Sartre fail to see this? Why does he argue that a non-self-conscious consciousness would be unconscious? Clearly because for him, in *Being and Nothingness* as already in the *Emotions,* the *cogito* has been taken as the unique and indispensable starting point of all philosophy. And the *cogito,* unlike Husserl's *cogitationes,* is self-referential. In moving the content of consciousness out into the world, Sartre has nevertheless retained the Cartesian thesis that the first unique moment of thought must be thinking about thinking: consciousness, to be consciousness, must be self-directed and self-contained. This moment has indeed lost the lucidity of the Cartesian original, for the light of consciousness now looks outward. It is, in itself, contentless, merely, as Sartre puts it, "an operative intention"; but it must operate *on itself*, it must reverberate somehow within itself, else, he believes, despite the thesis of intentionality, it would not be consciousness at all. True, in Sartre's view, this merely operative intention cannot be cognitive, since knowledge is always directed to an object, not to itself. So it is prior to knowledge; indeed, Sartre concludes, it is the precognitive absolute, the transphenomenal being on which, as its being, consciousness as phenomenon rests. The consciousness of consciousness, not as thetic but as nonthetic, is "the immediate non-cognitive relation of the self to itself" on which the very possibility of consciousness depends. This pre-reflective *cogito,* then, is the condition of the Cartesian *cogito,* as of every *cogitatio.* It is the absolute beginning of philosophy.

But, again, it is precisely here, in founding philosophy on this immediate, non-cogitating *cogito,* that Sartre has foundered. He has cut off once more the bridge from thinker to thought that Husserl's method had established and has insulated the empty self against any impact, except through negativity, from or on the world. Yet the very example he uses to illustrate his pre-reflective *cogito* could have led him beyond this initial, and, for him, ultimate impasse. In counting my cigarettes, he tells us, I do not know myself as counting, witness the fact that "children who are capable of doing a sum spontaneously can not *explain* subsequently how they set about it." These tests of Piaget's, Sartre continues, "constitute an excellent refutation of the formula of Alain—To know is to know that one knows." [16] Indeed they do; but what they indicate is simply the tacit ground of all knowledge, not a tacit knowledge of one's *self.* They suggest that at the basis of knowing-that, there is a tacit knowing-how (an "operative intention"!) which cannot be made wholly explicit. They suggest a revision of the conception of knowledge to include that other-directed tacit base. But to follow this suggestion would mean denying both the self-referential being of immediate consciousness and the wholly positional character of cognitive consciousness. It would mean, moreover, denying not only these Cartesian principles, but their corollaries also: the concept of consciousness as wholly active and as instantaneous. But to all these theses, as we saw earlier, Sartre is committed from the start, too deeply committed to question them even at the hand of an example which so plainly illustrates their contrary. The child's "knowing how to add"—which he cannot specify—is nevertheless knowledge; it is directed to the numbers he is adding, not to himself; it is both something he does, as agent, and a giving of himself to a task, as patient. Finally, as the action-x-passion of an embodied being, it takes time; it is not, it does not even aim at being, instantaneous, as the *cogito* is alleged to be. On all these counts, then, the Piaget experiment should lead us to substitute a non-thetic vector toward and within the world for any *cogito,* even a "pre-reflective" one. That move, however, Sartre is unable to make; and so we will find his assimilation of themes from Hegel, from Heidegger, and from Husserl, as well as his own phenomenological descriptions, confined and cramped, over and over, by the barrier of this first Cartesian step.

To return to Sartre's argument: his search for the being of the percipient has led him, he believes, to a non-reflective awareness (of) self as a non-substantial absolute. This is, primally and originally, how consciousness is: it simply surges up as non-thetic consciousness (of) itself. It is its own beginning. That is why one can, and must, say of it that its existence implies, and precedes, its essence—not, indeed, as the particular realization of some abstract possibility, but in its very rising into being, consciousness creates its essence, that is, the "synthetic order of its possibilities." [17] Without the existence of consciousness, there cannot even be nothingness. Consciousness is limited only by itself. Yet its existence, of course, is far from substantial; it simply is as it appears: "it is precisely because consciousness is pure appearance, because it is total emptiness (since the entire world is outside it), it is because of this identity of appearance and existence within it that it can be considered as the absolute." [18]

So much for the *percipere.* We have found its transphenomenality in the concrete subjectivity of consciousness itself. Have we then founded, in consciousness, the being of the *percipi* as well? Far from it. As the lines just quoted indicate, consciousness has "the whole world" —that is, its object—"outside it." Granted, what is perceived is relative to the perceiver; it is passive, there to be acted on. But though passively awaiting the activity of consciousness, and though existing, as perceived, in relation to consciousness, it does not *derive* from consciousness, for it is, as perceived, *before* consciousness. Intentionality reasserts itself. The very being of consciousness, as non-thetic (self) awareness, points to its other as what, thetically, it is consciousness *of.* For consciousness, existence is primary; its essence follows from its existence. For being-over-against-consciousness, however, its very essence—to be over-against-consciousness—leads us to infer its necessary existence. Consciousness leads us to its object, the being of the phenomenon which confronts it, and the ontological proof leads us, dialectically, as noted earlier, from the essence of such a being to its existence.

This is the argument of sections IV and V (on the

being of the *percipi* and on the ontological proof), which is expanded, finally, in the tentative description of being-in-itself. Consciousness, we will find, exists as for-itself, in immediate, pre-reflective yet nevertheless doubling reflection *of* (not *on*) its being. But thetically it is of, and necessarily leads us to, its very opposite: being which simply is, is in-itself, is what it is. We have distinguished, therefore, two absolutely separated regions of being: on the one hand, the being of the pre-reflective *cogito,* and on the other, the being of the phenomenon, of which we had earlier been in search. Overcoming the dualisms of ontological tradition, we have reached the acme of all dualisms: the sheer, active upsurge of consciousness, against the meaningless plenum of sheer being-as-such. Nor can either idealism or realism help us overcome this gap. Idealism would derive being from consciousness; but being does not flow from consciousness, it confronts it. Realism would derive consciousness from being; but consciousness has no derivation. It simply springs up. "Nothing" is its cause. Its way of being (though not its being) is self-contained. It is in the way that consciousness has to be— and that, as we shall see to the point of satiety, is precisely *not* the way that being is. Sartre concludes:

A multitude of questions remain unanswered: What is the ultimate meaning of these two types of being? For what reasons do they both belong to *being* in general? What is the meaning of that being which includes within itself these two radically separated regions of being? If idealism and realism both fail to explain *the relations which in fact unite these regions which in theory are without communication,* what other solution can we find for this problem? *And how can the being of the phenomenon be transphenomenal?* It is to attempt to reply to these questions that I have written the present work.[19]

Yet philosophical questions seldom hide surprising answers. The answers to Sartre's questions are already packed away in the questions themselves. The dialectic that elicits them takes, from the start, an inexorable course.

The Major Movement of the Argument

Part I, "The Problem of Nothingness," forges the tool by which Sartre will connect—always in *dis*connection—his two disparate spheres of being. The problem is no abstract one. What the Introduction has led us to, out of the restriction of philosophy to the pure phenomenon, is the concrete reality of *this* man as being-in-the-world. For it is part and parcel of the very structure of being-human that it is, on the one hand, its own immediate, pre-reflective "self"-awareness and (but not merely additively "and") its relation to the other realm of being, the being-in-itself that it is not.

Paradigmatic for this relation—the relation of consciousness to being, or of man to world—is the attitude of the *question*. First, if I knew the answer I could not ask; therefore in questioning I assert the non-being of my knowing. Second, if the world had already given me the answer, I could not ask; therefore the question also entails the possibility of non-being in being itself. And third, the question implies the existence of a truth sought as answer. But this, too, Sartre insists, entails negation; for the true reply will be "thus *and not* otherwise." The positive delimitation of truth from falsity will therefore constitute, as much as a negative answer would do, an introduction of non-being into the undifferentiated plenum of being-in-itself. The very nature of inquiry, therefore, including *par excellence* the present ontological inquiry, leads us to negation as the theme we need to pursue in order to find the two great realms of being emerging in the concrete bond between them that constitutes man. Waiting for Pierre in the café, we find how "nothingness haunts being." Studying the conceptions of nothingness in Hegel and Heidegger, we move toward an insight into the origin of such negation. It is through man that nothingness comes into the world; and, indeed, that *is* the reality of man: that through him nothingness comes into the world. But the reality of man is freedom; and freedom is in fact, Sartre tells us, the human being putting his past out of play by secreting his own nothingness.

Nihilation as a *cleavage* between my immediate psychic past and my present is the act by which I make myself as free. The consciousness of that cleavage is *dread:* the dizzying mood in which I recognize myself, not only as not being what I was, but also as being, in the mode of *not* being it, the future that I will, or ought to, be. This is the mood from which, in my everyday, "serious" existence, I am everywhere in flight. Evading the nihilating revelation of dread, which exhibits me as an emergent freedom, responsible in this very instant for my own being, for the values which "start up like partridges before my acts," [20] I hesitate in the false instantaneity of bad faith. Thus Sartre asks at the close of his first chapter, "what consciousness must be in the instantaneity of the pre-reflective *cogito,* if the human being is capable of *bad faith?*" [21] The inquiry which follows in Chapter Two, however (the chapter entitled "Bad Faith"), already makes it plain that it is in fact bad faith which is the predominant alternative. Social role-playing, for example (the way the waiter *is* a waiter, yet without *being* so in the straightforward way in which the inkwell is an inkwell), invariably exemplifies the "inner disintegration" of my being, not the transcendence of that disintegration toward the in-itself which, were it possible, would be its correct alternative. Thus we are already moving toward the final question of the book, not whether bad faith is possible, but whether some attitude different from it can in fact be realized. Man is freedom as nihilation, but is that freedom ever achieved? Can being as for-itself and being-in-itself ever be reconciled in the free act of a being which achieves its being for-itself as truly being? The thrust of the ontological inquiry initiated in the Introduction and the pathos of the self-destroying vision of man that this inquiry generates will emerge inseparably through the intervening variations on the central theme.

In Part One, then, the study of the "question" has opened up the perspective of nihilation, found dread as the instrument of self-recognition, and bad faith as its apparently inevitable alternative. Out of the initial positional consciousness of an object, supported by a non-positional consciousness (of) myself, the contrast of the in-itself as plenum and the for-itself as opposing that plenum—as a "hole in being"—has opened up. Part Two proceeds to examine the structures of the (in the first instance nonthetic but non-reflective) for-itself.

First, let us deal with its immediate structures. We discover the "presence to itself" which "supposes that an impalpable fissure has slipped into being. If being is present to itself, it is because it is not wholly itself. Presence is an immediate *deterioration* of coincidence, for it supposes separation [my italics]." [22] What brings about this separation, however, is precisely nothing: this *is* the "fissure," the "hole in being," the "fall of the in-itself to the self," "by which the for-itself is constituted."

How can such nothingness come to be? Only by what Sartre calls an *ontological act,* the "perpetual act by

which the in-itself degenerates into presence to itself."
Sartre describes this act as an absolute event in which
nothingness—that is, consciousness—comes to being
and is sustained by being; it is the very putting into question of being by being. As being is complete in itself, isolated in its plenitude, it cannot, for Sartre, be caused by
any other being, nor can anything affect it. Its unique possibility is nothingness, which, as nothingness of being, is
sustained by being. This being we see in human reality,
which, since it is defined by the "original project of its own
nothingness," is a being whose being is founded on nothingness.

Out of this original foundation of nothingness, then,
Sartre elicits the further structures of the for-itself. First,
its facticity, its character as *an unjustifiable act*. Secondly, its character as *lack:* human reality is the being
which has to not-be what it is and to be what it is not. It is
the over-against-being through which negation, through
which lack appears in the world. To assert this lack, it
must itself *be* a lack. But a lack of what? Of "the impossible synthesis of the for-itself and the in-itself." [23] Making
itself as a *lack* of being, human reality is *on principle* both
the aspiration to *be* (what it is not) and incapacity of such
being, since it is precisely as *not* being that it *is*. To anticipate a later formulation, "we are condemned to be
free." [24] We choose ourselves, we make ourselves be, as
the unrealized and, by the very logic of our being, unreal-
izable completion of ourselves.

In this nihilating act, thirdly, consciousness not only
posits value, it is *as* value. Value is the lacked which the
for-itself lacks. It is the empty "for" of the for-itself: "The
being of value qua value is the being of what does not
have being. . . . Value is beyond being. . . . Value taken

in its origin, or the supreme value, is the beyond and the *for* of transcendence . . . the meaning and the beyond of all surpassing." [25]

Notice, we are still with the pre-reflective *cogito*. Value at this stage is not *known;* it is not an object posited before consciousness, but rather is itself this non-thetic transparency, this consciousness of being which exists everywhere and nowhere. Value is lived concretely as my lack, which constitutes the meaning of my being, continually present, always out of reach. Thetically, as the object of consciousness, value must be grasped reflexively, and along with it the for-itself it accompanies. In this reflective consciousness, Sartre distinguishes two elements: first, the *Erlebnis* upon which we are reflecting is posited as a lack; and second, value is thus seen to be the unattainable meaning of what is lacked. It is in this way that Sartre can term reflective consciousness, moral consciousness; for whenever I reflect, I am concerned with the meaning of what I lack as for-itself. Here again, Sartre ensures human freedom, for as reflective consciousness I am free to consider certain values and to ignore others, to occupy myself with this or that object, yet my more or less studious attention to these values does not in any way affect the fact of their existence. Note also that by implication the all-or-none of honest and unhappy dread or of the relaxation into bad faith is already given as our only pair of alternatives. Either on the level of reflection I shall rise to face myself as pure lack—in freedom, anguish, total responsibility— or sink into a complacent taking of my values (which are *really* lacks) as substantive realities.

Short of the ultimate statement of this duality, Sartre adds here to facticity and value the concept of *possibility* as *"the something* which the For-itself lacks *in order* to be itself," [26] a something already shown to be unattainable in terms of its starting point. Finally, the dialectic of the for-itself and the possible (*its* possible) is shown to produce the "circuit of selfness" in which the self seeks itself by its own surpassing, and in which the *world* appears as the fugitive structure, "haunted by possibles," which I *live*.

The argument has been confined, so far, to the limits of the pre-reflective *cogito;* yet it has transcended these limits in that direction towards its possibles, which constitutes the for-itself's nihilating upsurge. It becomes necessary, therefore (in Part II, Chapter II), to elicit the temporal structure of the for-itself. Given the instantaneity of the *cogito* from which it started, however, Sartre can find in temporality only *flight,* "the refusal of the instant." [27] Consciousness temporalizes itself as what it *was,* in sheer contingency, and *is not,* and as the future which is its lack, and which again it is not. Yet even so, as the very being which has to not-be what it is (was) and to be what it is not (yet), the for-itself, even as denial, is nevertheless primarily present. In this Sartre differs from Heidegger, for whom the Future is the dominant dimension or *ekstasis.* Thus Sartre argues that the Present, although it is conditioned by the Past and the Future just as much as it conditions them, forms the nothingness essential for the negation of the Past (when the for-itself discovers it is its Past as that which it has to surpass) and the Future (when the for-itself discovers itself as lack, as what it is not and has to realize). The present is "the mould of indispensable non-being for the total synthetic form of Temporality." [28]

All this, in the life of consciousness, is still primarily non-thetic. I may try, in pure reflection (this is presumably what Sartre is attempting here), to seize on the character of original temporality itself: on the nihilating, empty eruption of the for-itself as *historicity.* More frequently, however, consciousness falls prey to *impure* reflection, where, with their shadowy being, the structures of duration, of psychic life, of the "person" are spun out.

In Chapter III of Part II, "Transcendence," Sartre returns, in the light of the exposition of the for-itself, to the question he had posed in the Introduction of the phenomenon and its knowledge. ("Transcendence" here, it should be noted, is not the transcendence to the future, Heidegger's "existentiality," referred to in the "Temporality" chapter, but the transcendent relation between the for-itself and the in-itself.) We are now moving from the for-itself as the non-thetic *conscience* (*de*) *soi* to the thetic consciousness of—an object. What does the being of the for-itself have to be in order to be knowledge of the in-itself?

There is, Sartre announces (and as I have already mentioned) only intuitive knowledge, and intuition is the presence of consciousness to the thing. But presence-to —is, we have found, essentially negation. The for-itself puts itself in question as *not* being the being of the object. Knowing, though opposed to being, is also a form of being; it is the for-itself as realizing its own being, and its otherness than being, in its internal negation of itself. We meet, in other words, in the clear light of positional consciousness, the exacerbation of the for-itself/in-itself, *pour-soi/en-soi,* conflict. The world as known refers us either to absolute being, when we consider knowledge to be subjective, or to ourselves, when we want to grasp this absolute. Consciousness is everywhere surrounded by being: being which is itself and nothing else. When the for-itself attempts to grasp being, it is thrown back on itself. Knowledge, rising between the for-itself and the in-itself, between non-being and being, is itself defined in terms of what it is not; to know being as it is would mean to be the thing itself. Yet, if I were to be the thing, then the whole question of knowledge would vanish, for the "such as it is" would have no meaning and according to Sartre could not even be thought. He denies that this is either skepticism (for this would place the "such as it is" on the side of being) or relativism (for there is truth in knowledge). But, although in knowledge we find ourselves in the presence of the absolute, the truth of knowledge is a human truth. "The world is human." [29]

Within this to-and-fro, all-or-none context, Sartre has handled, in this chapter, a surprising number of traditional (and some untraditional) epistemological categories and problems: quality, quantity, abstraction ("the revelation in profile of my future"), space, time, and perception ("a conductor in the circuit of selfness"). He has elaborated, with a slight twist, Heidegger's theory of the instrumentality of things. And he has returned to value, the in-itself-for-itself, which, as the "perpetually indicated but impossible fusion of essence and existence," [30] is apprehended as beauty. The beautiful is, for Sartre, the ideal, the completion and perfection of the world which would correspond to the totalization of the for-itself, the identity of consciousness and being. It is because we apprehend our own being as a lack, and thus long for plenitude, that we are able to apprehend the world itself as incomplete, as lacking beauty, and can transcend the actual state, positing its ideal realization in the realm of the imaginary. Ordinarily, Sartre argues, we do not thetically posit beauty, but rather, as he has already said of value in general, we grasp it intuitively, discovering it through its absence, as something lacking, as the imperfection of the world. This is a *Symposium* emptied of content. It is true for Sartre, as for Plato, that only he who has seen beauty itself will breed true virtue, because he alone is in contact not with illusion but with truth; and, indeed, that all others are imitators of imitations. But the Sartrean ideal is vacuous, even self-contradictory. The for-itself is in its very being the nihilation of being, and its ideal reunion with being—the for-itself-in-itself—is thus by its very nature the self-canceling denial of itself. Could it come to an issue—which it cannot—it would be the pinpoint-being, the *un*being of A.~A which it had achieved. Wittgenstein at the close of the *Tractatus* threw away his ladder: exact speech issues in total silence. Sartrean existence *is* the ladder, forever aimed at its own extinction, or, in the downward direction, forever fleeing it. Indeed, on the ground of the *cogito,* of the claim to wholly self-contained and wholly explicit knowledge, that is the only existence we can have, or can be. Human reality, temporalization, is, and can only be, flight, deterioration, from the eternal perfection of an unattainable ideal. This is historicity confined within the iron grip of the *cogito;* but the *cogito,* deprived of supernatural or rational support, has itself collapsed into nothingness.

From this ground, further, in Part III, the compulsive dialectic of the Other and of the body necessarily follows. True, Sartre sometimes mentions a non-thetic awareness of body, which would, if he had started with it, have led him, as it did Merleau-Ponty and Marcel, to a different and more hopeful issue. But he begins, fatally, as we shall see in more detail presently, with the body as the known; and on his premises—and on the premises equally of traditional rationalism or empiricism, on the premises also of phenomenology—that is where he must begin. The pre-reflective *cogito,* being purely self-directed, is impotent to reach the body; it is only through thetic consciousness, through "knowledge," that the body comes into view. It appears as the alienated aspect of myself, the congelation into a thing of my facticity. But as object, secondly, it comes into view essentially as what the Other knows. Indeed, even taking my body as myself, my brain as my mind, as a materialist like J. J. C. Smart would do, I therewith take myself in effect as known by another. And as the Other's object, finally, my body becomes the opener for me of the dizzying spectacle of another's subjectivity: of another for-itself which degrades me to mere being, unless in my turn I succeed in so degrading it. (I shall deal with these matters in more detail in the next chapter. I want here only to indicate how this problematic develops within the overall structure of the work.)

Finally, Part IV is a deepening and elaboration of the ontological foundations laid down in the argument so far. The for-itself, totally free, responsible even for its own being, and indeed for the meaning of being itself, in the teeth of its ineluctable contingency, of the fact that it is not its own foundation, is essentially agent, actor, and maker. Yet for Sartre action in the last analysis is possession. Being sheer activity, as sheer nihilation of the alien object and the alien Other, it seeks to absorb the in-itself into itself, and so to escape its own non-entity. Even knowing, the act by which the for-itself posits its negation in the object, becomes a kind of having, a digestive process by which I seek to devour the alien world. Yet the for-itself, being in its nature nihilation, cannot possess its object; whether in practice or theory, the in-itself forever escapes it. So I either strive vainly and absurdly for an empty authenticity or relapse into bad faith and "the spirit of seriousness." Either way my action is suffering, my aspiration failure: man is a useless passion.

The upshot, in summary, is this: we are a negation, a hole in being; our manner of existing is a disintegration of a unity, a flight from ourselves, and, inexorably, a failure.

And in this condition the only honest attitude is dread: a mood which swings, it seems, between blind arrogance —*I* am responsible, *I* give meaning, *I* make the world— and blind despair—I am nothing, an unjustifiable fact, a contradiction, prey to the Other's look, a mere means to the Other's end. Wherever we turn, we find an impasse.

Yet, as we noticed in discussing the pre-reflective *cogito,* there might have been a simple way out of that impasse. Non-thetic consciousness is essential, not only to the being of the for-itself, but to knowledge—that is, to the relation of the for-itself and the in-itself. It is not pre-reflectively reflexive, but outward directed; it directs the for-itself toward the in-itself. To see this, however, would have meant for Sartre a radical denial of his Cartesian starting point. And then he would not be Sartre. That is not to deny the power, or even the greatness, of his argument, both in *Being and Nothingness* and elsewhere, nor, for that matter, its direct and dramatic bearing on our own philosophical problems. For if the tragic outcome of Sartre's philosophy stems from its Cartesian beginning, we have after all, since 1641, all begun there. And if we can succeed in evading once and for all the consequences of Cartesianism, we owe a debt to Sartre for the appalling honesty with which he most of all twentieth-century philosophers has faced the consequences of our common crisis.

chapter five: the problem of the other

the other, the body, the emotions

In the preceding chapter
I presented in profile, so to speak,
the argument of *Being and Nothingness*,
analyzing the Introduction in some detail
and sketching very briefly the main movement of
its dialectic. Now I want to look more closely at some
of its special themes, in particular the problem of the
Other and in relation to it the problem of the Body.

Fundamental to both these expositions, however, is the theory of the emotions which Sartre has carried over from his early work—and to which he returns explicitly in Part IV of *Being and Nothingness*. Indeed, as F. Jeanson emphasizes in his book on Sartre, the themes of both *The Imaginary* and *The Sketch on the Emotions* are still operative in *Being and Nothingness*—and Sartre himself suggests as much in the opening sentence of Part III. We have been working so far, he says, with the *cogito* by means of a study of negating action and have thus come to understand consciousness as for-itself.[1] But "negating" is the move undertaken in the study of imagination—the image is what is not—and as we have seen, it is, in *Being and Nothingness*, the force of negativity that makes the dialectic move. Moreover, the pre-reflective *cogito*, Sartre's variant of the Cartesian original, *is*, I think it is not too much to say, the magic consciousness identified with emotion in the earlier essay. This identity should become clear as we proceed—and I shall return to it finally in connection with Sartre's exposition of action in Part IV.

The Second Cogito

In the chapter on "Transcendence," Sartre has completed his study of the structures of the for-itself, grounded in the discovery of the pre-reflective *cogito*. Then in the same chapter he goes on to consider some structures characteristic of reflection as well. The whole movement, however, has been confined to *one* consciousness, whether thetic or non-thetic. We have not yet evaded—or even discovered in our path—what Sartre calls "the reef of solipsism." Nor, as I noted above, have we discovered the body: since the body, Sartre insists, is in the first instance "that which is known by the Other." We must first learn (1) how there can be the Other; and (2) how my being is related to the being of the Other.[2] These questions, in Sartre's view far more difficult than any he has asked so far, must be answered before we can understand the body, whether "for-itself" or "for-others." Thus Part III is entitled "Being-for-Others," and "The Body" is sandwiched between the "Existence of Others"—since it appears first as known by others—and the "Concrete Relations with Others," of which the body serves as vehicle (and victim). Meantime, at the beginning of Part III, we are still in the realm of the *cogito,* interpreted (with the help of the study of negation) as for-itself.

Having set the problem, Sartre proceeds (in Section 2) to consider the reef of solipsism, noting the inability of both realism and idealism to steer their way past it. "Realism" in the Cartesian tradition is a philosophy based on intuition; but it provides (as Gilbert Ryle, too, has argued) no intuition of the soul of the Other. Thus, as far as knowing a real Other is concerned, it gives way to idealism. But idealism, at least in its Kantian form, also fails to deal with persons; it gives us no critique of social experience. Nor can the Other be explained as a Kantian "regulative idea," a mere guiding maxim: the Other has to come precisely from *outside* my experience, as no item in Kant's cognitive landscape is allowed to do. The Kantian "solution," therefore, ultimately gives way, in its turn, to an ungrounded realism. So both these positions fail: both (Cartesian) realism and (Kantian) idealism have had to leap to the Other by an unintelligible and purely external negation. Or if philosophers have tried to substitute an *internal* relation, they have moved, like Leibniz or Spinoza, to God as foundation of the I-Other relation. What we must do, however, Sartre argues, is to find some positive solution which neither falls back on God as all-absorbing reality nor surrenders to solipsism.

Sartre now looks (in Section 3) to his predecessors for guidance. He finds in Husserl a purely cognitive approach which still leaves open the road to solipsism. Hegel has recognized rightly that the problem is one of *being*, not of *knowing*, and these two categories will stand in sharp contrast throughout Sartre's own argument. But despite this seminal insight, Hegel too fails, Sartre insists, since he neglects the place of the individual in the inquiry, and therefore the place of the *cogito*. Heidegger too neglects the *cogito;* yet even his existent, for all the emphasis he places on *Mitsein,* remains isolated. From these historical reflections Sartre draws four conclusions. We must start from the *cogito,* though of course from his *pre-reflective cogito,* which is prior to knowledge. If I am seeking the Other in a sphere anterior to the worked-up thesis of a knowing attitude, moreover, I am seeking him somehow *not* as object. Yet at the same time I am seeking him, further, insofar as he reveals himself as not being me, even though this "not-being-me" is not the familiar in-itself of the knowable material world. On the contrary, this is a new kind of not-being-me: not that of the cup-which-is-not-myself but that of the One Who, though neither myself nor my object, yet looms up, before and behind knowledge, as uncannily Someone Else.

The most important lesson Sartre gleans from his investigation, however—most important, at least, for our understanding of the argument to come—is the one he lists first, before the three just mentioned. The Other must be approached, he tells us, not by any abstract argument (all these have failed), but *by a second cogito.* And this move, from the original *cogito* to the *cogito* by which I apprehend the Other, he likens to Descartes's move in the Third Meditation from himself to God.

The parallel is worth thinking about. *Via* the methodological doubt of the First *Meditation,* Descartes moved in the Second *Meditation* to his indubitable starting-point, the self-guaranteeing awareness of his own existence in any moment of awareness. Whenever I pronounce it, the sentence "I think, I am," cannot fail to be true. And this pellucid moment of self-contained self-awareness is the unique beginning of philosophy. But what comes next? As he explains in the *Regulae,* Descartes's method consists in establishing a first and simplest intuition, "an act of a plain and attentive mind, so clear that no doubt remains concerning that which is apprehended," then in moving step by step from this first intuition to the next simplest and so on, until he has covered, surely and carefully, the whole range of human knowledge. At the outset—until a goodly portion at least of the whole system is established —he must proceed, he insists, in this heuristic manner, not, as ancient mathematicians pretended to do, by the method of axiomatization and proof. And he has himself confirmed in the *Replies to Objections,* that it is this method of discovery—the synthetic method, as it was traditionally called—that he is using in the *Meditations.* As the title of the work declares, he is going through a series of *meditations,* schooling himself to move, and moving, from one perfectly established, self-contained intuition to another. At the start of Meditation III he has reached the first of the series, and now needs to find a path to a second, which must be equally indubitable, equally susceptible to direct apprehension by the mind. If he is to achieve knowledge of an external world, moreover, this second idea must be something outside himself. And in particular, if he is to trust his clear and distinct ideas beyond the self-evident, momentary presentation of any one of them, it must be the idea of an all-good, all-powerful God. Now on the view of Husserl or any pure phenomenologist, the first of these two demands misleads him, since it takes him beyond pure consciousness to metaphysics. But the second demand, ever since the publication of the *Meditations,* has raised the question of the "Cartesian circle." Descartes needs God to guarantee his clear and distinct ideas, yet he has to use clear and distinct ideas to prove the existence of God. How, if at all, can this peculiar move be justified? For our purposes we may safely set aside the scholarly debate on this subject, and concentrate on one very simple point. All we need for our present purpose is to recognize that, logically speaking, this *is* a very peculiar argument, precisely because it is not so much an argument, in the logician's sense, as it is the *strategy* of a discoverer. The philosopher in his meditation must direct his attention from his first, self-contained, self-conscious intuition to another equally self-sustaining intuition. For all the complications of the Third Meditation, with its "formal" and "objective" realities, its modified causal principles, and so on, what the whole thing amounts to is *one* straightforward step from intuition I (the *cogito*) to intuition II (God). Once the thinker has that, once he has looked with total attention at the idea of God that his own mind innately contains, he will have what he needs to go on again: the guarantor of his clear and distinct ideas, the shield against error, the patron of a unified knowledge of nature and of man. All this will follow. But in itself the step from the *cogito* to God is simply the turning of attention from one direct presentation to another equally direct.

What of Sartre? The external world is already with him in the in-itself whose negation the for-itself is. And he is certainly not moving from his (pre-reflective) *cogito* to God; for him God is not only non-existent but impossible. That solution to solipsism, which he has rightly recognized as typical of the tradition, he certainly cannot adopt.

Moreover, his original *cogito,* being non-thetic, was not *known,* as the Cartesian *cogito* is; it was only *lived.* Nor is the move to the second *cogito,* the *cogito* of the Other, a cognitive move. As I have already said, Sartre contrasts throughout *being* and *knowing,* and the move here is from *being* to *being,* not, as for Descartes, from one moment of knowing to another. In all these respects the situation here is very different.

Yet the parallel Sartre draws between his argument and Descartes's is exact. He has been working so far, if with far-ranging dialectical instruments, on the ground of *one* self-contained, unique beginning, the pre-reflective *cogito,* the consciousness (of) self which is, for him, the fulcrum of all intentionality, of all outward-directed, and indeed all reflective, thought. It is this first and unique *cogito* which supports all the structures of the for-itself. But the for-itself, like Descartes's moment of self-aware-ness, is, and must be, *alone.* Another for-itself would be for-*itself.* How then can the for-itself discover such a con-tradictory double of itself? Only by a new, separate, equally absolute "intuition," or quasi-intuition, which looms up in experience as direct and overwhelming, but not for-me. Descartes has first discovered an idea of him-self; he has secondly—has always had—an idea of an all-good, all-powerful Deity. With reverence he looks at this idea, and behold, God *is.* He has but to inspect this idea and all that he needs will follow. Sartre has first dis-covered a different and non-thetic *cogito;* and he has no idea of God to which he may next proceed: he cannot re-cover the old gentleman who receded from the Parisian rooftops so long ago. But he does have, as Descartes does in Meditation III, an experience which reveals to him directly a second directly apprehended presence. That presence is the presence of the Other, and the experience through which he apprehends it is the experience of *shame.* Although he acknowledges three Other-revealing emotions—shame, fear, and pride—in the course of this chapter, it is shame he starts from, not only in the description of the Look—in the scene at the keyhole—but in the very beginning of the argument. I make an awkward gesture (say, picking my nose), and suddenly I find myself observed. The Other is there. In the *Meditations,* the believer looks with reverence to his God and acknowledges His being as the source of all being. The for-itself is ashamed, and the being before whom he is ashamed is discovered to him as the Other, the monstrous for-itself that is not *my* for-itself, which by its very being threatens me with degradation to objectivity. Just as the intricacies of the Meditation III reduce to one move from the *cogito* to the apprehension of the idea of God, so the complexities of Sartre's argument on the Other reduce to one move from the first, pre-reflective *cogito,* the *cogito* of the for-itself, to the "second *cogito,*" the *cogito* that reveals the Other.

Shame, Fear, Pride

We have already looked at the main steps of Sections II and III, on solipsism and on Husserl-Hegel-Heidegger. In Section IV, The Look, Sartre returns to shame as his starting-point, and asks in detail his two original questions: on the Existence of the Other, and on my relation to it—both, remember, as questions of *being,* not of knowing. In other words, the problem is not, as philosophers often put it, how I *know* other minds. On the level of probability I could manage that as I can the inferential knowledge of any other object. But the scandal is this: the world is organized around me, while the Other as Other claims to organize the world around him. Yet if, as it is, the world is my world, made the world it is by my self-projec-

tion, how can such an Other *be?* And how, in my being, do
I relate to him? These are the questions Sartre has to ask.

There are three main divisions of his exposition.
First is the phenomenology of the Look, which reveals the
Other and my relation to him. Second comes the ontology
of the Other: who is the Other, what is his being and the
being of my relation to him? Finally, there is the metaphysical question, why is there an Other, a question which
leads us back to the temporal dimensions of past, future,
and present, and introduces briefly the problem of
"mind" as an (im)possible totality of consciousnesses. I
shall not try to trace in detail this complex and often obscure argument, but shall only stress some of its chief,
and debatable, themes.

The description itself is among the best known sections of *Being and Nothingness:* the jealous watcher at
the keyhole (let's call him Pierre), wholly engaged in
spying out those within. This is the paradigm of the "situation" as Sartre here defines it. Pierre's jealousy *is* his absorption in the conjecture that Thérèse may be in there in
bed with Paul. That is Pierre's world; the fact that he is the
lover of Thérèse, who is having an affair with Paul is what
makes him jealous, and thus makes his jealousy, makes
him as a jealous man. But these "facts" are facts of a
human situation only through his jealousy. Were he wholly
indifferent to Thérèse and indeed away making love to
Annette, they would not be the facts they are. Situation always has this dual character. I live the world in and
through my (non-thetic) consciousness (of) self—in this
case, for Pierre, through *being* jealous. But, on the other
hand, my consciousness (of) self, in this case Pierre's
jealousy, *is* projected, through the keyhole, into the room
where Thérèse and Paul may be in bed together.

This duality of non-thetic consciousness, reflecting

the way I am in the world through my emotion, so that my emotion is just my way of being-in-the-world and yet at the same time makes the world what it is, makes the grapes sour or my mistress unfaithful—this duality of situation is universal, as we shall see later when we return to Sartre's treatment of the emotions in Part IV. But there are certain emotions which uniquely reveal the Other, reveal him not as a probable object in my world, but as lived by me in his very being. These emotions, once more, are shame, fear, and pride: in the keyhole case, of course, shame. Pierre has been looking through the keyhole; suddenly he feels himself looked at; someone is coming; he freezes; instead of the impassioned mediator of an all-absorbing situation, he becomes—a spy. Suddenly he is degraded to an object, a puppet with a role, the nasty role of sneak. He acquires a "character": a man who doesn't trust his mistress. And that degradation happens, not just through a change of mood, from jealousy to shame, but through the upsurge of the Other whom his shame reveals. Shame is shame of myself before the Other; through it the Other is there as He Who Makes Me Ashamed. Of course jealousy, too, it may be objected, is jealousy of Another. But, Sartre would insist, it is not other-related in the same way as shame. In jealousy I am conjuring away through my emotion the escape of one of my possessions—wife or mistress. A loved object is, in Sartre's terms, just that: an object, and no more. Jealousy, therefore, is my magical way of keeping what is mine. But shame takes me from myself —and my possessions—and drops me, dizzyingly, into a place in the Other's world: he sees before him—a jealous lover. Thus I become a character in his drama, an object in his world.

Fear, too, reveals the Other directly and immediately as there. It transforms the world I was engaged in into the Other's world, in which I may be a victim. A soldier reconnoitering in a valley feels himself looked at from a farmhouse on the hill, and is afraid. He is afraid because somebody may be looking; and somebody's being there —eyes looking—is what is revealed through his fear. Before that, he was curious, on the lookout. Suddenly he is instead a possible target for a sniper's bullet. That is what it *is* to be afraid. In other words, the Other, seeing me, also sights me; I am no longer myself, but the target in his sight. As the Other looms up as He Who May Shoot Me, so I become, in fear, He Who May Get Shot. And with this revelation I lose my freedom. For it is the predator who freely stalks his prey; the prey, on the contrary, however fast he runs, is prey, not out of his own free choice, but because the Other makes him so. Thus the Other reveals himself by robbing me of my freedom: it is, suddenly, his freedom I have to live, not mine. That is why, Sartre follows Gide in saying, the Other plays the Devil's part. That is why, to quote Sartre's own familiar maxim, "Hell is Other people." The revelation of the Other is the loss of freedom, the fall of the self into the Other's world. This is the second *cogito* Sartre was seeking:

> Just as my consciousness apprehended by the cogito bears indubitable witness of itself and of its own existence, so certain particular consciousnesses—for example, "shame-consciousness" bear indubitable witness to the *cogito* both of themselves and of the existence of the Other.[3]

And this second *cogito,* it must be emphasized once more, is still—or again—on the level of being, not knowing. Although, admittedly, the character the Other gives me, that is, the object I become in his world, is an object of knowledge, it is primarily something *he* knows. I may indeed know it, too, and even accept it as "my" character. Yet it *is* not I. It is separated from me by an infinite gap: the gap between my projection of my possibilities and the Other's projection of his possibilities, including this strange double that is "me." Thus as being-for-Others I am radically, inalienably alienated from myself. Over against the Other, in the light of the second *cogito,* that is how I am. Moreover, the whole of Sartrean sociality consists in attempts to evade this fate: in ruses to make the Other keep his objectivity in the world of my freedom, and so to prevent my relapse into objectivity in the world that *he* freely constitutes. From instant to instant of the for-itself's existence, one or other of two I-Other relations is bound to prevail: either the sadism that objectifies the Other or the masochism that perversely accepts my own reduction to an object through the Other's Being. A third possibility—namely, that *we* are together—is, on Sartrean premises, wholly impossible. We shall have to examine later the question whether Sartre has really changed his position in the *Critique,* but in *Being and Nothingness* there is no question: the Other is the Devil, he is out to destroy me, either he wins or I do.

All this is crystal clear from Sartre's examples, shame and fear, as well as from his exposition of the being of the Other and from his cryptic metaphysical remarks at the conclusion of the chapter. But he has listed three basic passions through which the Other is revealed. The third, pride, he expounds briefly, but does not illustrate. Perhaps before we go further we should ask abouts its nature too. Shame, we have seen, is my being as I live it in the Other's look which degrades me to an object in his world. Fear, too, is my being as I live it in the Other's look, as the look exposes me to his power. He has not yet torn me from myself, but on principle he can, through humiliation or even death. Thus in either shame or fear the Other is the permanent possibility of my destruction. But in pride, on the contrary, I seem to assert myself. I rise up over against Others and glory in my Being. This too may come as a sudden upsurge; out of absorption in the world, accompanied by non-thetic awareness of myself, suddenly I become aware of the Others as spectators, not of my humiliation, but of my prowess, of my success. The runner running a mile is (thetically) intent on getting to the goal; non-thetically he is living his own effort, he is that effort; nothing else in all the world is there. He wins —and the commending, acclaiming Others appear. He grasps the coveted cup, holds it aloft, is himself held aloft on Others' shoulders; proudly he acknowledges his own being as Winner before the grateful crowd. This sounds straightforward; but is it? If our Winner really objectifies the Others, they have lost their Otherness and become merely objects in his world; so they have not revealed themselves as Others acclaiming him, but as the tools of his own aggrandisement. This is surely not pride, but vanity. And in fact in Sartre's own terms, vanity is the use of my objectivity for this purpose: my beauty or prowess, what the Other finds objectively in me, I use to objectify him. But where in all this is pride?

Let us reflect again. I fear the Other's look, on principle, as the possibility of my fall. When the Other, this one Other, does in fact look at me, I fall into shame. But pride, it seems, arises as the converse of shame: it is my superior look against the falling Other, my self-assertion which responds to his by threatening him. And Sartre does indeed insist that pride arises on the foundation of "fundamental shame." It is the attempted reaction to it, turning the force of my free existence against the Other's freedom. But pride is also transitional and unstable, for in fact

I must either defeat the Other and so become wholly my own freedom, or succumb to shame and alienation before him, abandoning freedom for thinghood. Moreover, for Sartre, pride, like vanity, is necessarily in bad faith. It is in bad faith because it has allowed the illusion of objectification to creep into my self-consciousness. My consciousness, formerly absorbed in the effort to reach the goal, is now somehow made focal, taken as a being I can put before Others and "be proud of." But that is to make my freedom thing-like, to flee the dreadful self-making, the nihilation of the in-itself that is the for-itself. The runner running has winning-the-race before him as a not-yet-being whose non-being he has to nihilate. Winning, he becomes the one who has won. The others acclaim him, in his pride he seems to lift himself above them; but this thing-like being-the-winner is nevertheless a betrayal of his pure freedom. Moreover, it is a relation to anonymous Others, to the crowd, not to the Other. Only a non-denumerable, generalized Other can be before me in this fashion. To one Other I can be only victim or destroyer. Pride, in short, is the fleeting resurgence of the For-Itself against the Other-in-general, unstable, and, in its delusive use of self-objectification for self-assertion, necessarily in bad faith. In its revelation of the Other, therefore, it seems to be secondary to the basic emotions of shame and fear. It is ephemeral, abstract (directed to Others, not the Other), and self-deceptive. Basically, it is shame and fear that reveal the Other. Pride is an attempted, but impotent, alternate to shame.

For-Itself and For-Others:
An Ontological Excursion

Sartre has discovered, then, a second *cogito* which supplements the first and defeats solipsism. As Descartes moved from reverent inspection of his own innate idea of God to the revelation of the Divine Other who founds his—and all—being, so Sartre has moved through the experience of shame to the discovery of a Satanic Other who, by his existence, threatens to undermine and subvert the being of the for-itself that has discovered him. This is not so much the "refutation of solipsism" as it is the discovery that though I have to be myself alone, there is, against me, an Other who will not let me be— because *he* would be instead. Such, for Sartre, is the ground of all community: language becomes a form of seduction, love becomes an alternation between sadism and masochism, solidarity becomes class struggle. Although much in his account is subtly and convincingly observed, and although his argument, on his own premises —on the foundation, as he proudly acclaims, of the *cogito* alone—is irresistible, one wants nevertheless to question it.

What grounds have we for doing so? We may of course simply invoke the testimony of experience: the rare but still indubitable experience of mutual understanding, of the reciprocal look of peers; or the look of mother and infant, where the one protects and the other is protected. In its immediate appearance there seems no internecine warfare here. Or we may rely on an empirical generalization as counter-example: the fact that human infants deprived of a family setting develop more slowly, and deprived of some simulation at least of an affectionate initiation by Others into the human world, become retarded perhaps beyond recall. But counter-examples, though useful, are not sufficient to answer philosophical questions. We may still ask, in general, what philosophical objections we can raise to Sartre's position and to what alternative they lead us. There are, I believe, three different junctures in his argument, all interrelated, at which he clearly goes astray, and his phenomenological or empirical narrowness, his failure to *see* the counter-examples that invalidate his "solution," stems, philosophically, from the wrong turnings he has taken along the way.

The first and most fundamental error we have already noted: it is the confinement of the pre-reflective *cogito* to consciousness (of) self. Piaget's example of children who can do arithmetic but can't say how they do it illustrates, as we have seen, not in fact Sartre's consciousness (of) self, but a non-thetic consciousness that carries us away from self to the world. The usual thrust of non-thetic (or as Polanyi calls it, subsidiary) awareness is *from* clues within myself *to* something out there, for the understanding or performance of which I am relying on those inner clues. For Sartre, the for-itself develops as the negation of the in-itself, but this uncompromising negativity obscures the positive relation that binds me to the world. All that I appropriate from it, all that becomes part of me—like the child's skill in arithmetic—becomes at the same time a repertoire of attitudes, of incipient actions, through which I attend to my present concerns out there in the hope of achieving my future goals. There is a flowing reciprocity here of inner and outer, non-thetic and thetic, past and future. If Polanyi, with his distinction between focal and subsidiary awareness, has best described the epistemological core of this situation, Heidegger in *Being and Time* has best described the fundamental character of human being which makes this relation possible. Being-in-the-world is prior to "consciousness" and shapes it. Human being from the first is out there with things, just as the things are from the first "there" as stuff (*Zeug*) of interest or of use to human being. There is no cut between a consciousness (of) self and an external world which it denies and by whose denial it is. On the contrary, there is a primary and pervasive tension from "self" to world and back again—a tension through which, and through which alone, "consciousness" develops. Husserl has christened the forward and backward aspects of temporal consciousness "protension" and "retention." I suggest that the term "tension," with its connotation of tautness, of a stretch from—to—, would best characterize in general the concern-for, the being-out-there-with-, that founds the relation of man to world, and so the being of man himself.

Now if, as Heidegger and Polanyi have jointly shown, we are, in all the varieties of from-to awareness, out there with things, we are also always—perhaps first of all—already out there with other people. Being-with-others is an essential aspect of being oneself. Sartre, of course, resists this Heideggerian insight, which does, indeed, beg the question of solipsism. But it begs the question precisely because at long last we are not starting from the *cogito* but from a very different beginning: the everyday existence of human being before methodological doubt. And when we look carefully, without Cartesian prejudice, at the structures of this everyday existence, at the way in which human being is in the world, with things and other human beings, we find no reef of solipsism. We find, on the contrary, structures which eliminate the very question of solipsism. To put the question at all in these circumstances is to join Russell's correspondent, who wrote to him, "I am a solipsist; why isn't everybody?" In a refined and reflective intellectual posture, one can indeed wonder about our "knowledge of other minds." But in its fundamental way of being, human being becomes what it is in and out of its being-with-others. It is being-with that is primary and being-alone, being against the world and others, that is a negation, through philosophical contrivance, of that primary being.

One passage in the chapter on the Other shows clearly how, at this juncture too, Sartre has taken a fatal misstep—a step necessitated, indeed, by his initial misreading of non-thetic consciousness. Specifying a number of ontological theses suggested by the phenomenology of the Look, he declares: "being-for-others is not an ontological structure of the For-itself. We can not think of deriving being-for-others from a being-for-itself as one would derive a consequence from a principle, nor conversely can we think of deriving being-for-itself from being-for-others." [4] Now of course it is true that the for-others cannot be *deduced* from the for-itself nor the for-itself from the for-others. But what Sartre fails to see—and, given his Cartesian starting point, could not see—is that both the for-itself and the for-others depend for their very possibility on what we may call the among-others (to adopt for the moment his Hegelian style). For-itself and for-others are both expressions, and developments, of the fundamental structure of being-with-others-in-the world. To put it in ordinary language, the human individual is, in his humanity and in his individuality, necessarily and essentially an expression of a social world. Were he not among-others, in a world made by others, he could not become, and so could not be, himself. A human individual acquires humanity, not just by being born a member of *homo sapiens,* but by learning to participate in a given social world, which in turn, however he may rebel against it, he expresses in his very existence. Without being-among-others there is no human reality of any kind at all.

To admit this, however, would be to abandon, not only the primacy of the *cogito,* with its threat of solipsism or alternatively of annihilation by the Other, but also its corollaries: the ideal of the instant and the conception of freedom as pure activity. I mentioned earlier, in the discussion of Sartre's predecessors, his adherence to the Cartesian concepts of time and freedom. But let us consider here, very briefly, how his account of situation is affected by these preconceptions.

A situation, Sartre says, is wholly out there in the world and is the situation it is in view of my way of being in it. The watcher at the keyhole is "beside himself" in the scene he is watching and yet the scene is the scene it is because he casts himself into it. I throw myself into a situation, and so make it one. Looked at this way, the situation has two contradictory aspects: it is all in the world and at the same time all in my (non-reflective) consciousness. How can this to-and-fro be stabilized? Only by the appearance of the Other, who objectifies it. Only the Other, and my relation to the Other, Sartre recognizes, create a public world of objective space and time. Yet in terms of the for-itself, which is primary, the giving of myself to these organized totalities is always flight from myself. To act now, in here, this instant, would be freedom. To move out there, by means of the "character" I have "for others," from the situation into which I have been cast toward the future situation I envisage: all this can happen only in bad faith, as the flight of consciousness from itself. Only the present could be authentic, and thus free, if anything could.

Yet Pierre has not been dropped from heaven to watch and listen at the keyhole. His past, Thérèse's past, indeed the past of Gallic sexuality, combine to constitute his present preoccupation and reverberate in it. Besides, to watch or listen is to anticipate what may be happening on the other side of the door. The past into which I have been cast, the future possibilities to which I am attending, these make my present, make the spatiality that surrounds me. The present is a precipitation of the past through its direction to the future. Its spatial dimensions, however ample or however narrow, express, in the mode of simultaneity, the stretch toward the future that is mediated by the past. And that past is social. True, it is my past, as the future is my future. But it is "mine" in a perspectival sense: as the narrowing to one sector of a constant stream of interactions. Moreover, the future, too, will be not only mine but ours and theirs: the stream that founds the past of future projects, both my own and others'. Only out of this interplay of future and past, temporality and spatialization, can the present situation of this individual emerge as such. Social time and social space are already presupposed as necessary conditions for the existence of the for-itself. Thus the concept of a pure detached instant as the model for the existence of consciousness is illusory. On the contrary, human being is social precisely because it is historical. I have come "to myself" in and out of the tradition of some particular social world into which I happen to have been born. Human time is built out of historical stretches, not instants of pure consciousness.

If the moment is illusory, however, the moment of pure freedom, *a fortiori,* is illusory also. Human freedom is never instantaneous and complete. It entails the interiorization of standards, themselves socially—that is, historically—developed, standards in free submission to which I have learned to act responsibly, even if I often fail to do so. Indeed, the very concepts of "success" or "failure" imply submission to standards by which achievement or its denial can be judged. And again, however idiosyncratic one's standards may become, they must be communal, and thus historical, in three senses. First, they must have grown out of a social world. Secondly, as standards they must claim universality: they entail what Polanyi calls "universal intent." They express, not just my "subjective" preferences, but rules by which I judge my own performance and judge that any other person in my circumstances should judge his. Thus the very concept of free action demands a relation to others; I as a free agent am this unique center of action and choice that has developed through participation in, as well as expresses, the standards of this culture, accepted by me with universal intent. Acting as free agent, in other words, I act not only as myself, but as he-who-would-do-so-and-so-in-such-and-such-circumstances. It is this possibility of *de*tachment that makes an action free. For it is characteristic of a human person, as Helmuth Plessner has emphasized, to be able to put himself in another's place and another in his. Thus the human present, too, the moment of action itself, has a social extensiveness. In this sense role-playing is not as such a betrayal of freedom as it is with Sartre's waiter, who does not exist as waiter but only plays the part; it is rather—the instantiation of freedom.

Finally, if freedom arises out of a social past and exists through generalization (spatialization?) of the present, its primary thrust is to the future, but a future which reverberates beyond my own possibilities; it will be the stuff of others' actions as well as of my own. Now admittedly, Sartre himself, like Heidegger, stresses the futurity of human existence: I am my possibilities. But his all-or-none dialectic, combined with his Cartesianism, leads him to interpret this being as a non-being: a possibility is what is not (yet), and so to be a possibility is to be what is not—and thus to not-be, to be only in the mode of nihilation. To be in the mode of possibility, however, is also to be: to be as a protension, a stretch to the future; to follow Merleau-Ponty's metaphor, a "fold in being" rather than a "hole." The present situation, once more, becomes what it is through the *pro*specting of possibilities founded on, and limited by, the development of a retrospected past. The introspection of a for-itself is the condensation into a relatively instantaneous stretch of consciousness of these primary temporal relations. But those relations, too, as I have been trying to suggest, also entail sociality. The history out of which I act is the history of a culture; the future into which I act is social both as the stuff of history for future actions, whether of myself or others, and as demanding, in its character of responsible action, reference to standards that are socially derived, and universal in their intent—applicable to myself at other times and to others as well as to myself.

The Body

In all this "beating about the neighboring fields" I have been commenting on Sartre's statement that the for-Others is not an ontological structure of the for-itself. I have been arguing that, on the contrary, the for-itself (and *a fortiori* the for-others) is an expression of the among-others, the primary relation which Sartre, in his commitment to the *cogito* and associated concepts, fails to see. This was the second misstep I wanted to point out. The third, equally apparent in a number of passages in the same chapter, is equally fundamental, perhaps even the most fundamental of all. For it concerns that most basic Cartesian error: the division of consciousness from the body.

In the text explaining his first Rule for the Direction of the Mind Descartes distinguishes between the unity of mind and the plurality of bodily skills. Thus his method from the very start rests on the separation of a pure and self-contained consciousness from the extensiveness of bodily existence. In the Third *Meditation* also—which corresponds, as we have noticed, to the place Sartre has reached in his argument in the chapter on the Other— Descartes is still operating wholly within the sphere of consciousness; the body in its real existence only reappears in the last Meditation. Sartre, it is true, has already admitted the in-itself as the target of intentionality, that plenitude from which the for-itself rises up as nihilation. The Other, however, we have seen, far from being the passive exteriority of the in-itself, is, menacingly and paradoxically, an-other *consciousness.* It is not, Sartre insists, the Other's eyes that look at me, but the gaze "behind" them, the consciousness that threatens to organize me into its world. So, through an-other consciousness, I fall from being for-myself toward the inertia of mere corporeality; thus it is that through the Other's look I discover my body. That discovery, however, is founded, Sartre insists, on the for-Others as an upsurge *in* consciousness. Even my relation to the Other is a relation between consciousnesses, in which the objective fact of his looking at me is "a pure *monition,*" [5] the occasion of my *feeling* of being looked-at. Indeed, I can be aware of the Other even when "in fact" he is not there. Thus, in the keyhole scene, Pierre may suspect someone is watching him watching and experience that watching as (or in) shame, and even though he finds himself mistaken—it was only someone leaving by the street door, there is no one there at all—his shame may linger.

Now of course it is indeed true that I may be aware of my presence to others even when in fact no Other is at hand. But is this experience therefore disembodied? Is it pure consciousness-of-peril-as-for-itself-before-the-

Other's-possible-gaze? Sartre's own description betrays the untenability of this view. My shame, he says, "is my red face as I bend over the keyhole." [6] In other words, the emotion through which I find myself before the Other is at the same time a state of bodily being. My shame *is* my red face. . . . Similarly, Sartre has described earlier the fear that reveals the Other to a reconnoitering soldier. He hears crackling over there in the undergrowth—and becomes vulnerable, a body that could become another's target. What happens here? In Sartre's terms, I fall from thetic consciousness of the surrounding territory, sustained by non-thetic consciousness (of) self (I am curious, interested, alert), to thetic consciousness of my body as an object in another's world, carried by the special non-thetic consciousness (of) self that is called fear. Now what is correct in this account, it seems to me, is that I do, in shame or in some kinds of fear, become aware of my body in a new way. But that is not to say that I was not in any way aware of it before. My shame *is* my red face as I bend over the keyhole. But my jealousy, too, my intentness in watching, was, not just non-thetic consciousness (of) self as such; it was non-thetic consciousness of my embodied self, it was the stealthiness of my posture, the quiet with which I breathed, the way I strained to see what was going on on the other side of the door. I exist as embodied being-in-the-world, and in no other way. Of course Sartre knows this; he is no believer in a Cartesian *res cogitans* or disembodied soul. Then how, on the one hand, does he see my relation to my body prior to the Other's degradation of me to an object in his world, and, on the other hand, what really is the bodily aspect of my being that the Other reveals to me?

To answer these questions we need to examine the next chapter, on "The Body," and we can then return to the question, how Sartre's view of the body / consciousness relation has helped to mislead him in his view of the Other.

In general, we have seen, Sartre's philosophical method in *Being and Nothingness* is one of flights and perches. He passes by dialectical moves and counter-moves from one phenomenological description to another. But sometimes he also adopts the Heideggerian habit of piling up oracular pronouncements, so that the argument all but vanishes beneath their weight. This holds especially of the discussion of the body, and most of all of its first part. Thus the argument is difficult to disentangle; but let me try to summarize its main theses and, as I see it, its major difficulty.

Sartre expounds in turn three aspects of the body: the body for-itself, the body for-others, and the body for-itself as known by the Other. In all three sections he is re-working themes we have already met. Thus the body for-itself is the concrete expression of my facticity, of the necessity that I be born *some* where, *some* how. It is the necessity of my contingency, the condition for all possible action on the world. In other words, it is simply the necessity that there be *a choice*. It is the choice that I am. As for-itself, however, the body is consciousness. It is the non-thetic consciousness through which, thetically, I act out and into the world. And at the same time that consciousness is wholly body. For it is, again, precisely the necessity of my contingent existence, born thus and so into a world, that body for-itself is. Secondly, the body for-others is what results when the Other consciousness, emergent into my consciousness as alien transcendence, is in turn transcended. What enters my consciousness first, to be sure, is not the Other's body, but the Other as transcendence, as Other-consciousness and threat; but in responding to this threat I can in turn transcend his transcendence and so make him—flesh. That is how I live the Other's body for-himself, through my demotion of him to the protoplasmic quivering of mere life. Not, mind you, to the in-itself: that would be to know the Other's body just as I know inanimate things, to know him as a corpse. No, the degradation to flesh is the transcendence of his transcendence, which still entails reference to his transcendence in my very conquest of it. It is the means by which I reduce to the level of mere living the spontaneity by which the Other organizes his world, his world including myself in it as transcendence to be transcended. "Out, out, vile jelly!" Gloucester's eyes are not pieces of gelatinous matter, but the instruments of another's gaze, the accusing gaze of a wronged father and friend. It is that sort of transcendence that torture aims to transcend. Thirdly, I live my body, not only as for-myself, but as known to the Other. I live my body as alienated, as slipping from me into a place in the Other's world. This is the root meaning of alienation for Sartre, on which his social theory will be built. All these aspects of bodily being, finally, Sartre sums up in a final phrase: "The body is the instrument which I am." [7] This summarizing statement, he holds, lays to rest once and for all any problems that the body, appearing to the for-itself, might have evoked.

Yet it also summarizes, in my opinion, both the impasse to which Sartre's approach to the body has brought him and the way out he is, thanks to his own premises, unable to take. What is it to *be* an instrument? It is to be a means, but to what end? The end is the for-itself's project, the nihilation of what is in favor of what is not, the nihilation that I am. But how can I be at the same time my possibility and the means to that possibility? And how can I know that I am so?

The answer to both questions is a single one. Sartre has been operating all along, we have seen, in terms of a strict dichotomy between knowing and being, or knowing and living. Knowing is a thetic confrontation with the object of thought; contrasted with it is the non-thetic awareness of the fashion in which, the passion by which, I relate myself to that object. The Other looms up not as the object of knowledge, but as lived by me as threat to my own being. Similarly, the body, for myself, is lived and not known. Sartre makes this crystal clear in a brilliant analysis of the traditional philosophy of sensation, in which he moves from the will-of-the-wisp "sensation" (or sense-data), to sense and sensible objects, and then to action as the necessary correlate of sense. His argument leads him to the insight that our sense-mediated interaction with the world, and therefore all our information about the world, is necessarily tied to its point of origin, the point of view that is my bodily being. The cup is not just on the table, it is to my right, from where I sit, beyond the pencil, and so on. If I remove from such relations all perspectival reference, I remove their content. Thus my body is the instrument that I am, the instrument of instruments, because it is my point of view. The body, Sartre says again, is the neglected, the surpassed. Precisely. It is the surpassed because in and through it I act out onto the world and am acted on by things (and people) in the world. It is also, and for that reason, the indispensable ground of knowledge and of action. Without it knowledge would vanish into contentless relations. For suppose the body, instead of being a non-thetic ground of action, were itself known. Such knowledge would be empty. Sartre writes:

> In this case . . . the fundamental tool becomes a relative center of reference which itself supposes other tools to utilize it. By the same stroke the instrumentality of the world disappears, for in order to be revealed it needs a reference to an absolute center of instrumentality; the world of action becomes the world acted upon of classical science; consciousness surveys a universe of exteriority and can no longer in any way enter into the world.[8]

Alternatively, therefore, for Sartre the body must be lived and not known. Thus, secondly, he continues:

> . . . the body is given concretely and fully as the very arrangement of things in so far as the For-itself surpasses it towards a new arrangement. In this case the body is present in every action although invisible, for the act reveals the hammer and the nails, the brake and the change of speed, not the foot which brakes or the hand which hammers. The body is lived and not known.[9]

And these two possibilities, he insists, are wholly disparate and mutually exclusive. Living is never and cannot be knowing; knowing is never lived.

Yet if the first alternative is empty and for us impossible of achievement, and the second full of all the concrete content of experience and, for us, necessary, why must we keep up the pretense that there is a dichotomy here? In fact, there is none—or rather, there is the duality of subsidiary and focal awareness, a duality inherent in all knowing and all action. But this is not the irreconcilable duality of living against knowing. It is the unity-in-plurality of lived bodily being as it bears on knowing and, indeed, on all rational action. Thus the body is present though invisible in the hammer and the nails just because it is through my subsidiary awareness of hammer, nails, hand, arm, that I am focally aware of placing the picture the way

I want it on the wall. All reasonable action on the world, all knowledge of the world, from perception to the grasp of the most abstract theories, shares this same structure. Read in terms of the concepts of focal and subsidiary awareness, then, Sartre's dicta on the body take on a different meaning. Thus, for example, he writes:

> My body is everywhere: the bomb which destroys my house also damages my body in so far as the house was already an indication of my body. This is why my body always extends across the tool which it utilizes: it is at the end of the cane on which I lean and against the earth; it is at the end of the telescope which shows me the stars; it is on the chair, in the whole house; for it is my adaptation to these tools.[10]

This is true. But it is not a description of living as against knowing; it is a description of the structure of knowledge itself.

Once more, however, this simple move is one Sartre cannot make. The pure act of consciousness and the tension of living must be for him wholly and ineradicably opposed. He declares early in the chapter, for example, that touching and being touched, the one purely active and the other purely passive and external, are entirely opposed to one another. At the close of the chapter he insists again: my hand as touched is a mere external object, my hand as touching is my consciousness in act. Two hands, both mine, belong to two worlds, and are forever separated by the total gap that isolates for-itself from in-itself, nihilation from reality, consciousness from the external world. It is, I believe, with the exposition of this chapter in particular that Merleau-Ponty was wrestling from *The Phenomenology of Perception*—which begins with a theory of the body—to *The Visible and the Invisible,* where he was still struggling with the mystery of the touching-touched, the seer-seen. And it is, in my view, Polanyi's distinction between focal and subsidiary awareness, and the theory of tacit knowing elaborated on the basis of that distinction, that provides the solution for the problem. Merleau-Ponty comes very close to it in *The Phenomenology of Perception* and, as we have seen, even Sartre himself comes close to it in many passages, especially in this chapter. But, as always, his Cartesianism continues to hold him in thrall. The step to enfranchisement of lived bodily existence as the vehicle of knowledge and of rational action he is unable to take.

But the crucial question for our present discussion still remains. I have been considering the account of the body as, in my view, the third place where Sartre goes astray in his approach to the Other. It seems clear to the point of truism that history and with it sociality are prerequisites to an understanding of our being with others, as distinct from Cartesian instantaneity and the isolation of the single for-itself. What has bodily being to do with this?

The answer is given, by implication, in Sartre's own argument. The Other for me, he makes it clear, is in fact the Other as embodied. Consider my perception of the Other. Suppose I see Pierre raise his arm. This is not, Sartre says, the perception of an arm raised beside a motionless body; what I see is Pierre-raising-his-hand. Thus, he concludes, Pierre's body is *in no wise* to be distinguished from Pierre-for-me: "The Other's body with its various meanings exists only for me: to be an object-for-others or to-be-a-body are two ontological modalities which are strictly equivalent expressions of the being-for-others on the part of the for-itself." [11]

Yet if this is correct, what has happened to the Other as Consciousness? Other as body, Sartre has insisted, is posterior to that first, hemorrhagic starting into being of the Other which threatens to organize the world around him and so drains me away from myself. The Other as body is secondary to this experience, just as my own living of my body for me is secondary to my being, the same being, but in a wholly other ontological dimension, as nihilating for-itself. But isn't Pierre-for-me Pierre in his *original* way of being in my world? Is it not bodily being-with that comes first, ontologically as well as empirically?

Sartre comes very close here to saying this himself —for instance, in his discussion of expression. In those phenomena mistakenly called "expressive," he insists, there is no hidden spiritual something behind what appears. The expressions are the phenomena: "These frowns, this redness, this stammering, this slight trembling of the hands, these downcast looks which seem at once timid and threatening—these do not express anger; they are the anger." [12]

Yet this is not behaviorism. The Other's expression and in it his very being are not given me as the inkwell is, as an inert piece of matter. What I see is *an angry man;* his mood is in his looks as their meaning. It is Pierre acting on the world through anger that is before me, directly and all at once. But this is just the bodily being of others through which, and in interaction with which, the for-itself develops. In the family, in social groups, in the workaday world, it is the bodily being-there-with-me of the others that enables me to become, among them, the person I am. Now for Sartre, of course, this being with others is always being against others. To perceive the Other in his bodily being is to perceive him as a transcendence transcended, as a center of meanings which I try to apprehend, and overcome, out of my own for-itself. It is to see his bodily presence as derived from that first clash of consciousnesses which is the original emergence of the Other. I make him a body in order to defeat him, to put him *out* of action.

Yet if we take the phenomena of expression as primary, and forget the compulsion of the *cogito,* the story is very different. For the Other's expression, and mine, may embody solidarity as well as conflict. Even in Sartre's example of anger, there may be mutuality—if, for instance, I share Pierre's indignation. And there are expressions which by their very nature exemplify, not transcendence transcended, but encounter. F. J. J. Buytendijk has analyzed in this sense, for example, the child's first smile, and Plessner the expression of the smile as such. Starting from the for-itself as solipsistic consciousness (of) self, such expressions can appear only as strategies in the internecine war of each against each. If, on the contrary, we start from bodily human being in the child's first year of life, we find the human person emerging in and through, not conflict, but love. It is affection, as the ground of encounter, and encounter itself, that shape the space in which the for-itself can grow, in which it can develop its own consciousness and its own freedom. But affection as much as anger is the bodily being-there of another with me. Thus if Pierre as a body and Pierre for me are correlative ontological indices of the same reality, I being-with-Pierre am also equally myself as body and myself for Pierre—and I myself-for-myself, in turn, am the inward resonance of those outward relations. I argued earlier that both the for-itself and the for-Others are expressions, and developments, of the among-others. We can now add the further thesis: that the among-others, like the for-itself and the for-others, is indistinguishable, in its root nature, from the bodily being—in this case the being together— of persons. The space I live in is the space created, however indirectly, by such bodily being-with. It is created in the first instance by maternal affection; it is developed and deepened, cramped or cut off, by the human presences, whether directly given, or mediated by cultural artifacts, that mark each personal history. The Other is there, as Sartre, too, notes, even in solitude. It is only with the others that I can have the breathing space to be myself. Thus, however inward and immediate its feelings, the for-itself is not a pure, self-dependent negation of an alien in-itself, but a bodily sedimentation, subjectively experienced, of the among-others.

Finally, if, as I have been arguing, the phenomena of expression illustrate the principle just stated, its best instantiation is the most institutionalized, as well as the most comprehensive, form of expression: language. For language is not only the primary medium in which we dwell together; it is perspicuously *both* mental and physical at once. "Man of words" though he is, Sartre's philosophical account of language is minimal and, indeed, absurd. True, language can be used as a "form of seduction"; in terms of Sartrean sociality that may well be its only use. But an adequate philosophical account of language must have at its disposal both a concept of human community that transcends Cartesian solipsism and a concept of a psychophysical unity that transcends Cartesian dualism. On the one hand, language demands for its possibility speaker *and* hearer; and on the other hand, language *is* the mediation of thought through a physical medium. Speech is indeed the primary vehicle of reason; yet it exists only in utterance. It is sounds or marks on paper with meanings *in* them. In this context, Merleau-Ponty's chapter, "The Body as Expression, and Speech," is the culmination of his dialogue with Sartre in *The Phenomenology of Perception.* Reference to it here must suffice to indicate where Sartre's view of bodily being-for-others has received its most definitive refutation.[13]

The Emotions

Sartre's account of the Other depends largely on his account of the passions of shame, fear, and pride. And the passions, for him, exemplify the non-thetic consciousness (of) self which is the under side, so to speak, of the thetic awareness by which the for-itself intends, and negates, the world, and so, by its nihilating activity, constitutes its own fundamental project—to be what it is not and to not be what it is. As I noted at the start of this chapter, this account of the emotions, and of the pre-reflective consciousness in general, carries over from Sartre's early essay on the same subject. Although worked up differently, at first sight, it continues in essence the analysis of consciousness initiated there. The example he had used in the early sketch was the way, in a puzzle-picture, I look for the figure (say, a gun) which the superscription says is there. It is the gun (which I do not yet see) that I am searching for; I'm not thinking about my searching, but sideways or underneath, so to speak, I am aware of what I am about. Emotions, then, are intensifications of this generic non-thetic consciousness. And in *Being and Nothingness,* as we have seen, starting from the cigarette example, the non-thetic consciousness (of) self, christened the pre-reflective *cogito,* stands firmly at the head of the whole argument.

It is worth looking briefly, in conclusion, at the fate of this theory in Part IV of *Being and Nothingness,* for we see there, that it is, paradoxically, not so much the irrationalism of which he has often been accused that prevents Sartre from breaking out of the impasse to which his argument has led him, as it is his thoroughgoing and incurable rationalism.

In the last part of *Being and Nothingness* Sartre is trying to found ontologically the structures which he has so far discovered phenomenologically. He is trying to establish the kind of reality that I have (or am) in and against the world, my body and the Other. But of course he is still working within the Cartesian distinction between human freedom, the unfettered choice of myself as my own project, and a passive, non-free, determined nature. Thus for him man must be either wholly free or wholly determined: for-itself and freedom, or in-itself and utter passivity—those are the alternatives. But what then of the passions —literally "sufferings": surely if I run away from danger, let alone fainting at the sight of it, it is because I am *overcome* by fear? No, says Sartre, I choose myself as fearing. I choose to exorcise the fearful magically, by running or fainting, instead of coping with it instrumentally and rationally; I make myself that kind of person and my world that kind of world. This is the same disjunction established in the *Sketch:* rationality or magic. Yet even when I act "rationally," I do have "subjective" "motives" as well as "objective" "reasons" for what I do. I have a goal which can be accounted for in both ways. Suppose my end is to help minority groups. Why? Because our society is divided and must be healed. But why do I want to help overcome this division? Because I am indignant at the unfairness with which minorities have been treated. Which is the real reason: the objective situation I want to see changed, or my feeling about it? Evidently, Sartre says, we are dealing with two radically distinct layers of meaning. How, he asks, are we to compare them; how can we determine the part played by each of them in the decision under consideration? This difficulty, he insists, has never been resolved; indeed, few have so much as glimpsed it. Thus historians, he points out, assign an objective reason where they can and where that fails point to an "irrational" motive as an alternative. If Clovis became converted to Catholicism, he points out, the explanation could be "objective"; we would say that since many barbarian kings were Arians, Clovis saw an opportunity of getting into the good graces of the episcopate which was all-powerful in Gaul. Here, then, the objective "reason" for his decision is characterized as a rational account of the historical situation. The reason for Clovis' conversion, in short, is the political and religious condition of Gaul, including the relative strengths of the Christian episcopate, the landowners, and the people. But for Constantine's conversion, on the other hand, one historian can find no such objective reason and so says: "he yielded to a sudden impulse." [14] If this were a correct analysis, Sartre suggests: "the ideal rational act would . . . be the one for which the motives be practically nil and which would be uniquely inspired by an objective appreciation of the situation. The irrational or passionate act will be characterized by the reverse proportion." [15] This dichotomy seems on the face of it to correspond so far to his own theory of emotion. Rationality and rational techniques or irrationality equivalent to magic: take your choice—and it's you who take it.

Now, however, Sartre wants to build this dichotomy into his account of freedom, and since both kinds of action, rational and magical, are after all action, he needs freedom on both sides. Let us look again at the reason: it is objective, but it is so only as "revealed to a consciousness" and in particular to the project of that consciousness as positing through the world what it—and the world —are not. Thus, it is *objective,* he tells us, that the Roman plebians and aristocracy were corrupted in the time of Constantine; it is objective that the Catholic Church was ready to favor a monarch who at the time of Clovis would help it defeat Arianism. Yet this state of affairs could be revealed only to a for-itself—"since in general the for-itself is the being by which 'there is' a world." Indeed, it can be revealed only to "a for-itself which chooses itself in this or that particular way—that is, to a for-itself which has made its own individuality." [16] For it is the for-itself, in its particular choice, that makes, not only itself, but the world of instrumental things as instrumental things. Thus, Sartre suggests, a knife is objectively an instrument to cut with; but if I had no hammer, I could just as well take up the knife and use its handle to hammer with. This apprehension of the knife would be no less objective than the view of it as a thing with a blade and handle, a thing to slice with. The same situation obtains for Clovis and the Church. That a certain group of bishops should assist him is merely probable; what is objective is what any for-itself could establish: the power of the Church over the people and its worry about Arianism. But what makes these particular "facts" a "reason"? Only their isolation by Clovis himself and their transcendence toward the possibility of his kingship. In short, Sartre concludes, "the world gives counsel only if one questions it, and one can question it only for a well determined end." [17] Reasons, therefore, are relative to ends. But the ends are made such by the project of the individual consciousness, and the very same project, as subjective, as felt, is a "motive." Clovis was ambitious. How shall we interpret that statement? "Ambition," Sartre says, has here the role of filling, giving its peculiar tone, to the non-thetic consciousness which carries inwardly, sideways so to speak, the outward thrust of consciousness. We are dealing here, he tells us, with one particular case of being-in-the-world. And just as it is the upsurge of the for-itself which causes there to be a world, rather than the meaningless exteriority of the in-itself, so here too it is the being of the for-itself itself as a pure project toward an end which causes there to be "a certain objective structure of the world, one which deserves the name of reason in the light of this end." [18] The for-itself therefore appears now as *the consciousness of this reason.* That is the positional side of consciousness. At the same time, however, this positional consciousness of the reason is also a *non-thetic consciousness of itself as a project toward an end.* It is in this sense that it is a motive. It lives itself non-thetically, as a project toward an end, a project, Sartre asserts, "more or less keen, more or less passionate," and this non-thetic, impassioned consciousness occurs, of course, at the same instant at which the for-itself is constituted "as a revealing consciousness of the organization of the world into reasons." [19] Thus through the recognition of the pre-reflective *cogito,* the apparent dichotomy of reasons and motives, or rationality and magic, has been assimilated to what seems to be a single theory of free action: reason and motive are correlative, exactly as the non-thetic consciousness (of) self is the ontological correlate of the thetic consciousness *of* the object. Just as the consciousness of something is consciousness (of) self, so the motive is nothing other than the apprehension of the reason in so far as this apprehension is consciousness (of) self. It follows, then, that the reason, the motive, and the end are "three indissoluble terms of the thrust of a free and living consciousness which projects itself toward its possibilities and makes itself defined by these possibilities." [20] So "reason" and "motives," rationality and magic, appear to be united as the single, yet double, upsurge of one consciousness in the apprehension of a determinable end.

How then does it happen that psychologists (and historians) can separate out "motives" and assign them as pre-existent determinants of action? It happens because of the nature of temporal consciousness. I make myself each moment out of nothing. But what I *had* made before takes on in memory a pseudo-thinghood: this is the illusory "circuit of selfness," in which, through a flight from ourselves, we make ourselves into things. It is in fact the production and the expression, not of original freedom, but of bad faith. Clovis sought the help of the Catholic bishops; that is the objective fact. What more is involved in saying he was ambitious? One may either be referring to an illusory "self" with properties, a pseudo-thing precipitated by the flight of time; or, more truly, to speak of the affectivity that accompanied his action, his "ambition," is simply to describe the feeling tone, the unreflective consciousness (of) self that carried his objective behavior on and in the world. It is still that pure moment of choice, the positing of a given end—in Clovis' case, the choice of conversion for the sake of possible kingship—that in the last analysis made the action what it was. Thus emotion is really the irrational converse of reason, which appears as a force of its own only through the illusion created by history. At the instant of choice, however, it is the reason that matters; the irrational "motive" is only its non-thetic other side. We have an objective end, a thetic positing of it which is a reason, and a non-thetic awareness (of) ourselves as so doing, which is a motive.

Two consequences seem to follow from this account. On the one hand: reason is primary. If passion is emancipated from its non-thetic role, if it moves on its own, it can be seen in two ways, either of them self-deceptive. It is either sheer magic, a surrogate for impotence—Sartre still accepts this formulation. Or it is a delusive hypostasisation into thinghood of what can, by its very nature as a kind of consciousness, deserve no such ontological stability. On the other hand, however, the reason itself which Sartre here elevates to primacy in the for-itself's existence—that reason has been emptied of all content. For "determinate ends" cannot after all stand on their own; it is simply the act of pure freedom that *makes* them ends. Thus if Clovis must isolate the facts from their context in order to aim at them, he can only do this—as any for-itself can only do—by nihilation. The possibility he aims at, the possibility that the church will support a Christian king, can be revealed to him only if the facts as they now are are transcended toward a state of things that now is not: he must surpass the present situation *toward a nothingness.* He must imagine himself crowned king, but to imagine is to posit what is not. He must see his lack as subject, that is, as non-monarch, and seek the lacking, kingship, and the bishops' support. Only in that nihilating choice does his reason assert itself as free. Thus we have at bottom either choice as subjective and irrational but illusory, or choice as rational and objective but empty. Determinate ends, seen as positive, would again issue in bad faith. The demand of reason, the primacy of positional consciousness, is absolute. But its content is—nothingness. If Sartre has banned Cartesian substance, if he has reduced extended things to the mere spread of a meaningless exteriority and "mind" to the moment of thought, positional or non-positional, he has also reduced Cartesian reason to Cartesian will, drained it of positive content for the sake of its autonomy. In the last analysis, it is the demand for total rationality in the instant of total freedom that forces him to turn the non-thetic, the less than luminous, mode of consciousness back into itself. It cannot, for him, give itself to the world, it cannot guide its possessor to the world, because to permit this would be to contaminate pure reason with feeling. Sartre, like his master Descartes, seeks a state "free of all cares and disturbed by no passions." He has not found, and cannot find it: for him, man is a useless passion, who tries to become God and fails. Only a radical rethinking of the concept of rationality could overcome this impasse. If passion is to be more than useless, it must be seen to have an end that is less than the pure reason of a *causa sui,* an end that is both known and lived, that is founded in history and fellowship, and in the embodied being out of which it takes its growth.

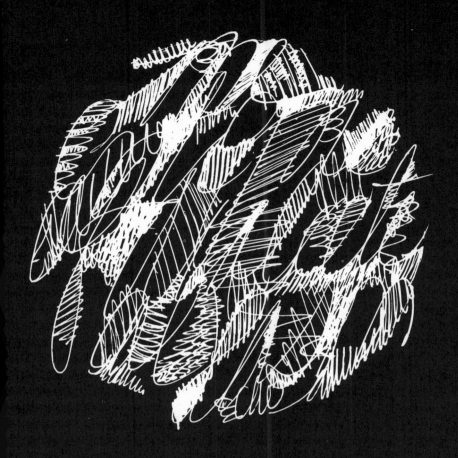

chapter six: the critique of dialectical reason

I. the development of sartrean dialectic

the critique: volume one, 1960

Being and Nothingness
was published in 1943. Sartre's
second major philosophical work, Volume One of the *Critique of Dialectical Reason,* appeared in 1960. Although I have referred
in passing to the *Critique,* my exposition so far has
been chiefly concerned with the sources of *Being and*

Nothingness, its argument, and some of its special problems. For many, however, including Sartre himself, the *Critique* marked a definitive step forward from his earlier work. Even an introductory essay, therefore—which makes no claim to giving a comprehensive analysis even of Sartre's philosophical work—must take account of the *Critique,* and especially of the question, whether and how Sartre's basic views have altered.

Although at this writing the *Critique* is not yet available in translation, its argument has been summarized for English readers in a number of places, notably by Wilfrid Desan in his *Marxism of Jean-Paul Sartre,* by R. D. Laing and D. G. Cooper in their *Reason and Violence,* and by Joseph MacMahon in his recent detailed study of Sartre, which is chiefly concerned with his literary work. Although I am not entirely happy with any of these summaries, I hesitate to embark on yet another. For one thing, the reason one feels one ought to present a summary of the *Critique* is relatively trivial. Seven hundred and fifty-five badly printed, scantily paragraphed, and altogether headache-inducing pages are furnished with the following guide:

Table des Matières	Pages
Questions de Méthode	13
Critique de la Raison Dialectique	113
Libre I	163
Libre II	379

That is all! So after one has laboriously made one's own table of contents, one would like to make it available to other readers (Laing and Cooper and MacMahon have done so, though MacMahon has failed to catch Section C4 of Book One!). This egocentrism on the part of Sartre and his publisher, Gallimard, doubtless will be rectified in the forthcoming English translation. Besides, on the one hand, the overall structure of the argument is perspicuous, and, in representing it one can only repeat what others have already said; and on the other hand, the contents, and even the method in its details, burst out, so to speak, in a number of directions, so that every reader seems to have his own *Critique* and his own perspective for the comparison of this work with the earlier one. Thus any attempt to recapitulate beyond the barest outline is bound to seem idiosyncratic, and had better be presented as criticism rather than mere summary. I shall offer here, therefore, only the sketchiest outline of the work's structure, and go on to look at some facets of it in the context of the question of Sartre's philosophical development— giving due warning that I am focusing on those puzzles that happen especially to fascinate me. To others, other problems and other concepts may seem of overriding interest.

The *Critique,* Volume One, is preceded by the essay "Questions of Method," published separately in English as *Search for a Method.* Here Sartre makes two major methodological points. First, he acclaims the exclusive, and victorious, candidacy of Marxism for the title of *"the* philosophy of the twentieth century," and claims for existentialism the ancillary task of reinstating the individual existent within an ossified pseudo-Marxist dogma. I have already discussed briefly Sartre's relation to Marx and Marxism, and can only echo here Aron's remark that in this connection Sartre behaves very much like the *pour-soi* of his own analysis: he seems to be a "Marxist" in the spirit of being-what-he-is-not and not-being-what-he-is.[1] In all his professions of faith, and despite the care with which he expounds or takes issue with some classical

Marxist texts (notably with Engels) in the *Critique* itself, Sartre's "Marxism" appears as somehow strained and artificial. I must leave it to better connoisseurs than I am to explain in detail why this is so. Secondly, Sartre outlines in this introductory essay what he calls the "regressive-progressive" method, in effect a rewriting of his theory of existential psychoanalysis, but with a more explicit emphasis on the role of social factors in providing the conditions for individual self-choice. Existential psychoanalysis was the method introduced in *Being and Nothingness* for studying the way a person makes, and has already made, himself. In the new version, based on a formulation of Georges Lefèbvre, one goes back, it appears, to the individual's beginning and then seeks to build up his history, progressively, from the origin thus understood. As he has approached his hero, Genet, in these terms, in *Saint Genet,* so now Sartre suggests the same method for the study of his favorite anti-hero, Flaubert, to whom, indeed, he has since devoted the first two volumes of a projected four-volume analysis under the title *The Idiot of the Family.* In the *Critique* itself, however, it will be society—and ultimately human history as a whole—that will be dealt with by this dual method of retrospective analysis and prospective reconstruction.

The groundwork for this vast project—to make the whole of history intelligible—is prepared in Volume One (all that exists to date). Book One of this volume moves from individual *praxis,* the act of what Sartre here calls "the practical organism," to the *practico-inert,* the movement, generated by human response to human need, which perpetuates itself as inhuman and anti-human. Sartre analyzes in detail two cases: the drain of gold from sixteenth-century Spain and the deforestation of China. In the latter instance, for example, the need for timber has let loose a chain of physical events from which an even more urgent need, the need for water, arises. The consequences of human action turn inhuman, and demand, in self-defense, new actions—which will again bring in their train new threatening results. This is in effect the for-itself, translated into "praxis," in interaction with the in-itself, now conceived, not as sheer exteriority, but as the network of material events and entities which both delimit and negate the agent's intent. Activity, in itself free—for, whatever befalls, man is still sovereign—is contradicted by passivity, or, better, by a kind of passive activity that runs away with it and threatens it with extinction.

It is out of this fall of *praxis* into its inertial consequences that Sartre sees arising what he calls "collectivities." These are mere "inorganic" collections of practical organisms, organized from outside by the demands of material needs and the scarcity of means to supply them. We depend on "worked matter," and it in turn sums us up, through its presence and its power, into additive totalities. The simplest case of this effect is the series, which Sartre illustrates with the (by-now famous) example of the queue at the bus stop at St. Germain des Près. There is not room for all—who will get a place? Only the limited dimensions of this material object serve to unite the would-be passengers, each of whom has *his* destination and *his* reason for going there. In terms of the abstract dialectic of the *practico-inert,* moreover, class too belongs to this category of collectives. In industrial society, for example, it is obvious that the machine, external to the worker, organizes him from outside himself. And, in general, the materials we work up to satisfy our needs revenge themselves by imposing a mechanical quality, a non-human organizing principle, which by its nature undermines our freedom. It is this external relation which determines class, as it does other "serialities."

This first major move, from *praxis* to the *practico-inert,* establishes an abstract and negative dialectic. Book Two of the *Critique,* "From the Group to History," is supposed to move toward the concrete and so to lead us to history itself—although at page 500, Sartre announces that we are still at the abstract stage! The first step, moreover, is not *from* the group, as the title suggests, but *to* the group, for we have not yet seen how there can be a *positive* dialectic of social reality or social action. Sartre looks first, therefore, at the "group in fusion," from which, if from anywhere, such a reality can be seen to rise. The case he studies is—almost *a priori*—the storming of the Bastille. Out of this classic instance of spontaneous action there comes in its dialectical turn the oath, which binds the joint actors into a brotherhood where each is "third man" to all the others. In the group that results there is thus a genuine, if mediated, reciprocity between each and among all. So far, so good. But the *practico-inert* must not be forgotten: as groups solidify and become traditional they become institutions. These, however, generate their own inertia, so that the threat to freedom, the self-denying consequence of action, returns to plague us. The constituting dialectic of group-formation gives way, thanks to the *practico-inert,* to a *constituted* dialectic, which is, not pure *praxis* but a mixture of *praxis* and *processus.* "Taylorism," a forerunner of time-and-motion studies, is an example Sartre analyzes at length in this connection. One expects at this stage a recurrence to the tragic to-and-fro of *Being and Nothingness;* true, man here tries to become man, not God, but here too he fails. Yet Sartre's conclusion is optimistic: he has laid the ground for a "structural anthropology," he declares at the close of his long and labored argument, and, on that foundation, for an account of history as intelligible: intelligible in the sense that free men understand it as the meaning of their own free actions. This would indeed seem to be a new message, written in the language of a new, and more hopeful, vision.

Reason, Analytical and Dialectical

With this sketchiest of sketches behind us, let us look now at some aspects of the *Critique* with the question in mind of whether, and how, Sartre has changed his position since *Being and Nothingness,* and first, the question, how he has changed his method. Here there is, at least in the first movement of the *Critique,* a striking innovation, and at the same time a development—or, to use a favorite term of Sartre's, a "totalization"—of the dialectic already characteristic of *Being and Nothingness.*

The novelty concerns the method of physics, or of the exact sciences in general, as Sartre understands it. Dialectic paired with phenomenology gives way to the "hypothetico-deductive method" with "dialectical reason" first as its explanation and finally as its source.

From his Cartesian beginning, we have seen, Sartre first discovered phenomenology, and applied it, according to his lights, in the *Emotions,* the *Imaginary,* and the *Transcendence of the Ego.* In *Being and Nothingness,* while he is fundamentally loyal to Cartesian method— and even, in some basic respects, to Cartesian metaphysics—he has set phenomenological description into the frame of a dialectical movement from which the power and direction of his argument derive. In the *Critique,* however, phenomenology has all but disappeared. There are, indeed, immensely detailed descriptions of historical events, and lengthy analyses of historical phenomena. An example of the latter (to which I shall return later) is the role of the radio in modern (chiefly pre-television) society. But these are either empirical accounts, subsumed under Sartrean dialectical categories —as with the Bastille—or abstract social analyses, again constructed with dialectical tools. One may indeed conjecture that, since phenomenology deals with the solitary consciousness, the turn to social themes was bound to involve a turn to other methods. Yet if one recalls the work of Alfred Schutz and his school, one must admit that phenomenology has in fact proved especially fruitful for the description of social worlds and the rereading of sociological problems. To turn phenomenology to this purpose one may of course have to abandon the transcendental ego—the ultimate I, still lonely in its sovereign power, that "constitutes" the whole panorama of "reduced" experience. But the transcendental ego was what Sartre had firmly exorcised in his earliest work: the "ego" is empty; indeed, it doesn't exist. Yet, at the same time, as we have seen, Sartre's phenomenology, like Husserl's, was still Cartesian, and therefore, as I have argued, still impotent to conquer solipsism. A Cartesian, and therefore a Sartrean, social phenomenology is inconceivable. Hence in Sartre's case it is reasonable that a deeper concern with the problem of social reality should entail a diminished interest in phenomenology as a philosophical method.

What is striking in the *Critique,* however, is not the absence of phenomenological description, but Sartre's new relation to a very orthodox conception of "scientific method." In *Being and Nothingness* the positivist conception of science and of the method of science is entirely marginal to Sartre's concerns. In that work he had argued tersely—and convincingly—for the meaninglessness of a pure "objectivity" which would be equivalent to pure exteriority—a Cartesian pure extension without its substantial base. The for-itself, though always out there with the in-itself, bestows on the in-itself whatever meaning that indifferent plenitude of being may acquire. "The world is human." Neither the in-itself in itself, nor the "objective" methods by which physicists study it, are of interest in the context of this ontology. Now it is otherwise. For one thing, a major model for understanding social life is drawn from physics: human action generates its own inertia, the *practico-inert*. Tariffs, or a price index, for example, "lived individually as impotence," constitute as an external "common material object" a *social* reality, a force which is "the practico-inert power of hundreds of thousands of men as *potential energy*." [2] Thus social reality is conceived on the analogy of physical reality, as distinct from the *praxis* of the individual. Sartre's use of this analogy, and its relation to the earlier conflicts of for-itself and in-itself, would be worth a detailed study. In the previous work the social world appeared as a vast network of techniques for my own aggrandisement (or for my fall into bad faith). Here, however, physics, not engineering, serves as the source for Sartre's explanatory model, at least of one major and recurrent aspect of social reality.

What I want to stress here, however, is another side of Sartre's new reliance on physics: his actual use of what he conceives to be the style of scientific reasoning, the so-called hypothetico-deductive method. In *Being and Nothingness,* as a phenomenologist aiming at ontology, Sartre is sucked into dialectic despite himself. In the latter work his attitude is critical: hence the title. Far from plunging into dialectic at the start, he relies on analytical reason to inquire whether dialectical reason exists. That is what he does not yet know. He asserts it as a hypothesis, then (as scientists have traditionally been thought to do) deduces consequences from his hypothesis and tests them empirically. Over and over he reminds us (and reminds himself; dialectical thinker that he is by nature and second nature, it is hard for him to remember) that we have not yet ascertained, are still trying to ascertain, whether in fact there *is* "dialectical reason" at all.

The hypothesis, of course, is vindicated, and in the end we see clearly, or so Sartre believes we should, that indeed our critical method is but one consequence of the all-inclusive power of dialectical thinking. Once established, therefore, the thesis first hypothetically entertained explains the very method by which it is discovered. But the tentative and experimental nature of our approach to its assertion is emphasized again and again. The whole argument is explicitly presented as one vast experiment.

Two brief comparisons may help to illuminate this Sartrean methodology. This work is a *Critique,* as massive and as ambitious as the *Critique of Pure Reason* itself —indeed, in a sense more ambitious than Kant's *Critique.* But Sartre's method differs radically from Kant's. First, he begins as an empiricist. He is trying to confirm a conjecture. He is experimenting, not moving among *a prioris*—a procedure Kant would radically reject. Clearly, then, he ought, moreover, to claim for his conclusions no such apodeicticity as Kant insists upon. Admittedly the dialectic will turn out, as we shall see presently, to be both "necessary" and "intelligible," but this will be an ontological, not a logical necessity—not even a necessity of "material logic," as Kant calls it. We are moving from the *a posteriori,* the realm of experimental investigation, to some other plane. Finally, when we arrive there, we stay there:

dialectic takes over. If we can enter into the self-understanding process of history as an intelligible whole—not a totality, indeed, but a "totalization," a whole process made of *praxeis* which understands itself from within—we shall see our initial method of analysis and experiment as one tiny, and pitifully abstract, offshoot of the concrete immensity within which we have found our intellectual home. True, the method is circular, in so far as its last stage founds its first; and Kant's method is circular, too.[3] But the first stage in Sartre's argument appears at its later stage to have been a taking-off place only, a springboard into a deep sea of significances. Kant's transcendental method, on the other hand, is much more modest in its circularity: for the justifying principles discovered by it and the experience, or the objects, they justify are precisely coterminous as well as interdependent. If there is no informed matter of experience, neither is there any form except as the form *of* the experience (or object of experience) whose form it is. The circle, though not vicious, is serenely static. Sartre's argument, by contrast—the reader will have seen it coming—is a rapidly expanding Hegelian spiral. If we follow Kant we rest secure in the knowledge of why things are as they were already. If we follow Sartre—or better, if we *could* follow him—nothing would ever be the same again.

Before we look at Sartre's Hegelianism as developed in the *Critique,* however, we might well compare his analytical method and its scope with another familiar theory of the method, not of science in general, but of social science. Since the turn of the century numerous philosophers and social scientists, accepting the positivist ideal of pure objectivity for the exact sciences, have argued that the study of man, in contrast to that of nature, demands "understanding" (*Verstehen*). In the first in-

stance the purpose of history was said to be not the formulation of general laws but insight into unique events, and
then the social sciences too were said to demand this kind
of insight. Such "understanding" was usually presented,
if not as a kind of empathy, at least as somehow more direct, more immediate than the highly abstract and impersonal scientific knowledge with which it was contrasted.
Now Sartre, too, in the *Critique,* speaks of "comprehension," which appears to be the equivalent of *Verstehen*.
Yet in the main, "comprehension" or understanding
seems to be, for him, a highly reflective attitude, to be
achieved after the labors of analytical reason, and even of
the dialectic, and on a new logical level. True, in "Questions of Method" he equates understanding with "existence itself." Thus he seems to be taking it as direct and,
as such, contrasting it, as existentialism's offering, with
the impersonal, objectifying attitude of an ossified Marxism. Existentialism, we are told, will inject human self-understanding into the bloodstream of Marxist social and
historical theory. When the life-giving elixir has done its
work, it will disappear; Marxism, revivified, will reign
alone. Yet even in this very passage, where understanding, acting, and the project are identified, understanding
is nevertheless described, not as immediate or intuitive,
but as an "indirect non-knowledge" which must found the
immediate knowledge of the intellect.[4] We seem to be offered, in other words, knowledge as a purely intellectual
operation of immediate apprehension, and understanding as its reflective, non-cognitive, but nevertheless "rational" supplement. As physics has treated nature wholly
"objectively," so, Sartre tells us, anthropology, too, has
treated man as object. That was wrong. Yet this error is
not to be corrected by turning aside to some more immediate awareness of man by man. It is to be corrected by a

more complicated process. First we have the field of "knowledge" which is equated with the scientific or "analytic," yet "immediate," apprehension of a subject-matter: still the Cartesian ideal of totally explicit self-generating truth. Then, hypothetically, we embark upon the labor of the dialectic which will ultimately [5] bring us to the stage where we see as a "permanent possibility" the reflective understanding of human organizations by human agents who observe them. Only by this devious route can we move from the single agent—if re-christened, still in effect the isolated for-itself, rising up as negation against the in-itself—to a social organization understood as such by a social observer who is himself an agent. The task of the social scientist—and even of the member of a social group—seems hard indeed.

Totalization

Hard, too, it appears, is the task of the dialectician who, taking over from the experimental reasoner, must prepare the ground for such social understanding. Nothing less than the total sweep of human history will do as his domain, and he must exhibit that vast totalization, Sartre insists, as both "necessary" and "intelligible." Such, he argues, is the indispensable prolegomenon to history—or to a critique of history?—itself. But if, as I have already suggested, Sartre's relation to dialectic here is more reflective, and, at the start at least, allegedly hypothetical, still the power of the Hegelian method over his thought, already evident in *Being and Nothingness,* is ready to display itself again—and more vigorously than ever. However wordy the text, however abstract its analyses, the Dialectic, once initiated, will carry us like a torrent, over any intervening rocks and boulders, to its inevitable close.

Again, I shall not venture to attempt here anything even approximating an exhaustive analysis of Sartre's dialectic as exhibited in the *Critique.* But an enumeration of some of the chief counters out of which it is constructed should sufficiently indicate its scope and style, and its difference, as well as its likeness, to the earlier dialectic of *Being and Nothingness.* I shall focus on three concepts: totalization, necessity, and intelligibility.

First, "totalization." The for-itself comes to be, and exists, as nihilation; it seeks to realize its own instant of action as pure freedom. Sartre has never abandoned this ideal; in the *Critique,* for example, he baldly denies that there is a "problem" of sovereignty. Man—each man—is sovereign; there can be no problem. But in contrast to the total independence of each individual-in-action, his social world is not only the wholly other, it is the whole of the wholly other. The world as worked up by others' actions, a humanized-dehumanized in-itself, must be seen as total in order to be denied as total, in order to serve as ground for the expression of *my* values—that is, of *my* lacking what I lack, and thus of myself as lack. If Sartre looks at society, therefore, starting, as he must do, from the for-itself, he can only "totalize." He *must* swing over from the pole of empty inwardness toward the other pole of indefinitely extended, totalized outwardness. True, he cannot reach it *as* totality, any more than Sartrean man could in fact achieve the glorious instant of his own free act. But if totality is unattainable, *totalization* is the only process by which what is other than instantaneous, free self-choosing can ever be understood. Granted, also, that, in the *Critique,* the concept of "lack" is abandoned for that of "need," with its more explicit (and allegedly Marxist) foundation in material situations and material wants. Still the skeleton is the same: for-itself / in-itself or individual *praxis* / totalization. If the trend toward the broader, almost all-engulfing category is more pronounced, the ingredients of the dialectic are analogous to, if not identical with, their earlier counterparts.

Moreover, that trend is already foreshadowed, I should like to suggest, in some puzzling passages in *Being and Nothingness.* The concept of truth is not one of Sartre's explicit concerns in either of his major works; but when he does touch on it in *Being and Nothingness,* he sets it in contrast to "reality," almost as "universal" is traditionally contrasted with "particular." The truth of being Jean-Paul Sartre, it seems, is being a Parisian, the truth of being a Parisian, is being a Frenchman, the truth of being a Frenchman is being a European, and so on. Or, to take Sartre's other example: here is a man doing a particular skiing figure. He does it Norwegian style—that is the truth of his performance; and the truth of *that,* in turn, is skiing as such. For reality, however, the series goes just the other way: the reality of being a European is being a Frenchman, and so on; or the reality of skiing is skiing Norwegian style, until in each series we come to this particular event here-now, Jean-Paul Sartre as *pour-soi* choosing, say, to reject the Nobel prize; this skier executing a christiana just here on this particular slope. For essence and existence the same inversion holds: Jean-Paul Sartre exists, his essence is to be Parisian, the essence of being Parisian is being French, and so on. Thus it seems that step-by-step impoverishment is the process by which, from the real or the existent, truth or essence are obtained.

But is "truth" really obtained by starting with the real and subtracting successive properties? Are even "essences"—*un*real though they may seem—to be discovered simply by stripping the existent, one by one, of its particularizing attributes? Man, we are told, has no essence; he exists first, and must make himself what he is (not). Does he achieve that goal simply by this sort of abstractive generalizing? Ultimately, along this line of reasoning, both the "truth" and the "essence" of anything at all will be—Being, which, existentially speaking, is as good as nothing. What is Sartre after here? One might suppose that, in his emphasis on existence and the concrete reality of this nihilating *pour-soi* here and now fleeing *its* past into *its* future, he is intentionally draining "essence" or "truth" of *any* content. But existentialism began with the cry, "Subjectivity is Truth." Is that not still its clarion call? To read individual existence into Marxism, not to generalize it into universal "truths" and "essences," is supposed to be Sartre's mission in the *Critique.* Yet, as we saw in the last chapter, there is an indefeasible impulse to rationalism in Sartre's thinking which runs the other way. The individual real, the existent, has its truth, its essence in the general—and even, it seems, in the most general. Remember that in the First *Meditation* it is the most general things of all—*generalissima et universalissima*— that Descartes finds it hardest to doubt! But an apter comparison here is Spinoza's third kind of knowledge: only when we have grasped its roots in the all-encompassing can we understand the particular a right. Only in full, independent, total Being-itself does the truth of *this* finite mode reside.

Is this Spinozism, latent in *Being and Nothingness,* given free rein in the *Critique?* Yes and no. Totalization does indeed take over: it is the context through which alone the individual's *praxis* becomes intelligible—and therefore true?—to the historian, to the social scientist, or even to himself. But the totalization Sartre envisages, of course, is human, not divine. It is a pan-humanism, one might say, that Sartre is after. Man, the nihilator of Being, the being whose very being is to say no, can find himself only if he nevertheless places his nay-saying, dialectically, within the context of Being itself.

Yet that is precisely what Sartre had not succeeded in doing in his earlier work—it is even what he proclaimed could not be done. *Causa sui* is impossible, the for-itself cannot become for-itself-in-itself; man tries to become God and fails. Thus, in the Hegelian terms already characteristic of *Being and Nothingness,* let alone of the *Critique,* the dialectic of existence appears to be one of pure contradiction, repeated thesis and antithesis lacking a synthesis to put the two contradictions to rest. What has happened to Sartre's negative dialectic in the *Critique?* Again, the role of "synthesis" in that work merits a special study; there are complex relations to Kantian as well as Hegelian synthesis which the historian of philosophy finds tantalizing, but which neither space, time, nor the reader's patience allows one to embark on here. But, crudely and as a first approximation, I think we may hazard the statement that the *Critique* differs from *Being and Nothingness* in permitting, and even in conclusion stressing, the possibility of synthesis: hence the optimistic, even triumphant, coda at its close. And we may see this new outcome either as a development of Sartrean dialectic, or as a change. To borrow another Hegelian slogan, quantity has turned into quality: more dialectic has turned into a different dialectic after all.

Or nearly so; even this statement I hesitate to make dogmatically. Let me qualify it a little. *Praxis* vs. the *practico-inert,* the group in fusion followed by the oath vs. the group institutionalized, itself becoming *practico-inert;* these are the poles of a dialectic which seems, either on the "constituting" or the "constituted" side, to reach no resting point. And, indeed, the Hegelian issue in an "organic" state Sartre emphatically and repeatedly rejects. The only organism is the practical organism, the individual agent. Otherwise there are organizations, which are made by men and, as material centers of resistance, come, negatively, to control men. But the possibility of any hyper-organism is decidedly rejected, over and over again; that is one of Sartre's major polemical themes. Yet both for the constitutive dialectic of the group in process of formation and for the constituted dialectic of a social organization, once formed, Sartre opens the way for synthesis. Thus, in discussing the role of "thought"—of controversy on the current issues—in the formation of subgroups, he writes:

> It is a question of a dialectical transcendence, by a practical project: that in turn supposes *a synthetic grasp* of all the contradictions, in brief, the living reunification of the group by the third man, taking the dissensions themselves as the instrument of reunification.[6]

In that sentence there is, after all, hope for mankind. Admittedly, the "living synthesis" [7] of a new community will always regenerate its own contrary, its seriality, its practico-inert. Yet even in the "constituted dialectic" that results Sartre sees not only contradiction, but also synthesis. True, the members of every generation are cast, willy-nilly, into groups already formed, which press on them from without and so limit, even deny, the upsurge of their freedom. Nevertheless here, too, where *praxis* has become enmeshed in *processus,* where truly communal action has relapsed into institutional compulsion, Sartre speaks of a "totalizing synthesis of diverse circumstances." [8] "This plurality of temporalizations," he writes: "and this temporal unification (*a synthetic unification* of the antecedent by the consequent, an actual reunification of the novel multiplicity through [*à travers de*] the older *cadres*) constitutes in fact the evolution of humanity as the *praxis* of a diachronic group, that is, as the temporal aspect of the constituted dialectic." [9]

Both diachronically and synchronically, indeed, there is alienation in such "objectivized" *praxis*—in the action of the individual within an extant tradition and within an organized society. But now, it seems, there is not only the to-and-fro of for-itself / in-itself, freedom / bad faith. From the perspective of dialectical reason, it now appears, a broader vision is possible. There is an "evolution of humanity" which embraces the double alienation of the individual—in the factual history of his nation and in the levelling seriality of his institution or his class—within the grandeur of a synthesizing whole. There are no Hegelian states, no hyper-organisms; yet the synthesis of History is in sight. Thus totalization appears no longer as an empty ideal, but as a concrete possibility: the concrete issue which the huge abstract "experiment" of the *Critique* has all along had as its aim.

Necessity

So far I have been talking about "totalization" as an intensification and expansion of Sartre's Hegelian method. Since his express goal is to understand history, and since he believes that a "totalizing" view of human action is the necessary forerunner to such understanding, totalization is the overarching dialectical conception that controls the work. But his other conceptual tools, too, are characteristic of dialectical thinking from Hegel onward —in particular, his use of modal concepts and their cognates, and especially of the concept of *necessity*.

Analytical reason atomizes, dialectical reason totalizes. Sartre sees this contrast—as we noticed earlier—
politically: he equates positivism, liberalism, and
fascism, and opposes to them all the all-inclusive truth of
Marxism (as he understands it, and of course with the
injection of an existentialist core). But back of this contrast there is also a contrast in philosophical method, a
contrast between "logic" as traditionally understood and
dialectic as its alternative. "Analytical reason" appears
as the method of positive science understood in the sense
of positiv*ism.* It appears to rest, in the last analysis, as
most empiricist philosophy has done, on the occurrence
of actual individuals. Its operations are indeed those of
deductive logic, and hence necessary. But logic in its
canonic form is conceived as purely extensional; it is
truth-value logic. Although it tells us nothing about the
real world, its connectives depend entirely on what there
is or is not. It works with atomic particulars, a, b, c, or their
variables, x, y, z, or with statements of atomic facts, p, q, r,
related solely in terms of their truth or falsity. Even if it
takes the leap from "x Phi's" to "(For all x) (x Phi's)," an
indefinite aggregate of "facts-that" is still what it refers
to. "Formal implication," as Whitehead and Russell
called it, is no more "totalizing" than "material." It still
rests on indigestible, itemizable, unintelligible particulars. Thus the contingent "that" or "that not" appears to
be the ultimate foundation on which the calculations of
analytical reason rest. But surely logic provides rules of
necessary reasoning? So it does; given its contingent
premises, it does of course trace deductive relations
among them. Indeed, the "analysis" of "analytical reason" consists precisely in finding such relations: relations that are necessary just because they consist in connections already given among the items to which they

refer. Given that p.q, or ~ p. ~ q, or ~ p.q, then necessarily p ⊃ q, because ~ (p. ~ q) is all that p ⊃ q says. Thus what follows by logical necessity doesn't really "follow" at all; given what is given, it just is. Logic necessitates emptily. It provides analytical connections between meaningless givens. It is a mere content-less skeleton of thought. So we have indeed the dichotomy Hume gave us: bits of mere givens which are contingent, never necessary, and necessary statements which are empty, necessitating not what they say but only how they say it.

How can thought overcome this disability? The answer of the dialectical philosopher, as we have already seen, is to get thought moving. Far from resting content with given counters tautologically connected, the dialectician ruminates upon his concepts so that they themselves change their shape and nature as his reflection proceeds. Thought is not a game with fixed pieces, but a process of development, of growth. And in particular, dialectical philosophers have felt the need to overcome the dichotomy between contingency and necessity. Our experience makes sense only if on the one hand "mere" facts are somehow assimilated to reasons, and if on the other the connections between data are shown to be demanded on some real and rational ground, not only tautologically. Thus the modal concepts, possibility, actuality (or contingent givenness), and necessity need to be reflected on and reassessed in relation to one another. The contingent must be absorbed into the rational core of reality, not left dangling as *mere* given, yet its necessitation must be neither external compulsion nor the *petitio principii* of deductive argument—it must be a *reason,* a principle that makes sense in some comprehensive way of the whole process of which all contingencies are now seen to form parts.

All this, admittedly, is a highly speculative piece of non-history. The thesis of extensionality in logic is a modern one, and by now may even be said (*pace* Quine) to belong to a phase only of the development of that discipline. But taking off from a particular philosophy of logic—or even from a caricature of it—I have been trying to suggest a context for—what *is* historically the case—dialectical philosophers' concern with modal concepts. Textually, the tradition goes back, I suppose, to Kant, where the three modalities, possibility, actuality, necessity, appear as the final three in the table of categories, and represent in the Dialectic the fourth antinomy—the attempt to prove a necessary Being. This impasse, like the others Kant had presented, Hegel must then evade by working into the destiny of his Absolute Spirit the necessary transition from the possible to the actual, and to the actual as necessary—in some grander sense of "necessary" than the humdrum one of formal logic.

In the case of Sartrean dialectic, modal concepts already figured prominently in *Being and Nothingness.* The for-itself *is* its possibilities; it is as its possibility—its not-yet-actual—that it is what it is not and is not what it is. My body, on the other hand, is "the necessity of my contingency": the sheer facticity that absurdly underlies my freedom. As making myself, I *am* my possibility, but as situated, as this body in this fashion at this time, I am necessarily, not what I may be, but what I happen to have become. The two-pronged dialectic of nothingness and being is at the same time a two-pronged dialectic of possibility and actuality-as-necessity. There is no escaping *either* the burden of freedom, the whole future as my possible, the *un*making of the present which is the very quintessence of the upsurge of consciousness, *or* the irresoluble facticity of what has been.

As we have already seen, however, *Being and Nothingness* offers no synthesis of its dominant contraries. I am always free, yet the die is always cast; there is no way out. But in the *Critique* we are offered, in the concluding movement of the argument at least, some hope of an all-embracing resolution. And this new outcome is mediated by the concept of necessity, which now plays a new and dominant role in making the dialectic work. Let us see, again very schematically, how this comes about.

The *Critique,* we noted, is an experiment. Starting from analytical reason, we are asking whether dialectical reason exists. The two givens we observe at the outset are: on the one hand, individual *praxis,* which here replaces the free act of the for-itself, and on the other hand, the fact of scarcity, the limited supply of goods on which and with which to perform our acts. The stage-set is different: we have, not consciousness as for-itself and the target of its intentionality, the in-itself, but the "practical organism" and the material it needs—but can find only in scarce supply—for the fulfillment of its wants. We shall have to consider later how deep an innovation this change of concepts constitutes. Clearly, if only out of respect for Marxist truth as he conceives it, Sartre *has* to locate the human condition more concretely in the material world than he had earlier seemed to do. And clearly he is here concerned with the generation of social structures, not of the individual's destiny as such. But for our present purpose—of tracing the argument in terms of modal concepts—we can still (as we did above) take *praxis* and the *practico-inert,* the human agency and the anti-human inertia it has generated, as the analogues of the familiar contraries of *Being and Nothingness.* On the one hand, there was already in the earlier work an attempt to make the for-itself "material." In other words, consciousness, in the chapter on the body, was already seen as "all body," although at the same time body was said to be "all consciousness." So now, similarly, the practical organism's *praxis* is man as sovereign, the individual's free act, but in the material world. And on the other side, scarcity, which generates the *practico-inert,* seems here to take the place of the individual contingency, the facticity, of *Being and Nothingness.* Scarcity, one could say, is the social body: it is the contingent necessity, or the necessary contingency, on which and against which, the individual, cast among others, has to work. Sartre seems to recognize this analogue when he writes:

> The contingency of scarcity (that is, the fact that immediate relations of abundance between other practical organisms and other environments are not *a priori* inconceivable) is reinteriorized in the contingency of our reality as men (*la contingence de notre realité d'homme*).[10]

Indeed, this is not so much an analogue as an identity. He continues: "A man is a practical organism living with a multiplicity of similar (organisms) in a field of scarcity." [11] Scarcity is the contingency, the facticity of the given, identified in *Being and Nothingness* as the body, but now seen, across the fact of social multiplicity, as the contingent limitation of the materials on which the satisfaction of bodily needs depends.

The starting place of the experiment, then, is, though in a social and more explicitly material setting, still possibility (free action) versus contingency (limited givenness, facticity). We see the human generate the anti-human—cutting down trees makes drought. Further we see the multiplicity of human agencies generating—in relation to worked matter—*human* inhumanities, the passive collectivities of series or class. Being a worker, being a member of the idle rich: these are external impositions, as passive in relation to my action as a lack of water. But this, Sartre tells us, is an anti-dialectic. What is needed for dialectical reason is not just this to-and-fro. What is needed to generate a proper dialectic is a movement of totalization, but, further, a totalization seen as the movement of *necessity*.

That the concept of necessity plays a crucial role in the discovery, and vindication, of dialectical reason is clear from a brief but pivotal section in Sartre's argument. He has first considered individual *praxis,* in relation to need, as totalization: my environment becomes a total field in relation to the needs I exteriorize in it (Book I, A). Next he has shown how it is that human relations arise as mediation between various segments of matter (Book I, B); in other words, it is matter, related to their respective needs, that mediates between individuals and so generates their social relations. (Consider, for instance, the postal system, or the "delivery" of health services.) Now (Book I, C), we have to derive from our view of matter as "totalized totality" a first constatation of the *necessity* of the movement we are considering. This section of the argument has four parts. First (C, 1), Sartre studies "scarcity and the method of production" [12] then (C, 2) "worked matter as alienated objectification of individual and collective 'Praxis,' " and in particular the phenomenon of interest.[13] Then, before he comes to the description of "social being as matter" (C, 4)—that is as the expression of the *practico-inert*—"and particularly the being of class" [14] and, further, to (Book I, D) the study of "The Collectives," [15] that is, of serialities in general, the passive externalities generated as constraining aggregates by human activity itself, he injects (C, 3) the concept of necessity "as a new structure of the dialectical experiment."

What does this mean? We have discovered the dialectic, or the anti-dialectic, generated by the "behavior" of worked matter over against the needy individual. This totalizing relation is "intelligible," [16] that is, it is transparent: like the *cogito*. My action simply *is* a totalizing movement, by which I constitute my environment as a whole-for-my-action; in terms of *Being and Nothingness,* I make my world a world. This is a clear self-referring act and therefore, Sartre points out, indubitable. But the indubitability of self-evidence is not "necessity" in the sense in which dialectic demands it. Dialectical necessity must be, not intelligible with the pure translucent self-identity of an immediate intuition, but in movement: it must be *the external interiorized and made necessary by means of such interiorization.* But this does not mean that necessity is compulsion simply from without. It is compulsion *made* mine and felt as such. It is the internal necessity of external action. Sartre's argument is carried here by the ambiguity of the French *"expérience":* the dialectical experiment becomes dialectical experience, or both in one. What we have so far seen, via analytical reason, in the anti-dialectic of man and matter is now made dialectical by the experience of man himself, who discovers *within* himself the necessity of his action *out there.* And it is this experience of necessity that confirms the hypothesis of the dialectical experiment. For the necessity so discovered is neither external constraint as such, nor the static "necessity" of the logically evident: it is *destiny.* When Oedipus takes into himself the need to have fulfilled the oracle, what had appeared as arbitrary compulsion becomes *his fate.* It is that awareness of an overriding necessity, which is nevertheless my own, an awareness which must be learned—and learned through suffering —that confirms the existence of dialectical reason and at the same time makes the dialectic real. It both confirms the experiment and embodies it in a real development.

Dialectical necessity, then, is destiny. Or, conversely, as Sartre puts it, necessity is *the destiny of freedom in exteriority.*[17] It is the necessity *that I act out there.* Note that this is not, as in *Being and Nothingness,* the necessity of my contingency—to recognize that is to recognize ineluctable constraint, the inevitable contrary of freedom, unalterably opposed to freedom itself. Nor is it, again, the self-containment of the indubitable: that would be logical truth, self-evident because self-referring, but incapable of development. No, dialectical necessity is neither the stubborn resistance to freedom by the contingent and unintelligible, nor is it the quiescent self-evidence of the intellectually indubitable. Dialectical necessity is the necessity of freedom itself: it is freedom destined to act out there in the world, and understanding its own nature as destined so to do.

The perspective of *Being and Nothingness* is different. There it is the factual that is necessary, and that is the total other of freedom. If I *am* my red face at the keyhole, it remains absurd that this should be so. Moreover, that it is the factual, or the contingent, that is necessary is itself absurd; for the "contingent" is precisely the non-necessary; in revealing itself as necessary it contradicts itself. On the other hand there is in a sense a necessity of freedom, but again a self-contradictory necessity. I *have* to be free: indeed, I am "condemned" to be so. But the condemned prisoner is precisely the person *without* a destiny: society has misjudged him, robbed him of the destiny a free agent ought to have. Thus freedom as what we are condemned to is the contradiction of freedom. *Being and Nothingness* presents us, therefore, with a double contradiction: the non-necessary—that is, the contingent—is what is necessary; the free, which should not be necessary either, is compelled, and so unfree, a necessity imposed from without.

But now, in the *Critique,* necessity appears neither as constraint nor condemnation: it is the successful interiorization of the external action that embodies freedom. Man really does act freely out there in the world and recognizes as his destiny that this should be so. It almost seems that role playing has become authentic, that the waiter can serve us with a waiter-like flourish without thereby falling into bad faith. Perhaps he really *is* a waiter, and freely so.

This issue of Sartre's argument will become clear in Book Two, where "freedom as necessity" and "necessity as freedom" will emerge as the vehicles of the group-information, that triumphant we-subject, evanescent but glorious, in which each must act freely with each other, so that out of this mutality they do for once act as one. What makes them do so? Again, the dialectic of modalities instructs us. *The impossibility of the impossibility of freedom:* that is the common need from which their common action flows. The populace is starving, it is impossible for each to live—that is, as practical organisms, to act. But each is a human agent, for whom such an impossibility is impossible; therefore, each uniting the others as their mediating third, they together storm the fortress that represents their oppressors, the agents of that impossible impossibility. They take the Bastille. For the Faubourg St. Antoine, indeed for the French nation, that was destiny.

But of course this is Sartre, and the solution is not quite that simple. The Bastille gave way to the Terror, the Directory—the *practico-inert* took over again. Still the new place given to necessity in the *Critique,* to necessity as *belonging* to freedom, not as *denying* it: this is certainly a crucial step on the path to Sartre's new synthesis, if such it be. For only if freedom is vindicated as truly necessary will the totalizing process of history prove *historical:* a pattern of human action in the world, not just of human suffering or of the fall into inertia and absurdity.

Intelligibility

Totalization and necessity are two of the concepts which function in the *Critique* to give Sartre's method new scope. But a third is needed to effect the synthesis he appears to have in view. He introduces "necessity," we have just noticed, as the supplement to the "intelligibility" of the anti-dialectic that was his first experimental discovery; but this intelligibility seems to be a first and abstract surrogate for the dialectical intelligibility which crowns the whole. Indeed, each necessary step in the dialectic demands its matching intelligibility. Necessity as destiny may be obscure to those it overwhelms. It must become intelligible, at each stage of the dialectic, to the agent himself. The "become" of that statement, of course, is "abstract": we have not yet reached history. But with the conceptual movement of dialectic it must be shown that each phase of social development ultimately has its own mode of being, not only in the *praxeis* of individuals, but in their consciousness. Each member of the crowd storming the Bastille not only adds to the number. He acts *as* one of the crowd and thus as other to all the others. He is mediating third to every other pair; if there are a hundred, it is he who, as the hundredth, makes it so, and so does every other. The group-in-formation comes to be, therefore, not only from the impossibility of the impossibility posed by the enemy or the oppressor; it comes to be from the joint action of agents who express the impossibility of that impossible, not only in their movement as crowd-storming-the-Bastille, but in their intent—in their mutual, interlocking awareness that they *are* a group-in-the-making. As such, indeed, Sartre declares, they may even be called a "We-Subject," [18] an example of that social reality whose existence in *Being and Nothingness* he had emphatically denied. The second dialectical development Sartre traces, the oath, again clearly binds the members of the emergent group in solemn awareness of its meaning. Performative utterances entail knowing what one is saying and therefore knowing what one is doing, as well as, by saying, doing it.

But what of the group once stabilized, the institutional group, with its impulsion back to seriality and the *practico-inert?* The industrial worker is alienated by definition from himself and his work; how can his action and his consciousness be identified? The answer is complicated. On the one hand, Sartre discovers, in an analysis of rights and duties, an intelligibility of social *function,* and even, for organization as such, an intelligibility of *structure* (*à la* Claude Levi-Strauss).[19] In such rituals as baptisms, for example, members of an organized group perform a "second oath" which marks their acknowledgment of "the necessity of freedom." [20] Now this necessity, Sartre tells us, is the inverse of the practico-inert. The *practico-inert* was characterized as *passive activity:* the consequences of our acts take off and run away with us, despite ourselves. But organization, as "exteriority structuring interiority," has precisely the character of *active passivity.* This category characterizes, in fact, the performance of social functions [21] as well as the ritual occasions of the passage just quoted. Thus it seems that in general through my commitment to a social structure and through my institutionalized action in it, I give myself to it. I seem to acknowledge its goals as my norms, to accept it—that is, to accept the *praxis* of its members —as the ubiquitous medium of my existence.

This appears indeed to be an astonishing transformation of the Sartre of *Being and Nothingness*. There, activity was activity, passivity passivity, and that was it. What metamorphosis has the dialectic wrought? It has been suggested by one of Sartre's commentators that his earlier dialectic advisedly dealt with the single for-itself only, and that he is here filling in the social framework whose existence—and whose power—he would all along have acknowledged. In other words, he might be read as using, like Kant, a method of "isolation," in which strands of a synthetic whole are sorted out for reflection, but no claim is ever made that they exist apart from that synthetic unity.[22] But this explanation really will not do. The author of *Being and Nothingness* clearly believed that all social role playing is in effect bad faith, that there is no We-subject, that the act, to be free, must be totally active. The very idea of active passivity is, in Sartre's earlier terms, inconceivable. The notion that a human being can *ever* freely and without self-deception give himself to anything but his own freedom is for him truly a discovery. Had this not been so, indeed, the road to this point in the *Critique* would not have been as long and devious as it has been. For some one who had all along acknowledged the social being of man, the rootedness of freedom in society, there would have been no need to invoke the immense apparatus of these five-hundred pages to demonstrate its possibility.

Besides, the victory of a socialized freedom is far from complete. For one thing the "second oath" of ritualized commitment belongs, it appears, to the "constituted dialectic" only, to the institutionalized dialectic which is always ready to degenerate once more into the *practico-*

inert. This dialectic must be held subordinate to the "full intelligibility of the constituting dialectic" [23]—that is, to the generation of the truly "common individual" in the group-in-formation and then in the original oath. Apart from these unique situations, then, we are almost back with the old alternatives—the impossible wholly free act or else the fall into bad faith. Thus norms, for example, result from an "ossification" of the group, such that the agent "loses" [24] his comprehension of his own action and that of others. Only the resultant gap between act and understanding gives them their "normative" character. So the individual's concrete self-giving slips after all into the abstract recognition of an external apparatus; he is alienated and betrayed.

Yet the change is there; active passivity, as characteristic at least of the constituted dialectic, is a phase of dialectical reason, abstractly considered. It has even its concrete reality in the exercise of social function or on the occasion of the "second oath." Moreover, the intelligibility of each stage of the dialectic—the emergent group, its solidification in the oath, and even, to a degree, the exercise of a function in the organized group, or the re-enactment of its birth in social ritual—marks a "synthesis" impossible in terms of *Being and Nothingness:* a synthesis of *being* and *knowing.* Indeed, to mark this synthesis at each appropriate stage along the way is, it appears, the chief function of the concept of intelligibility in the discovery and development of dialectical reason.

At key places in the argument of *Being and Nothingness,* on the other hand—as we saw in tracing its course —"knowing" and "being" or "knowing" and "living" are sharply and irreconcilably contrasted. The pre-reflective *cogito* is the for-itself as lived, but only on the detached intellectual level of reflection can there be knowing, which is neither lived nor of the living: it is instantaneous intuition of its purely external object, the in-itself. (Even when we "know" ourselves it is our quasi-objective "selves," our "characters," that we know, not the non-thetic "conscience (de) soi" that underlies such, and all, knowing as its real being.) In Sartre's view of emotion ("passion"), moreover, the affects are the irrational alternative to reasons, the hidden under side of action. Even though, as Cartesian wills, we do in a sense choose passion, choose to find the grapes sour, or the enemy unconquerable, we do so unknowingly, excusing our own failure by the resort to magic. To understand our own self-surrender, and yet by that very act of understanding to give ourselves freely —that is, for Sartrean man, a radical innovation. It springs, if you like, from an intensification of the rationalism and the idealism already present in the earlier work. There, however, these motifs were kept in check by the radical dualism of Sartre's starting point. Despite the dialectical structure of its argument, the reason of *Being and Nothingness* remained analytical: knowledge was pure inspection, the static contemplation of the self-evident, being was its Other, the object of intuition, never at one with it. Only the demonstration (by analytical reason!) that dialectical reason exists can give us the perspective from which this duality can be seen as one. Only if we see that human reality does in some typical circumstances necessarily—yet freely—act in the service of something more than the act itself, can we bring together consciousness and its object into a viable whole. That "something more," of course, must be human—that is, social. There is neither Deity nor substance on which we could rely for its source. The world is still human. But neither is it, despite the Hegelianism of Sartre's method, Hegelian "objective mind" or "world mind" that provides the new synthesis. There is no hyper-organism; it is always individual *praxis* to which we return—but individual *praxis* intelligible, in the appropriate context, in its bearing on, and meaning for, a social whole. Now even the material—the social matter of the *practico-inert*—comes to mean something *to* the individual; and in that awareness knowing and being *can* be reconciled.

His *Critique,* Sartre says, is meant to introduce an existentialist foundation into Marxist philosophy. The reiterated return to intelligibility shows us what he means by this—for it is, as we have seen, the intelligibility of his own action to the individual agent that he has in mind. The dialectic, however totalizing, will develop only in and through the individual "practical organisms" who, apart from "matter," are all there really is. So we read the individual existent into the social, and eventually historical, dialectic of the whole. That is how, on Sartre's own account, his message should be read. Yet on the whole—and in view, too, of his own confession—we may also, and better, read the story the other way around. Sartrean existentialism was a brilliant exegesis of the failure of humanity; only the Marxist dialectic of history, as Sartre conceives of it, can rescue us from that "tragic finale." Not existentialism supplementing Marxism is the heart of the story, but Marxism giving a social-historical frame that makes possible a more fruitful issue than Sartre's existentialism in its own terms could have allowed. The old ingredients are still there, but they have been literally translated, and in their translated form and place, there may be some hope, sometimes, of escape from what had been previously ineluctable catastrophe.

History: Sartre and Kierkegaard

It is "the place of history" that Sartre has been seeking in Volume One of the *Critique*. All *praxis,* he has argued, is *totalizing,* at least in relation to the "passive activity" of the *practico-inert* which it initiates. To become the locus of history, however, such totalization must in addition prove both *necessary* (in the sense of "destined") and *intelligible* (in the sense that the agent's action is assimilated to his own awareness of that destiny.) These are the conditions for history which dialectical reason both institutes and discovers. But this conception of history stands in sharp contrast to another dialectical view, that of Søren Kierkegaard as presented in the "Interlude" of the *Philosophical Bits.*[25] Before we leave our reflections on Sartre's dialectic, therefore, we may put it into perspective by comparing it briefly with Kierkegaard's argument in the "Interlude."

On two points, to be sure, they agree. Both follow the Hegelian method, yet deny Hegelian "absolute mind" in favor of the concrete human individual. And, of course, both make heavy use of modal concepts in their reasoning. But to how different a purpose! For one thing, "totalization" is not a Kierkegaardian concept at all. Starting, like Sartre, with individual existence, he needs to arrive, not at social reality (which does not concern him), but at the confrontation of the finite individual with the Infinite Being who made him—in this case at the still more vexing paradox of the historical Christ, that is, of God in history. So his whole dialectic is one of individuals, finite and infinite, temporal and eternal. The other two Sartrean concepts we have been looking at, however, are dealt with in the "Interlude," the first explicitly, the second by implication. For his two major questions are these: is the past necessary? (and, as a corollary of this, what is the historical?), and what is the sense of the past? (how can we "know" history?). The first exactly parallels Sartre's speculations on necessity, and the second certainly bears on the problem of the intelligibility of human action seen in a historical context.

For Sartre, action, to be matter for history, must be, not only indubitable or factually undeniable, but necessary. For Kierkegaard, the historical can never be necessary. True, what has happened has happened, one cannot deny it; but—and Sartre would agree—that is not a sufficient condition for necessity. But here the ways part. Sartre seeks the ground for a historical dialectic, and this means to him that there must be an inner necessity to the structure and the consequences of human action—otherwise there would be only a fragmented, meaningless aggregation of mere facts, and no dialectic at all. To Kierkegaard, however, such reasoning would simply repeat the Hegelian error of confusing essence and existence, the abstract and the concrete. There may be, in the "System," some "ideal movement" of concepts, which is necessary. But this has simply nothing at all to do with what really comes about in the real world. Necessity was alleged to be the union of possibility with actuality. Nonsense! Necessity is, if you like, the actuality of the possible *qua* possible; it is Leibniz's possible worlds, the world of pure logic and mathematics, whose only being is that it doesn't contradict itself. But once something *comes into being*—instead of something else —it could have been otherwise. That is actuality, precisely the non-necessary. And in this respect, Kierkegaard insists, the future and the past are perfectly symmetrical. The one happened as it happened, that cannot be denied,

and the other has not yet happened; but neither is necessary. That is why it is correct to describe the historian
as a backwards prophet.

What, then, is the historical, the subject matter of
history? Here Kierkegaard follows Hegel in distinguishing the merely spatial dialectic of nature from the truly
temporal dialectic of history. Natural events simply happen, over and over, and proliferate spatially. But human
events introduce true novelty: they create a second dialectic within time. And within that re-creation there is always the marvel that it happened this way and not otherwise. This is never necessity; it is the marvel of the
coming-to-be of what might not have been. For Kierkegaard, in other words, the locus of history is time, not
clock time, indeed, but time as the mysteriously experienced medium of the individual's life. Now Sartre, too, follows Hegel in dividing nature from history. He stoutly
combats Engels' view that nature is dialectical, only
human action is so. But for him time is, so to speak, a late
comer. In *Being and Nothingness* "temporalization" was
flight, the fall from the perspicuous instant of action into
bad faith. In the *Critique* he is indeed seeking to vindicate
the "temporalization" of action as the work of dialectical
reason. The action of the group in fusion has its temporal
reality (July 14, 1789) and its temporal consequences
(ever since). Were that not so, history could not result. Yet
these events can be seen as historical, Sartre still insists,
only if the total flow of temporal development is assimilated to an inner pattern of necessity—and so *"aufge-
hoben,"* sublimated and wiped out in its sheer temporal
contingency. But that is, from Kierkegaard's point of view
—and indeed, I believe, truly—precisely to deny the historical. Human existence *is* temporalization, first, last,
and foremost. Time, existential time, the time of becom-

ing, is its proper medium: the medium in which our acts succeed or fail, prove right or wrong. The United States went into Vietnam not because of the necessary development of capitalist imperialism, but because it had made a series of stupid, immoral, and, indeed, horrible mistakes.

How, secondly, can we "know" history? Kierkegaard seems to agree with Sartre in insisting that knowledge, which must be certain, must therefore be immediate. It is presence-to, whether to intellect or to sense. But obviously the past is never present. Moreover, even the contemporary who "sees" the event happening, only sees it as there—he cannot see it *coming* to be. There is *always,* in the sense for what comes to be, a wrenching loose from sheer presence, and thus from the indubitability of knowledge. Indeed, the past carries with it, when we seek to grasp it, its own uncertainty. To face it is not, and cannot be, to know it, but to face the question: was it, how was it, why was it so and not otherwise, and so to face the alternative: doubt or belief. Time and existence are the place of faith or skepticism, eternity and essence alone are the media for knowledge. Thus from a Kierkegaardian point of view the search for "intelligibility" as the unity of knowing and being, the search for the kind of human action that knows what it is and why it is there where it is: that search results from a category mistake. There may be historical faith; strictly speaking, there can be no historical knowledge—whether in the self-knowledge of the agent or the hindsight of the historian.

Can we apply this Kierkegaardian criticism also to Sartre's view of history? Yes and no. If knowledge must be certain, if to know is to know that one knows, then history is beyond its range. If belief and knowledge are totally different human attitudes, then history belongs to the former, not the latter. Kierkegaard of course stresses the dichotomy because it is faith in the supernatural—in the historical foundation of Christianity—that he is after. But if, as I believe it is, all knowledge is belief—"justified true belief," in the modern phrase, but still belief—then historical belief should not be singled out as different in kind from the beliefs induced in other contexts, whether by our intellects or our senses. And in that case there is no absolutely special problem about the "intelligibility" of historical actions. We act within a human world, as well as on objects mediated by human actions. Sometimes we know what we are doing; sometimes we are swept along by currents we fail to understand; sometimes we think we know what we are doing and are mistaken. In science we act, in a more limited way, by putting to nature questions to which we may or may not get significant answers. Sometimes our questions are the wrong ones to ask; sometimes we misinterpret the answers. Yet sometimes we do pretty well. Since in history men are both agents, objects of inquiry, and questioners about those objects, the situation is more complicated. But it is not essentially different. We are trying to make sense of something in the world around us: sometimes we fail or partly fail: sometimes we succeed or partly succeed; we can never be sure. Still, we needn't stop trying. For Sartre, however, such a modest and compromising aim would never do (indeed, it smacks of liberalism!). On the contrary, his extreme rationalism, his demand for Cartesian clarity combined with Hegelian scope, forces him into the difficult course of the search for a Dialectical Reason which shall have a Total Intelligibility of the whole panorama of historical action as its outcome.

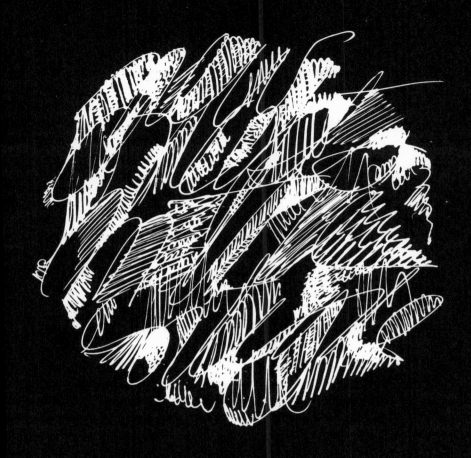

chapter seven: new concepts in the critique

the practical organism

Sartre's move from a
phenomenological dialectic of the
individual consciousness to a critical
dialectic of society demanded substantive
as well as methodological innovations. I want to
examine these innovations, or apparent innovations,
in three areas, all of which were neglected if not altogether

overlooked in *Being and Nothingness.* First, there is the problem of the biological nature of man, the relation of consciousness to the living organism that "has" consciousness. Secondly, there is the theme of individual development: the treatment of childhood—a theme that Sartre broods over in incredible detail in his recent work on Flaubert, but hinted at also in the *Critique.* Finally, there are concepts introduced by Sartre with the explicit purpose of explaining social reality, on the material side the concept of *scarcity* (which I have already dealt with to some extent in comparing Sartre's earlier and later dialectic), and on the human side *reciprocity,* the symmetrical relation between man and man. Be it said again, however, I am by no means trying here to expound all the major concepts of the *Critique,* nor even to look at those I am concerned with in their precise articulation in the argument. But I want to ask in each case: is there a substantive new development? Why or why not?

In an interview published in *The New Left Review* (and in abbreviated form in *The New York Review*) Sartre distinguished three stages in his philosophical growth.[1] In the early work—where Roquentin, Orestes, and, I would suggest, Mathieu, are the literary surrogates for his philosophical problem—it was the for-itself that was central. He was seeking an ontology of individual consciousness as pure activity in a purely passive world. With the turn to a social ("Marxist") perspective, he substituted for the for-itself the concept of the *practical organism.* In the last decade, however, from the *Critique* to *The Idiot of the Family,* he has been concerned with yet a new dimension, *le vécu, the lived.* This sequence suggests at first sight that Sartre has been moving away from his Cartesian point of origin—where pure consciousness is what concerns him—to a more biologically rooted view of man. It suggests, indeed, a rapprochement with the thought of his friend and enemy Maurice Merleau-Ponty. For Merleau-Ponty the "lived body" is a central conception: a human person is an embodied being, inescapably psychophysical, inextricably natural *and* cultural, an organism which achieves self-consciousness within the natural and human worlds, rather than a moment of consciousness rising up *against* the world as nihilation and as lack. Is this in fact the view toward which Sartre has been developing? This and the concluding chapter should provide us with an answer, at least from the perspective of the present, if not with a prognosis for the future. It will be, in effect, "Yes" and "No," but, for the *Critique* at least, more "No" than "Yes."

That the "practical organism" has replaced the for-itself as the central *persona* in the realm of dialectical reason already suggests a turn to a new emphasis on man as animal—a unique sort of animal, who makes himself by his *praxis*—but still an animal. This is a dimension of human existence, as we saw earlier, almost wholly missing from the Sartrean man of the earlier period. If I *am* my red face as I bend over the keyhole, this "being" expresses the flat contradiction of inner and outer, not the ambiguity of an animal life which, while remaining animal, has yet achieved humanity. As for Spinoza, so for Sartre, body and consciousness, as the two parallel aspects of one existent, remain utterly disparate, even though they express, in their disparate ways, one single nature. In Spinoza's view, I, as a finite mode, can approach the understanding of God or Nature, and therefore indirectly of myself, under the attribute of thought *or* of extension, but never both at once. So it is for the self-understanding of the for-itself in *Being and Nothingness*. Consciousness

and body are still Cartesian contraries, deprived of substantial status, but intelligible only as strict alternates to
one another. True, "consciousness is wholly body, body
wholly consciousness," yet an entwinement, an entangle-
ment, of the two is inconceivable—or conceivable only
through confusion.

Can an "organism" be understood at all in these
terms? I think not. An "organism" is not just a body, and
certainly not just a consciousness. If it is an organism sufficiently advanced on the evolutionary scale to be called
"sentient," it is both together, body and sentience, sentient body, or bodily sentience, both in one, and reverber-
ating to one another. It is neither unequivocally, but inalienably both together. Moreover, a *human* organism, a
"practical organism," capable of action in and upon a
world that is both human and material, both cultural and
natural, such an organism is still body-and-sentience, but
able also to take a stand within its natural-cultural setting
and self-consciously to appraise, and even, within limits,
to alter that environment. To express such a situation the
parallelism of Spinoza, or of Sartre in *Being and Nothingness,* is utterly inadequate.

In the context of *Being and Nothingness,* of course,
this may not matter, since Sartre expressly excuses himself there from any claim to found an "anthropology." Yet
one may surely feel uneasy about a phenomenology, or an
ontology, of human agency—and this the tale of the for-
itself must be admitted to be—which leaves out of account the biological, and for that matter also the social,
foundation of human life. Now the *Critique* does claim to
have founded an "anthropology"—that is, a general
theory of man—and it claims to do so in terms of a general concept, "practical organism," which seems to refer
to our animal as well as to our social nature. Has Sartre,

in turning more explicitly to a social perspective, also given more weight to the biological basis of human action? Merleau-Ponty, in *The Structure of Behavior,* distinguished three types of order—"physical," "vital," and "mental" (or human)—in terms of which behavior must be interpreted. Sartre, in the *Critique,* is working, as we have seen, between the physical or quasi-physical (the material and the *practico-inert*) and the human, or the social as the product of the human, notably the group in formation and the oath ("institutions" are indeed "social," but not wholly human, since they tend to fall back into the quasi-physical sphere of the *practico-inert*). If he sees men as "organisms," however, he appears at least to be giving recognition also to the mediating level of the *living,* as distinct from the sphere of physical inertia on the one hand or conscious *praxis* on the other.

To ferret out the reality behind the appearance, however, is extremely difficult. As I have tried to indicate in the previous chapter, the general tenor of the argument in the *Critique* is clear; the overall movement, from the question put by analytical reason, through the genesis of the dialectic, to its hoped-for issue, is plain to see. When one searches the text, however, with the aim of discovering whether and to what extent Sartre is treating the practical organism as an *organism,* one feels almost hopelessly at sea. Sometimes he seems to do so; sometimes his "practical organism" is indeed made of flesh and blood. But sometimes, on the other hand, it seems to shrink back into the abstract moment-of-action of the for-itself. Once more, as Iris Murdoch puts it, "The agent, thin as a needle, appears in the quick flash of the choosing will." [2] Let me try, if I can—though I am by no means sanguine of the issue—to sort out some of Sartre's references in the *Critique* to biology and to the biological nature of man, and see what conclusion we can reach.

In the *Critique,* as we have seen earlier, Sartre substitutes the concept of *need* for the more abstract *lack* of *Being and Nothingness.* What is "lacked" or "lacking" can be thought of in terms of a relation to consciousness alone, whether to the intentionality of consciousness or to the non-thetic consciousness (of) self that accompanies it. Indeed, "lack," "lacking," "lacked" form a trio that Sartre plays with almost as if the game were one of pure logic. But "need" suggests a relation more directly rooted in the real world. Hunger, thirst, sexual appetite are drives of living human beings, felt in and through their bodies, and assuaged only by bodily satisfaction. And in some passages Sartre does indeed stress the bodily nature of need[3] or the biological character of his "practical organism." [4]

Yet somehow the category of the biological hinted at from time to time is never wholly assimilated into the theory of social relations that the dialectic is to give us. This is clear from the first section of Book One, "On Individual 'Praxis' as Totalization," where Sartre gives his basic exposition of "need" and faces the question of its relation to its biological foundation. It is true, he admits, that if we consider "the body as function, function as need, and need as praxis," we obtain a first view of human work in which we see "the lived revelation of a goal to be reached as nothing but the restoration of the organism." [5] But this, he insists, is not a fundamental view. What matters in the last analysis is human *work*—that is, the organization by human agency of a field that lies outside the human agent himself. If I go hunting or fishing, if I gather fruit, I thereby organize my environment in virtue of my aims. It is in this sense that *praxis* totalizes. It not only negates the in-itself (it is still man who introduces negativity into the world), but makes of it a whole. The river or the forest with its game, the orchard with its fruit, are made the organized unities they are by the human intent that seeks in and through them the satisfaction of its needs. True, Sartre admits later, *praxis* takes place "within the general milieu of animal life." [6] But that is a mere contingent fact which lies outside the dialectic and remains obstinately opaque. Even if biology should succeed in "solving" the "problem" of the origin of life, he argues in the section now before us, this would be, like any scientific success, a purely analytical achievement, unassimilated and unassimilable by dialectical thought.[7] Life, once given, must be understood dialectically, in terms of the oppositions of freedom and necessity (or need?), external and internal, organic (that is, organized, or, better, organizing) and inorganic (that is, material and inertial). It is these fundamental contrarieties that will generate the whole series of interactions between *praxis* and the *practico-inert* and will thus provide the totalizing view which alone, Sartre believes, can serve as framework for history. Needy being that, by some unintelligible chance, I am, I act freely to satisfy my needs. In this way I interiorize the external world, and organize the inorganic. Sometimes, indeed, Sartre talks as though he admitted degrees of organization, rather than simply the organic and its absence. Thus, for example, need is understood, he says, in relation to "the unorganized or the less organized." [8] Thus also in one passage at least, in discussing the question of the permanence of the group, he remarks that so far we have found two kinds of permanence: that of the organic and that of biological integration (although it is not clear just where he has noted these two as distinct varieties).[9] For the most part, however, I think it is fair to say, "biological integration" is relegated to a purely background status. Life in the sense of animal life, it has been emphatically decreed at the very start of the argument—and in the context of the exposition of "need," the seemingly biological concept from which the whole movement of the dialectic will arise—life as animal life is merely the brute given which lies outside the reach of dialectical intelligibility. As against that indigestible and irrational fact, it is *praxis* as organized, and organizing, action, over against an "inorganic plurality" that is of primary interest. It is from the pair organic/inorganic, in the sense of organized/inertial, that the dialectic flows. Between action and inertia, organizing activity and the passive flow of the material, there is no mediating third. True, life cannot be understood mechanically. Given that it exists, we have to go dialectically about making intelligible what we can understand about it. What we can understand, however, is the interaction of human action as organizing principle and the inertial force of materiality, or of the quasi-material which action itself produces. As in *Being and Nothingness,* so here, the living as such is not a basic category of Sartrean thought.

This interpretation is confirmed, not only by the section on need, but by two passages in which Sartre refers, in passing, to the theory of evolution. In the first, a footnote to the discussion of Engels' "dialectic of nature"—whose "dogmatism" Sartre decidedly rejects—he remarks that biology in its present state is still "analytic and positivistic," and will not be able to provide a proper theory of the origin of life unless it moves to a "totalizing" view, which would envisage biological facts "in their interiority."[10] In this connection, he notes, it is strange that Marxists, allegedly dialecticians of Nature, tax with idealism those like Kurt Goldstein who try ("rightly or wrongly," says Sartre) to see organized beings as wholes. For what this amounts to, he remarks, is precisely to demonstrate, or to attempt to demonstrate, "the dialectical irreducibility of that 'state of matter,' life, to that other state—inorganized matter—which has nevertheless produced it."[11] Sartre's cautious reference to Goldstein is commendable; his position is indeed obscure. But what is remarkable about this note, it seems to me, is that it indicates how very peripheral to Sartre's own thinking is the whole question of biological theory and the philosophical issues it raises. Engels must be dealt with at length; but the biological problem of the (ir)reducibility of the living is worth only a sidelong glance. But how can one seriously attempt to develop a theory of human action on the Sartrean scale while ignoring almost entirely its basis in animal behavior and the biological nature of man? And what is this "practical organism" whose organismic character can be so blithely ignored?

The other reference is at least as peripheral to Sartre's argument, but revealing for his attitude to biology. In the section on interest (part of the section on "Worked matter as alienated objectification of individual and collective 'Praxis' ") he refers to the Darwinian struggle for life as equivalent to the so-called law of interest. Now he is clearly equating Darwinian theory here with social Darwinism, and hence with the utilitarian theory which, he argues, makes "human relations *a priori* antagonistic." He finds it strange, moreover, that even some Marxists should hesitate "between the law of interest and the Marxist conception of history, that is, between a sort of *biological materialism* and *historical materialism*." [12] Two points may be made about this very incidental reference. First, the equation of "Darwinian" with "utilitarian," etc., betrays an almost total want of interest in biological theory as such. And secondly, from the reference to the Marxists in question it is clear that Sartre's own materialist, and allegedly Marxist, theory of society is "historical" *as against* a "biological" view. Again, one wonders what a "practical organism" can be whose *"praxis"* can generate history in abstraction from its biological development. Is it, not in fact a new *persona* of Sartrean philosophy, but the for-itself rechristened?

Indeed, Sartre reaffirms in the *Critique* his earlier thesis: *there is no human nature*.[13] And in a sense, of course, he is right. Normal infants of our species are born, not human, but potentially so. To become a person is an *achievement* of a human organism, not a fact given from birth as such. And that achievement can be accomplished only through the infant's participation in a human social world. A person develops through learning to express his culture, the culture of his family, his neighborhood, his language, ultimately the subcultures of the interests he develops and that make him the person he is. As Sartre puts it in his reflections on Flaubert, it is through the human that the baby becomes human.[14] There is no simply given nature that he has, by genetic endowment alone, and which his history cannot shape in one direction or another. But on the other hand the development of a human being is not a springing into existence of a pure consciousness. A developed human being becomes so only through participation in a human world, in a network of human worlds, but in so developing he *embodies* that world or those worlds. And by that process, conversely, he *personalizes* nature. Thus a human person, one can say, is at one and the same time an *embodiment* of culture and a *personalization* of nature. True, there is no new "essence," no new stuff, added to the human neonate over and above, say, his simian cousins, that automatically makes him human. He has, for himself and uniquely, to make himself. But, on the one hand, as Adolf Portmann has demonstrated, his very biological nature prepares him for this self-making.[15] In his first year, in which he learns to speak, to stand upright and to perform responsible actions—that is, in what Portmann calls the year of the social uterus—the child takes into himself, into his very bodily being, the world offered him by maternal affection (or, if Sartre is right, in Flaubert's case, by the lack of it). Man is not *without* a nature; rather, as Helmuth Plessner puts it, he is *naturally artificial:* it is his nature to need culture, to need the sedimentation into a human world of the actions of those who have preceded him.[16] It is this need, the need for human meaning, built into our very ontogeny, which unites, in every human history, the organic with the social, the artificial with the biologically given.

For Sartre, however, the relation between these three—need, nature, and culture—is very different. He introduces biological needs, with the contingent fact of the scarcity of goods for their fulfillment, as the starting point of his dialectic. But this is simply animal need, not the need for meaning, which is uniquely human, and as we have seen it serves as the *unintelligible* base on which and beyond which the dialectic will take place. That dialectic, however, results solely from the interaction of *action* with *inert matter.* "Man," Sartre says, "is that material reality by which matter receives its human functions." [17] Action comes first; [18] through the inertial consequences of action, the "passive activity" of the *practico-inert,* alienation follows. But it is man "who has put into the thing his own action, his own knowledge." [19] This is no dualism, Sartre insists, but a monism, a monism not indeed of substantive matter, but of "materiality." Matter as such, he holds, could exist, only for "God or a pebble." [20] What we have instead is "worked matter," matter viewed, and handled, through the medium of human action. Thus ". . . worked matter, with the contradictions it contains, becomes *for* and *by* men the fundamental engine of History." [21] But this is still, I submit, the sharply dualistic "monism" of *Being and Nothingness:* first action, the for-itself (*now praxis*) springing up as the Other of the In-Itself, and then the In-Itself as its Other, as what by its very upsurge it nihilates; but yet, the other way around, the In-Itself (now the inertial) as the whole locus, the factual reality, in which and against which the For-itself tries to assert itself. Bereft of substantiality, these are still the Cartesian realities of the pure interior and the pure exterior, the *cogitans* and the *extensa,* only no *res.* The embodied human being in whom the dialectic is to operate is represented only as the contingent fact of need and scarcity, or in the reference to the "general milieu of animal life." Everything is material or everything is human—or (*contra* Descartes) both at once: hence the dialectic. But between these two there is still no place for life.

Granted, there are numerous passages in which Sartre does stress the biological reality of the human organism.[22] Indeed, in general, he seems to be playing on an ambiguity in the concept of organization itself. "Organization" may be understood as the ordering principle of any material aggregate, or for that matter of any collection of actions. Thus a corporation, a club, a school, is characterized by the way it is organized. But "organization" may also be used to characterize the structure—and the functioning—of certain natural wholes. It is the latter meaning which seems to be entailed in the concept of an organism, and sometimes Sartre acknowledges the existence of his "practical organism" in this sense. But more fundamental, for him, it seems to me, is the conception of the "practical organism" as the center of organization of action. As material, Sartre argues, we are infected with inertia, but as agents we also "lend to matter our power of transcendence toward organized action." [23] It is this power of organiz*ing* that Sartre is often—and misleadingly—referring to, I believe, when he contrasts the "organic" with the "inorganic," or with an "inorganic plurality." Thus he compares *praxis,* not with any animal behavior, but with a seal which imposes its figure on a receptive wax.[24] Pure agency shaping the purely passive, the revenge of passivity on agency through the *practico-inert:* that is his basic model. So for example the whole range of "collectives," the merely serial togetherness of human individuals, is described as "inorganic" in contrast to the organic unity of the individual agent, who really acts.

But there is a further complication here. As we noticed in the preceding chapter, one of the recurrent themes in Sartre's argument is a firm opposition to "organicism" as a theory of society. There is no such thing as a "hyper-organism" generated by the formation of social structures.[25] Social "organizations" are the creatures of *constituted* dialectic only,[26] the *constituting* dialectic stems from the *praxeis* of individuals alone. Only individuals can produce, by their mediating but individual actions, a group in fusion, only individuals can swear a solemn oath to be true to the group so formed. And constituted dialectic, as we have already seen, must be produced, and understood, under the guidance of the constituting, active, and fundamental phase. So, after all, Sartre has to insist, all *praxis* is founded on "man as *bio-*

logical unity." [27] "Organizations" are after all the product of "organisms" in the ordinary biological meaning of the term. Only this dictum can save Sartre's dialectic from a full Hegelian or idealist issue in some supersociety or superstate. The "intelligibility" of the dialectic also, we have already noted, consists, not in the self-containment of "objective" or "absolute" mind, but in the perspicuity to the individual, active consciousness, of the social, and ultimately historical, context of his act. But the individual agent, in this situation here and now, is the embodied human being, and no one else. Sartre has to fall back on the individual *life* as the locus of history. If there is history, it is individual human beings, "biological unities," who make it. Is not the biological then after all a fundamental category for his view of social action?

Not quite—perhaps even not at all. In his introductory argument ("Introduction B: Critique of Critical Experience"), Sartre stresses *life* as the object of his investigation, but this is "life" in the biographical, not the biological, sense. Referring back to "Questions of Method," he writes: "the epistemological starting point must always be *consciousness* as apodeictic certainty (of) itself and as consciousness *of* such and such an object" [28] —still the position of *Being and Nothingness*. And he continues:

> But it is not a matter of questioning consciousness about itself: the object it must give itself is precisely *life,* that is, the objective being of the investigator, in the world of Others, in so far as this being has been totalizing itself since birth and will totalize itself till death.[29]

The question is still: how can the *cogito,* non-thetic or thetic, pre-reflective or reflective, with its instantaneous upsurge out of nothing and as nothingness: how can this strange yet most familiar being grow? How can I, how can Sartre, how can any agent, totally free, imprint its project by its freedom on inert matter, and yet develop? How can totalization happen over time? Sartre seems to glimpse, at the close of the *Critique,* a vision of history as universally totalizing; yet the power of any one individual to "totalize," to shape his environment into a human life, remains a mystery. If anything is to be intelligible, Sartre seems to hold, the larger totalization, the totalization of *all* history, must reverberate in the individual life, the totalization of each practical organism, "no matter who." [30] And conversely, the individual life must totalize the universe: it must rise up into being as this unique expression of all history, of all humanity: for there is only each for-itself against *the* in-itself, as exteriority, as being as such and in totality. And all this must really happen, from birth to death, not in abstraction, but in the concrete reality of human hopes and frustrations, decisions and disappointments.

From the point of view of *Being and Nothingness,* all temporalization is flight. If that is so, there is no history, neither of individuals, nor of societies, let alone of humanity as such. That is Sartre's most fundamental problem, the problem with which, in *The Idiot of the Family,* he is still wrestling: how, out of the contradictory, and abstract, to-and-fro of for-itself/in-itself, or action/inertia, can a life—any single human life—develop? In the *Critique* he hoped, it seems, that the social perspective of Marxism, hopefully materialist and hopefully totalizing, would enable him to break out of his initial quandary and see the individual life as growing with the dialectical growth of a greater whole. The tortured reflections on Flaubert which have replaced, or at least anticipated, Volume Two of the

Critique, suggest that his hope was vain. It was so, I believe, in part at least because of his failure to assimilate the living in the biological sense to his conception of life as individual history, because he sees man still primarily in terms of thought *versus* being, consciousness *versus* the merely inertial. Granted, history, whether individual or social, is not to be identified with organic growth. But human development is nevertheless an extrapolation of growth, a diversion of the natural into new channels, not its denial. Man has to make himself within a human world, not only, like other animals, within a biological environment. But that development is the history of the human *organism* becoming human. Temporality originates, not in the stream of consciousness, but in the life-span of the embodied individual, who is born, learns to walk and talk and love and hate, grows old, and dies. Engels or no Engels, if nature were not dialectical, neither would we be so. Real human development is rooted in the real biological development of members of this species on this planet. That there are living things, that there are these hominoid living things, is, to be sure, a contingent fact: it might not have happened, it might soon be no more. But it is not a *mere,* unintelligible contingency. It contains, in the hierarchically organized functions and structures of life as it has evolved, the frame for all intelligibility.

Childhood

The passage I have just been considering—as well as the whole tenor of "Questions of Method"—suggests, secondly, a concern with biography, with individual development, which was conspicuously absent from Sartre's early philosophical work. Has he changed fundamentally since then in his attitude to childhood?

It is worth considering in this connection one of the

few explicit parallels Sartre himself draws between *Being and Nothingness* and the *Critique.* In a note at the conclusion of the section on necessity, he first reminds us that, in his present terms, and referring to the practico-inert, "the foundation of necessity is practical." [31] This means, he says, that "it is the for-itself, as agent, discovering itself first as inert, or, better, as practico-inert in the medium of the in-itself." Indeed, the very structure of action as "organization of the unorganized" first exhibits to the for-itself its own alienated being as in-itself: in other words, action generates the "circuit of selfness," the flight from freedom to objectivity or pseudo-objectivity. Thus Sartre can easily put the basic theme of his earlier work in the new terms: "This inert materiality of man as foundation of all knowledge of oneself by oneself is nevertheless an alienation of knowledge at the same time that it is a knowledge of alienation." [32]

But what about the pre-reflective *cogito?* It is still there: *"praxis . . .* is always consciousness (of) self," yet that consciousness is impotent against "the practical affirmation that I am what I have done"—or "made." As in *Being and Nothingness,* so here, the ambiguity of *"fait"* in this context is important, since it is by my action that I have made myself, and by making myself that I act on and in the world. What is crucial here, however, is the recognition that this *I* which I am as what I have done-or-made always escapes me, and does so "by constituting me immediately as *another."* [33] It was this relation, Sartre continues, that made it possible to understand "why man *projects himself* in the medium of the In-Itself-For-Itself." But the fundamental alienation flowing from such self-projection does not come, he insists, "as *Being and Nothingness* might mistakenly lead one to believe, from a prenatal choice: it comes from the universal relation of interiority which unites man as practical organism to his environment." [34]

Has Sartre changed his view in this respect? Aron seems to think that he has done so.[35] That is, he seems to take Sartre as confessing here an error of his earlier position. Previously he had thought of a "pre-natal choice." I make myself, yet wherever I stand, the die is already cast. Now he gives more weight to environment and its "interiorization" by the individual—presumably, as in the case of Genet or Flaubert or the young Jean-Paul himself, the developing individual at some crucial moment in his childhood. Yet basically, it seems to me, the paradox of the Sartrean free act remains the premise for both arguments. On the one hand, *Being and Nothingness* did not literally predicate of the for-itself a "pre-natal choice"; only one might mistakenly have thought that it did. And on the other hand, the very emphasis on social and material environment in the *Critique* makes a "pre-natal choice" inevitable: the child born into a class, into an institutionalized social niche, "is its victim before birth." [36] He cannot choose himself except as what he has already been made to be.

True, Sartre has acquired an interest in the decisive moment of a child's history which he formerly lacked. This is plain from *Saint-Genet,* with its detailed study of the moment in which the young Genet made himself the thief he was accused of being. It is plain from *Words,* with its slogan "Childhood decides." It is plain to the point of supersaturation from the new study of Flaubert. Of course, there is little said of childhood in the *Critique* itself, since its subject is the dialectic of social life in general; but "Questions of Method," which, Sartre has alleged, should really have followed, not preceded, the main text of that work, clearly foreshadows this type of interest. As I suggested earlier, the regressive-progressive method is especially well suited to the study of individual histories, rather than of "History" itself. And in the period of *Being and Nothingness,* on the other hand, a concern for such analysis and synthesis in depth of the individual life was certainly missing. Oddly enough, Sartre remarks in "Questions of Method," "Marxists care only for adults," [37] but so in the main do "existentialists" from Kierkegaard to Heidegger and, in the period of *Being and Nothingness,* Sartre himself. Even his "existential psychoanalysis," it seems to me, deals rather with the expression of my choice of myself in my present preferences than with the emergence in childhood of a process of self-making. That is one of the ways in which Sartre "corrects" Freud. All is consciousness, and consciousness is *now.* True, my hatred of viscosity, for instance, may stem from what my mother did to me in infancy; but what interests Sartre is the analysis of adult consciousness as self-projection and as the flight to bad faith, not its emergence out of the shadows of childhood in the individual life history. Even in Sartre's literary corpus of the earlier period childhood is conspicuously absent. The one striking exception, so far as I know, is the central figure in the story "The Childhood of a Leader," in which the child portrayed is a sort of empty shell and the point of the story is the speculative one made more directly and convincingly in Sartre's essay on anti-Semitism. Lucien's decisive act, moreover, the refusal to shake hands with a Jew, is that of a young man, not a child. *No* project had been initiated in that empty childhood; for this emptiness the young adult substitutes a typical pseudo-act, an identification of himself with a stereotype: I am a Jew-hater, therefore I am somebody. The interest in concrete individual life and its early development, therefore, seem on the whole to be an innovation, at least of emphasis.

At the same time, however, as I noted earlier for the *Critique* in general, the ingredients of the human condition are still the same: total freedom, yet total facticity. The I by its very nature as agent in the world *must* alienate itself from itself; cast into the world by Others, it makes even itself an Other when it acts, as it must do, in and upon that radical Other, the in-itself, whether the purely material or the dehumanized human, the *practico-inert*. If childhood has come to interest Sartre as it used not to do, that is because he is fascinated by the terrible—perhaps the insoluble—puzzle, how a Sartrean for-itself can in fact *come to be.* The for-itself *ought* to be instantaneous; temporalization is flight. Yet people *do* develop; how is this possible? What Sartre wants to know principally in the *Critique,* of course, is: how does humanity develop. But since humanity is an aggregate of individual *praxeis* —there is no social superorganism—that question leaves at its base the question of individual genesis. Mankind can develop only if men can do so; no overarching dialectic, however sweeping, can evade that truth. There is only one *Madame Bovary;* yet in a sense the problem of Gustave—the "idiot" as genius—is the problem of us all. To that problem we must yet return, as Sartre has done.

Scarcity

Meantime, however, the *Critique* was centrally concerned, not with individual biography, but with the social developments that make a history of humanity possible. For, as I suggested in the previous chapter, Sartre seems to have seen in Marxism, or in his own interpretation of

Marxism, an escape from the solipsism of *Being and Nothingness,* and the ground for a rational theory of society and social history. Here he explicitly claims to have introduced new concepts, which are meant to alleviate the bleakness of his existentialism—or, in his own view, to place it at the human center of a larger and therefore truer scheme. Two concepts in particular mediate this new development: *scarcity* as the basis for the interaction of man with matter and indirectly of man with man, and the *reciprocity* of I-Other relations, whether mediated by a third man or by matter, or (perhaps) immediate. Both these concepts are employed, it seems, to alter fundamentally the I-Other relation as set forth in Sartre's earlier argument.

First, scarcity. In *Being and Nothingness* the Other looms up as threat or victim. Logically or ontologically, there is no other possibility. Thus, it seems, every consciousness wants, *a priori,* the death of another, or wants, at least, the victimization of the Other, or, alternatively, of itself. This principle the Sartre of the *Critique* emphatically denies. True, the practical organism is threatened by the Other, but not directly—and not, it seems, in virtue of the very appearance of the Other as such. The practical organism, we have seen, is needy: it needs to be replenished by the inorganic. But, alas, the materials to satisfy its needs are *scarce.* That contingent fact generates the chain of events that will produce social structures: serialities, to begin with, in which each becomes himself part of an inertial aggregate, then groups and institutions, with the exploitation consequent upon them. Scarcity, however, might be defeated; so the ills of organized society are non-necessary. We can hope for a utopia.

There are a number of difficulties in this alleged "solution," even apart from the abstractness of the dream it offers. To begin with (as I noted earlier), scarcity when interiorized is simply the sense of contingency characteristic of the for-itself: it is the awareness that I am—and must be—just so and not otherwise, just here now and not there then. It is simply facticity all over again. Were it overcome, this would be, Sartre announces, the overcoming of man himself. Such, of course, is dialectic: self-devouring contradiction. But as a vision of humanity to replace the concept of the for-itself as "useless passion," it is cold comfort. The human condition rests on scarcity; some day there may be abundance and so no humanity!

Besides, why scarcity and only scarcity? Suppose there were room in the bus? The British, for example, would queue up in any case: they *like* to be orderly. The self-alienation, Sartre could answer, of members of the oldest industrial society! They have made themselves serial. There is something in it. But the point is: if you change the image, you see, not a crowd pushing for places, but a small number of people each using a material object for his own ends. It *serves* each of them; they are not (not necessarily or not always) enslaved by it. Things in the world, as Heidegger tells us, are "ready to hand" for our use. They can also be maddeningly *unready;* they can also be in short supply. But why must that be the basic fact? Because scarcity shows me the Other as competitor, and shows me to myself too in my Otherness than him. That is, for Sartre, what is most striking in the fact that there are Others at all. But suppose, as Rousseau suggested, we find in facing nature the need to cooperate rather than to compete? Think of a barn-raising in the homesteading days of the Midwest. Think of a dam, produced, not by the struggle for scarce goods, but by cooperation for plenty. Granted that the quest for power or profit may, and usually does, enter into all such projects; but that is no reason to make such motives exclusive—unless one is, as Sartre appears to be, already so Hobbesian in one's view of man that no other alternative seems possible.

This seems a strange analogy. Sartre rails against "liberalism" and "positivism," against the atomizing view of man and society taken by utilitarian thinkers. They are mechanical, anti-dialectical, unable to "totalize." Hobbes is the arch example of this kind of thinking. But why, unless he himself shares this atomistic style of thought, must Sartre find competition for scarce goods *the* source of social organization? The truth is, I suspect, that when he thinks about society he really *is* a Hobbesian. There are three passions, Hobbes told us, that necessitate the social contract: fear, gain, and glory. The upsurge of the Other, in *Being and Nothingness,* was also carried by three passions: fear, shame, and pride. Now pride, we saw, is the obverse of shame; shame, then, is pride (= glory) facing the other way: it is my humiliation before, rather than my triumph over, the threatening Other. So in the basic relation of any individual to any other we already had, in effect, two of the Hobbesian three. Now Sartre looks more directly than he had done at men as "material agents" and finds them, whether in want of bread or bus seats, vying with one another for the scarce goods available to satisfy their needs. They compete, not only out of fear or pride (and shame), they compete for gain as well. This vision of human interaction arises inevitably out of—and only out of—a thoroughly molecular conception of the individual. Like particles in a container full of heated gas (to speak anachronistically), or like self-impelled billiard balls, we go off each in his own direction, each pushed by his own appetites—and we collide. That blind inertial consequence necessitates society. And society is alienation: I give myself away to others, simply because otherwise I could not live at all. Society is necessitated by the impossibility of an impossibility. Not, of course, that Sartre would recognize the authority of the Hobbesian sovereign; shades of Rousseau, as of Descartes, forbid! Each man is sovereign. Yet all men can survive only through mutual alienation, only through the self-denying ordinances that institute society.

What most strikingly differentiates Sartrean from Hobbesian man, however, is Sartre's preoccupation, both before and after the *Critique*—though minimally in it— with the inwardness of the individual. Consciousness, and in particular the unhappy consciousness, is his true medium. Hobbes good-humoredly admitted human beastliness, content to engineer an obsequious survival in the face of the worse evil of violent death. Sartre, shut up in phantasms, suffers the alternate agonies of dread before his lonely freedom and remorse at its self-alienation in the world out there. "It's never fun to be a man," he says.[38] Dialectical reason, in its laborious course, offered, perhaps, hope to transcend that pain, or at least its temporary assuagement. In *The Idiot of the Family,* however, it has been, if anything, intensified.

But for the moment we are still with the *Critique* and its construction on the ground of scarcity. Scarcity is not, I have suggested, so exclusively the mediator of social action as Sartre would make it. Let me mention, finally, an example offered by Sartre himself which bears this out: his account of the social structure of a radio audience. To produce a series the member of the bus queue must be there. Those who stay home or go by Métro have no part in the constitution of the series. A radio audience, however, is defined by *absence.* There is a voice speaking; there is the *praxis* of language as its foundation. But the voice by its presence to me and to him and him and him . . . by that very presence indifferently to each makes impossible a common *praxis* for us all. Not only is it an object—a radio—that mediates the disembodied voice; that voice, received, dehumanizes. Indeed, it uses the original reciprocity of discourse *in order* to dehumanize. For it makes of its hearers "inert objects, subjected as inorganic material to the human work of the voice." [39] Of course I can turn the radio off. But that very action, Sartre argues, exhibits "the series defined by absence" constituted by the broadcaster's voice. For my exit from the listening audience makes no difference to its structure: the voice "will continue to sound in thousands of rooms before millions of hearers. It is I who precipitate myself into the ineffective and abstract solitude of private life without changing anything in the objectivity [of the broadcast]. I have not denied the voice; I have denied myself as a member of the crowd (*rassemblement*)." [40] Sartre analyzes the situation further for a political broadcast. Either I am convinced by the government's message (and they have constituted me as their Other), or I am skeptical (and every relation of doubt is one of Otherness), or I am already convinced of the falsity of their rhetoric, and then I either envisage Others as those I could relieve of their deception, or rely for my conviction on the authority of some Others who have persuaded me. But in any of these cases, here I am, listening in absence from the speaker, in absence from the indefinite Others objectified by his address. My powerlessness in this situation, my powerlessness to act on the Other listeners, Sartre declares, "makes of those Others my destiny." [41] Even if the speaker is introduced by name, the reciprocity of language has been destroyed—and it is *no one* speaking.

There is no need to fill in the voices—or, for television, the faces—to illustrate what Sartre is saying. His description strikes home. But does it justify his theory about scarcity as the origin of seriality and seriality as the origin of social relations? This seems to me more questionable, for several reasons. Sartre is arguing at least four points: (1) it is the scarcity of material objects that throws men into serial relations; (2) series are ordinal relations; (3) they are (as in the bus queue) irrelevant in any direct way to mutual *praxis* and so easily relegate human agents into the medium of the *practico-inert;* and (4) the group in fusion and so ultimately the group itself, Sartre will try to demonstrate, originates from the denial of seriality. In the case of the radio audience, (3) is clearly apposite. Mass media do objectify by means of an inertially organized multiplicity-in-absence. Sartre's account is apt, and aptly terrifying. But what of the other points? What has the radio to do with scarcity? Granted, each listener, or someone in his neighborhood, must have money to buy a set. But even if Big Brother endowed each infant at birth with his own set, the situation Sartre describes would hold. Scarcity, it seems to me, is not the definitive factor in the case. Unless of course power originates from competition for scarce goods—and so Big Brother was the product of scarcity. But that is too far-fetched. The point is: here is a characteristic structure of the practico-inert, of the dehumanized human, which in a world of plenty might still exist, might even be exacerbated. The very indefinite possibility of extending such anonymous audiences of disembodied voices—the potential globalization of the media—renders the vision *more* annihilating.

Nor can I see here any clearly *ordinal* character of the aggregate involved. The indefinite set of Others-absent-from-one-another appears rather to be a cardinal collective. Sartre tries to anticipate this objection. If I protest, he says, against a broadcast, and, for instance, write to the newspapers, thus making a public statement of my view, nevertheless each reader in turn must read what I have to say. But surely the contrary is the case. Newspaper readers read—as radio listeners listen—at one time. It is precisely a false network of pseudo-contemporaneity that the mass media constitute. We are together, now, in virtue of our very separation, each at his set, each in his armchair, but all at once. Why is Sartre so confident that not only this one, but all human collectivities, are generated from ordinal relations? Possibly his insistence that social relations are generated only by the plunge into series is related to his concept of temporality. It is still the bead-like moment of a single consciousness that is for him the fundamental reality; a mutual presence-to of one such consciousness and another would be impossible. So if we are to relate consciousnesses, as we must do in order to build society, we have to start by taking one such moment after another, and putting one consciousness after the other. But such an act is wrong, since *every* man is sovereign; society is based on an original fall. Were there a mutuality of human presences, however, this move would be unnecessary. Series exist, indeed, but they need not be *the* foundation of society.

Finally, the notion that groups arise only as the denial of seriality appears even more arbitrary. *If* scarcity were the sole mediating ground of human relations, and *if* seriality, with its transformation of agents into objects, were the sole response to scarcity, then, indeed, groups could emerge only as contradicting, in their turn, the serialized denial of individual *praxis*. But are there no other human relations, more direct than the mediating influence of scarce matter, through which society might originate? Taken at face value, Sartre's own example of language and its degradation through the mass media seems to suggest that there might be such. To speak, must not you and I be present to one another? To answer this question, or at least to suggest some reflections related to a possible answer, we must look, however, in conclusion, at Sartre's other chief innovating—or apparently innovating—social concept: the concept of *reciprocity*.

Reciprocity

By means of a "second *cogito*," the Other looms up as threat to my existence. *He* organizes the world, and so my world, which my for-itself makes mine, bleeds away into his, and—since I *am* that making—I bleed away too. The Other's appearance engenders a hemorrhage of my world toward his. I can reclaim my freedom, therefore, only by denying his. Simone de Beauvoir recalls in her memoirs how she and Sartre worried in their youth about "the problem of the Other." They used to invent life histories for strangers observed in cafés—never mind whether those stories were true. That is one way to put the Other out of action, by fictionalizing him. Then he, too, becomes my creature, powerless to harm me. But of course between myself and the Other there is, within this framework, no reciprocity. He and I, I and Thou, can never be *really* together. We may be united, indirectly, against a common Other, but we are never, as two freedoms, face to face. There can be no respect. Though Sartre did make one effort, in his popular essay "Existentialism and Humanism," to infer the freedom of all from that of one, and hence to provide a basis for human mutuality, his argument there is palpably sophistical and, so far as I know, he has never repeated it in that form. At this stage of his philosophical development at least, the only relation he could validly acknowledge between one human being and another was that of torturer and victim.

As he has turned to social and political concerns, however, he had had to seek, philosophically also, for some more adequate conceptual foundation for social life. If the whole human world of artifacts, the café, the Métro, the newspaper, the radio, is *my* set of instruments, and mine alone, and if this obtains, as it must do, for each for-itself making its world, how can this highly organized system have come about? There must be, there must have been, some actual cooperation in effecting some shared ends that has produced the institutions and artifacts I use. Besides, if one is truly concerned, as Sartre has been, with the oppression of others, one does respect those whose part one takes. One loathes injustice, not simply out of negativity, but out of respect for those who deserve justice and fail to get it. Somewhere, somehow there must be, not only mutual threat, but mutual respect.

It is in this context that Sartre believes he has found in "Marxism" the "true philosophy" into which his existentialism can be harmoniously assimilated. On the one hand, as we have seen, Marxism offered him a platform for revolution into which the concept of class struggle adumbrated in *Being and Nothingness* could be easily integrated. And it also offered the kind of "totalizing" perspective which the turn from individual consciousness to the world seemed to demand. Neither of these relations, however, bears on the fundamental social problem: how can one for-itself be positively and reciprocally related to another? How can there be, not only oppression, but brotherhood? How, except destructively—by the direction of each one's hatred to the common exploiters of all—*can* the workers of the world unite? It is in "historical materialism," as he understands it, that Sartre finds his answer. Each man acts to shape his own world: that is the existentialist insight which must be retained in any true account even of social action. But men act, and have acted, together to generate history: the rise and fall of societies, governments, institutions in general. And they are able to do this because their relations to one another are *mediated by matter*. The mutuality of men, their ability to respect one another so as to act together, *is made possible by the relation of each to material objects*. The dialectic of history is generated by the interaction of man with matter. Hence "historical materialism."

The first example of this process that Sartre presents is that of language. Language, he says, *is* matter: words must bombard my ear; it is through their material presence that they unite speaker and hearer. A phrase is "a totalizing in act where each word is defined by relation to the others, to the situation and to the whole language as an integrating part of the whole." [42] The language itself, then, is an indefinite network of such connecting links, a complex object through which particular subjectivities can relate to one another. But language cannot connect, Sartre argues, unless individual men use it. A necessary condition for the existence of language is that there be *particular* subjectivities to connect and who do the connecting. It is for that reason, he holds, that reciprocity fails in the case of the radio audience. Telephone conversations are another matter; here / speak, via audible sounds, to *you:* two for-itselves are in fact mediated by materiality. But in the case of radio or television it is no one subject that is addressed; therefore reciprocity fails, and the speaker too vanishes into objectivity. Hence the "vertiginous" character of the experience. In their proper functioning, words flow from one *praxis* to another.

Now this is clearly an advance on *Being and Nothingness,* where language was "a form of seduction." Not that it may not, but it need not, be so. On the other hand, there is still something forced about this account too. "The word is matter"? [43] It is true, of course, that language is necessarily embodied. It has always seemed to me rather a joke on Descartes that he makes so much of the uniqueness of language as the mark of man's possessing a disembodiable mind. For speech is perspicuously mental-*and*-bodily, all in one. Words are meanings and *are* only *as* meanings, but as meanings potentially heard or (in writing) seen. They *are* not matter; the same word repeated is not the same matter, but it is the same word. They could not exist apart from matter, and neither could the thoughts they carry. But neither can words be matter as such. They are classes of sounds, or marks, that signify—and signification cannot be reduced to any finite or specifiable series of particular objects. Sartre recognizes, to be sure, the necessary component of "signification" in language; but this comes, in his view, from the particular legislative enactment of each *praxis* (= each for-itself), who gives meaning to each word he uses as he uses it. Thus he adds to the dialectic of his individual action—making the world and being made by it—a dialectic of inter-individual relations: "a moving and indefinite dispersion of reciprocities." [44] It is upon the foundation of such "dispersed reciprocities" that Sartre will construct (or discover?) the dialectic of social organization which develops from them. Thanks to the mediation of material bits—words—there can after all be reciprocal relations between individual consciousnesses, there can be society.

But is language as the foundation of social life, is social life itself, as additive as this? Man lives *in* language, and therefore in a world; he is *in* a world, and therefore in language. Sartre is still hamstrung by his solipsistic starting point—and, clearly, in his exposition of language, by his nominalism, his conviction that only particulars are real. In *The Idiot of the Family* he suggests a more global view of the child's relation to his mother tongue, a view very close to Merleau-Ponty's, in fact; but that's another story. In the *Critique* there are still only active individuals, centers of sense-giving, and the purely inertial matter—phonemes—that can link these otherwise isolated centers to one another.

Hence the importance for Sartre of "the third man." Two individuals may work the same matter—for instance, speak the same language or dig the same ditch—but each is "interiorizing" what is out there in terms of his own project. How can they have a common project? How can there be shared *praxis?* Two workmen sharing a task —regulating a chronometer, Sartre suggests—each interiorize the same imperative; but for each it is assimilated as quasi-material. Each relates to it as an object which he either uses as the technique for his self-projection, or (and this is the usual case) submits to as the Other that has robbed him of his freedom. The dyadic relation of man to man, therefore, remains rooted in matter, in the *in-human.*

It can become human only when it is mediated, not by matter, but by a third *praxis:* by an agent who assimilates to his action the acts of the Other Two. Here Sartre envisages a situation in which he looks from a window at two country workmen invisible to one another: one a gardener, the other one working on the road. Each has organized his world around his work. But the urban intellectual looking at them both unites them: they are both workers and both rural. Though separated in space—that is, external to one another, as all practical organisms are—they are related internally through their relation to the spectator, and through this dialectical transformation he also relates, internally, to them. Thus the relation of two men through matter, "dispersed" and fleeting in its dyadic form, can become the foundation for a richer dialectical development through the injection of a third *praxis* who assimilates to his activity the matter-mediated relations of the other two. The dyad, realized by a third subjectivity: that is the "Trinity" from which social structures can develop. Of course there is always the danger that one of the Three will dehumanize the other-two-in-their-reciprocal-relation: hence the "anti-dialectic" of the *practico-inert,* from which history has (so far) never escaped. But hence also the possibility of the group-in-fusion, the possibility, even the necessity, of the constituting dialectic at the heart of social reality, and even the hope, in the long run, of an ultimate synthesis.

The question is: has this move to the dialectic of *praxeis* mediated by matter in fact enabled Sartre to overcome his initial solipsism? Is he able to move on, as he has promised to do, to the concrete reality of men in societies created by history? He has seen much: the *Critique* for all its deviousness and repetitiousness and for all its abstract Hegelian language contains a number of brilliant analyses, as for example in the account of the mass media or in the examples used to introduce the *practico-inert.* But something is wrong still. The net of abstractions by which Sartre would catch history never gets woven tight enough. The human reality slips through. I cannot specify in detail all the evidence for this statement, but several points of varying degrees of vagueness should suffice to indicate that this is indeed what has happened. Consider for one thing the strangely contrived character of the example by which Sartre introduces the "third," on whose *praxis* as assimilating consciousness depend both the development of society itself and of the social scientist who is to understand it. Two utterly separated laborers and an even more utterly detached observer: is that the sort of situation out of which social life is generated? True, human individuals are always, except pre-natally, external to one another in space (and presumably the unborn child can be ignored here, since it is not a "practical organism"). Moreover, that in consciousness also, not only in his spatiality, every man is an island, the Sartre of *Being and Nothingness,* and of the literary corpus of that period, has amply demonstrated. Starting from there, however, is exactly the way *not* to demonstrate the contrary. If one is to mediate successfully between the for-itself and the for-Others, as I have argued earlier, one must start from the among-Others—where we all start. And that is just where Sartre, looking out his country window, like his childhood forerunner looking out, I rue de Goff, over the roofs of Paris, is *not.* The indwelling of man in the human world, once exiled in favor of the sovereign Cartesian moment of self-contained clarity, cannot be drawn back into existence by any weaving of material links between a mulitiplicity of such isolated units.

Corresponding to the artificiality of this beginning, moreover, is the recurrent uneasiness of the reader (at least of this reader) throughout the *Critique* about the conceptual foundation of mediated reciprocity on which the whole dialectic rests. Relations between two *praxeis* are mediated by matter, then by a third *praxis* mediating the matter-mediated dyad, and so on. But Sartre's insistence on such mediation in social structures suggests, by contrast, an *immediate* reciprocity which, in the *praxeis-processus* that generate society, has been dialectically transformed. Is there such a thing? Late in the text there is at least one explicit reference to it—at least as an abstraction.[45] Moreover, the initial account of "human relations as mediation between different sectors of materiality"—the section in which the basic unit for the dialectic is laid down—suggests that there may be. At least an element in reciprocity is that "I acknowledge the Other *praxis* . . . at the same time that I assimilate him as object into my totalizing project." [46] The two "totalizations," Sartre says, "respect one another." [47] True, this mutuality never comes to rest in unity, for there are *two,* each of which still "integrates the whole universe." [48] But unstable though this mutual recognition is—and who can deny its instability?—it must exist if the whole superstructure is to develop. Yet if, on the other hand, as Sartre also insists they are, all human relations are solely mediated by matter—if it is a question of the for-itself, as a pure subjectivity, linked to other subjectivities by the intervention of the purely inertial, whether of the literally material and inhuman or the quasi-material inhumanity of institutions—then the foundation in mutual respect is missing. Even on Bastille Day the fleeting "we-subject" is an abstraction: triadic relations in which each dyad is indirect cannot themselves achieve concrete reality. Despite the brilliance of many of Sartre's historical descriptions, in short, Merleau-Ponty was right in insisting that he is too much concerned with "totalizing" to acknowledge the very limited, concrete realities on which in fact human history rests. Subjectivity, materiality, totalization: these three counters, so separated, cannot by any dialectical ingenuity reconstitute the human situation. Subjectivity is always already embodied, and our bodily being is always already embedded in a concrete whole, in a natural environment which is at the same time a human world—as (in Whitehead's term) a *concretion* of the universe, not the universe itself. And in this kind of wholeness there is always already some mutuality, however fleeting and however imperiled. Again language is the best example. If there could be no human understanding without speech, the converse also holds. Without mutual understanding there could be no speech, for there would be nothing to mediate, and no medium in which to mediate it.

That Sartre himself recognizes this difficulty in the *Critique,* finally, seems clear from the very fact that he has taken a long detour in his proposed path from the foundation of history to history itself and is trying in his study of Flaubert to reconstruct somehow a single life—a single life, to be sure, within a highly complicated network of institutions already mediated by countless thousands of past *praxeis* and countless movements of the practico-inert—but still a single life in which the immediate reciprocities underlying all these abstract complexities are somehow to become evident. Most tellingly, Sartre even envisages here the founding relation for a human life of a mother's affection for her child. That was what Flaubert lacked, he is sure, and what few infants, he is equally sure, have ever had. But nevertheless love between mother and child exists, and where it exists there is an unquestioning reciprocity between two subjectivities in which individual development can be rooted as in no other ground. So he seems to suggest, even more surprisingly, does sexual love, as distinct from the sado-masochism of *Being and Nothingness.* Whether, so late in the day, Sartre can really assimilate to his philosophy the astonishing phenomenon of love, and hence of a concrete, immediate reciprocity as the coping-stone of human relations, is another question. But its introduction in *The Idiot of the Family* brings into focus once more its absence in all his earlier work, in the dialectic of the practical organism as well as in the ontology of the for-itself and the for-others.

On the whole, then, the answer to our question:

whether in the *Critique* Sartre has succeeded in introducing subjective innovations in his view of man is, as predicted, "Yes" and "No," but more "No" than "Yes." His "practical organism" is still a subjective center of action, not an organism of flesh and blood. It has not been born and grown to human stature in a concrete human world, carried by human affection (as well as hate, which, Sartre admits, by the way, is "a recognition" [*"une reconnaissance"*]).[48] "A man," it has turned out,[49] is "a practical organism living with a multiplicity of similar [organisms] in a field of scarcity." [50] The "with" is still inadequate, and so the "man" in the case is not quite man. Too much is absent from Sartre's original premises; not even so laborious a reconstruction can restore what the initial vision had overlooked.

We have still to ask, in conclusion, whether the most laborious reconstruction of all will succeed where both earlier efforts have failed—and finally, how, as far as Sartre has gone till now, we are to see his philosophical work as a whole in the context, not of a "totalizing" history, but at least in the context of the history of philosophy in the West.

chapter eight: postscript

on first reading the idiot of the family

"Every great philosopher
has only one thought." Does this
Heideggerian tag apply to Sartre? Philosophy is a conversation about fundamental problems, a conversation going back to Thales, in
which, generation after generation, each person takes
his special place. Thus each great thinker, it seems, repre-

sents *one* position. Like any artist, he displays for us a comprehensive vision of the world, except that, unlike other artists, he states that vision in argument, and what makes him "great" therefore is the ingenuity of the premises from which he starts and their power to produce manifold and apposite conclusions. Yet no thinker can outrun the bounds of his own first principles, of his "one thought." However much we can mine from reading Spinoza, ultimately we come up against the impasse of responsibility versus strict determinism which his concept of substance inevitably generates. However many shrewd insights and intriguing arguments we discover in Hume, we run eventually head on into the problem of the person, which he himself admits to be insoluble in his own terms. Of course no one is perfect, and even great philosophers may be inconsistent: they can feed into their conceptual machine something that doesn't strictly belong there. But if a philosopher does this habitually, he makes a muddle, not a philosophy. To the ideal of "adequacy" he sacrifices "coherence." That is why, for most students of philosophy, John Locke is such a bore. Although in fact there is also a very great deal he cannot say at all, he can, within certain limits of superficiality, say almost anything, even if his premises, had he properly digested them, would have eliminated much of what he wants to tell us. He has of course a place based chiefly on influence, as well as on the way in which he represents for us the confusion characteristic of certain trends in a certain period.

Looked at from this perspective, Sartre appears as one of the great philosophers of coherence. Whatever he cannot see from where he stands, he denies; and there is much, in *Being and Nothingness* and still in the *Critique,* that he is blind to. But the stand he takes is firm and rigorous, and the searchlight he casts on what does come within his view is brilliantly penetrating. Above all, the stand he takes is not idiosyncratic but the expression of a destiny we all share. He is the ultimate and most consequent Cartesian, carrying what remains of the Cartesian either-or to its terrifying logical conclusion. We have seen how he does this by weaving together phenomenological *motifs* with dialectical methods, but always on the strict conceptual ground of Cartesian consciousness, Cartesian freedom, and Cartesian time. Thus it is that the Sartre of *Being and Nothingness* and even, in a way, of the *Critique,* represents for us the "tragic finale" of a tradition initiated in the seventeenth century—the tradition that conceived of a pure, and purely rational, center of conscious activity seeking to control a purely passive material world.

Twenty years ago, indeed, it seemed that Western philosophy in general, whether in the European or the English-speaking world, expressed in its differing styles this single tragic impasse. Cartesian mind had shriveled to the Sartrean pure act, and on the other side of the Cartesian dichotomy both early and late Wittgenstein embodied the frustration of the more outward-directed empiricist tradition. So we had either Kierkegaard without God or Hume without his eighteenth-century amiability. Hume had already reduced the external world to a series of mere bits. Wittgenstein first tried to use the new logic to revive the more objective, "picture," view of truth, but when this failed he fell back on linguistic therapy as philosophy's sole task. In the small space we are doomed to move in, we "circle round and round the same landscape," using our reflective efforts to overcome philosophical reflection rather than to practice it. We are where we are: why try to think as if we were somewhere else? Thus on the one hand subjectivity had emptied itself of substance and of content, and had become simply the negation of the external world; and on the other hand the external world, shrunken to a subjective series of impressions, was re-objectified in a fashion by taking our special "form of life" as if it were an unquestionable and objective given. Doubtless this is an unfair view of Wittgenstein, both in his early and late phases, but if so, it is scarcely unfair to the practice, some years ago, of many of his alleged disciples. If philosophy in the one demi-tradition was anguished, in the other sector it was trivial.

But things have changed. In its slow and gentlemanly way, even British philosophy has gained a little broader perspective. And, in its more dramatic style, so has the philosophy of the Continent. On both sides, the change has come through attention to the problem that defeated Hume, the problem of the person. Descartes *said* the "mind" was housed in the body more intimately than a pilot in a ship, but, starting where he did, there was little he or his successors could do to explain this mystery. It is here, in the philosophical description and understanding of human beings as embodied persons, that conceptual reform must take, and indeed has taken, its start.

The thinkers and the arguments that have started us on this new course need not concern us here. Our final question is: where does Sartre come into this story? Is it correct to set his philosophy as a whole, with its Cartesian provenance and its Cartesian foundations, in the historical place we have so far assigned to it? Retrospectively from *Being and Nothingness* and, on the whole from the *Critique,* it seems to be so. *Being and Nothingness* does indeed express paradigmatically the agony of twentieth-century thought; the *Critique* does embody in its strained and abstract reasoning the terrible effort of the Cartesian ghost to get out of the machine. But a philosopher may not only present in his *magna opera a* position or *a* crisis in the dialogue that is philosophy; he is a person too, and persons develop. Sartre is still twenty years younger than Plato was when he wrote the *Laws.* Where his whole work as philosopher will stand in the history of thought depends on where he is going now and where he will go from now on. So far the evidence is mixed; one can only hazard a guess.

The view Sartre himself takes of his own development, I have already mentioned in discussing the *Critique.* He has worked, he says, with three concepts: the for-itself, the practical organism, the lived. Basically, we found, however, the second of these did not represent a clear-cut advance on the first. The *Critique* could be translated without significant residue into the dialectic of for-itself / in-itself. There was, indeed, a hint of an "active passivity" inconceivable in the earlier mode; but this was unstable, relapsing, almost instantaneously into the "passive activities" of the practico-inert. Is there now a significant advance in the third stage: in the use of "the lived" as central concept?

The material which could—perhaps—supply us with an answer is massive: the first two of a projected four-volume work in which Sartre undertakes to reconstruct as *lived* the reality of one individual, Gustave Flaubert. It is of course a work of biography (though in part of extremely speculative biography), of psychoanalysis, of literary criticism, and not in the first instance a work of philosophy. But it contains, recurrently, glimpses of Sartrean philosophy—some familiar, some, on the contrary, surprisingly novel. What will issue from all this in the way of a developed new position is, it seems to me, still hard to say. The evidence, if I read it aright, is confusing and contradictory. Let me hazard some brief general remarks about it, and then substantiate my general impression by reference to three particular passages, one illustrating the constancy of Sartre's position, one its ambiguity, and one its novelty.

Sartre's aim in *The Idiot of the Family* is to reconstruct a single life as lived. Is the lived here really a new category? Looking at its usage throughout the two volumes one is inclined, on the whole, to think that it is not. If Sartre in the *Critique* had to march by the most ingenious dialectical detours toward the plain fact of human sociality, here he is straining even more ingeniously and exhaustingly to show how one consciousness can know another in its experienced conscious quality. For of course there *are* only individuals and we cannot pretend to know social action really unless we can demonstrate how one of these existents can somehow enter into the consciousness of another. Moreover, the conceptual units out of which Sartre's reconstruction is effected are the old familiar ones, a combination in fact of the two sets of earlier concepts. "Being" and "Nothingness" are fundamental, perhaps because they suit Flaubert—whose mode of existence is "irrealization"—but also, clearly, because they suit Sartre. The old Sartrean view of imagination is fundamental—again for the same twin reasons. Further, just as emphatically as in the earlier work, man is ideally action, action is *praxis:* acting upon passive matter, and *praxis* is rational. What ails Flaubert is that, first by the *fiat* of his father, who "made" a doomed younger son, then (in Sartre's "fable") by his mother's minute but unloving care, he has been constituted as *passive activity.* In other words, he *is* chiefly through Others and therefore also as Other than himself. We are to learn in a later volume how, in and beyond the seizure of '44, Flaubert freely made himself what he had been made: we are to know his liberty as well as his enslavement—for of course every man *is* freedom, however others may have enslaved him. But the point here is that in the framework of these all too familiar concepts, "the lived" beckons us like the light at the end of a long tunnel. It is something we have to try to get at with deviousness and difficulty as the underside of a life's rationale, the inwardness of an alien consciousness. It is still, I think, that consciousness (of) self which, however we assimilate ourselves to ourselves, escapes the reflective level and looms as emotion, as the magical aspect of our being-in-the-world. "Rational thought," says Sartre, "forges itself in action, or rather *it is action* itself producing its own illumination (*lumières*)." ¹ To act, to give reasons, to be free—and therefore to be properly a man—all these are one. From this vantage point I, as free agent, order my world. When rationality breaks down, on the other hand (and in Flaubert's case it had broken down *a priori:* father, mother, elder brother all had made it so), action collapses too (since they are identical). Things happen to me, chance reigns, and I suffer it. "Chance," writes Sartre, "the course of the world interiorized in passion." ² In other words, it is when I fail to make sense of things, and thus to act on them, that I fall back on feeling: why did this have to happen to me? Feeling is failure, the assimilation to my own consciousness of the horrid fact, the ultimate fact, that I am not my own foundation. In this context "the lived" appears as surrogate for the emotion of the early essay and of *Being and Nothingness.* In this context Sartre still appears as the arch-rationalist in fascinated pursuit of the irrational.

Persisting also, moreover, in the case-study of Flaubert, is the quasi-Marxist slant of Sartre's social philosophy. Not only Flaubert's father and mother made him, but the Family, with its solid bourgeois status founded on the nearly feudal sovereignty of his self-made father. The fact that Flaubert is a member of the bourgeoisie, committed through his father's decree to fealty to his class, loathing it yet inalienably one with it—and thus alienated from himself—all this, again, gives Sartre a theme on which he rings endless, and wholly familiar, changes. From *Being and Nothingness* on, it could have been foreseen, and it is illimitably boring.

Yet throughout the long discursive course of Sartre's reconstruction of Flaubert there are hints here and there of something different. There are hints that a man *might* be not only a mask—*"un personnage"*—but also a living person—*"une personne"*—that if the wretched Gustave was a "useless passion," [3] in search of an illusory and impossible in-itself-for-itself,[4] *man* is not necessarily so. In *Being and Nothingness,* for example, the instant, as moment of lucid self-knowledge and independent action, both in one, haunted the argument as the ideal from which all temporalization is flight. Now Flaubert is accused of allowing temporality (understood as Husserl's "inner time consciousness") to collapse into a succession of instants.[5] He is said to flee temporality toward the instant, not, as in the earlier work we all appeared to do, the instant in the direction of temporality. He cannot really grasp the future, he cannot live it really, but only in dream. Is there then after all in contrast to Flaubert's case, free action in the world that *really* makes sense?

To this reader, moreover, there is a tantalizing though wholly implicit suggestion of philosophic innovation in Sartre's references, throughout the text, to the work of Merleau-Ponty. I have elsewhere described the relation of Sartre's philosophy to that of his former fellow-student as a "dialogue"; but I had thought of the term as only half-applicable, or as metaphorical.[6] Much of Merleau-Ponty's philosophizing, both in his major work and elsewhere, is indeed "dialogue" with Sartre: he wanted, not only to transcend Cartesianism, but particularly to transcend the Cartesianism of Sartre. Over and over, all the way to the notes for the unfinished *Visible and Invisible,* it is an argument of Sartre to which he is seeking to reply, or a Sartrean concept he is seeking to modify. But never before, so far as I know, has Sartre (at least in his published writing) in turn listened and replied. Not only their quarrel, but even Sartre's tribute in *Les Temps Modernes* after Merleau-Ponty's death, suggest this want of response.[7] When they were first reconciled, Sartre reports there, Merleau-Ponty told him he was working on a project inspired by Whitehead's saying: "Nature is in tatters" (*"La nature est en haillons"*). Far from seeing the philosophical implications of this remark, Sartre interprets it in psychoanalytic terms as referring to the death of Merleau-Ponty's mother! Merleau-Ponty's struggle, the post-Cartesian struggle, to found a new image of nature, and of man in nature, seemed to elude him altogether. The "dialogue" of Sartre and Merleau-Ponty was a dialogue between two positions, not between two men. Merleau-Ponty was indeed replying to Sartre, but the reply was unheard. Ten years after his death, the case has altered. True, Sartre still does not reply to Merleau-Ponty's reflections; in *The Idiot of the Family* he is not in any case explicitly writing philosophy. But he quotes him recurrently, tacitly accepting his phrases as if Merleau-Ponty were a writer whose thinking he had wholly assimilated to his own. They are quotations very much by the way; not much is made of them. But that is just the point. Merleau-Ponty's turns of phrase are quoted as one quotes a writer to whom one is very close indeed, a writer whose language one uses because one thinks his thoughts. Yet at the same time Sartre is still speaking his own old language, whose over-abstraction, whose hopeless "totalization," Merleau-Ponty had, in the view of many of us, so tellingly criticized. What will become of this strange assimilation? After putting aside the *Critique* to embark on a four-volume Flaubert, will Sartre put aside the Flaubert to give us a new philosophical work? Will he himself change from the last great Cartesian to one of the pioneering post-Cartesians? Will he give us, what Merleau-Ponty never succeeded in achieving, a fully developed philosophy that will transcend the nihilism in which the Cartesian tradition necessarily issued and which he himself has most fully and rigorously stated? As of this writing, I think it is too soon to say.

Meantime, however, let me close this inconclusive postscript by pointing to three passages in the new Flaubert which illustrate the Janus-faced nature of the philosophical views it implicitly contains.

The first is an analysis of the comic, which takes off from Bergson and adds what Sartre says Bergson missed: the social function of comedy. Bergson was right, he holds, in seeing in the comic the demotion, in relatively harmless circumstances, of the vital to the merely mechanical. The individual who appears as funny is thereby reduced from agency to the level of the inorganic. The social effect of this, moreover, he believes, is to reduce the group to seriality. The comic is indeed "social" in that it is contagious; but it spreads, serially, from one laugher to another, and thus it loosens or even negates the unity of the group in action. This negation, however, is not skeptical in its import; it serves in fact to strengthen "the spirit of seriousness." This would-be eloquent politician stumbles on the platform; how amusing. But the social structure we each believe in is strengthened, not weakened, by his lapse. Dignity is confirmed by this small indignity. But what of the comedian himself? The comic *actor,* Sartre believes, is always felt as less than human. If you pass him on the street surrounded by his family, you get a shock. Can that funny man nevertheless be a serious person, like you or me? Surely not! For the comic, Sartre holds, works essentially by the twin means of *derealization,* from the reality of *praxis* to the imagined level of a pseudo-praxis that fails of its purpose: the conspirators overheard by their enemies or the clown who jumps into the river to get out of the rain; and *dehumanization*—the reduction of the practical agent to puppetry, of the vital to the mechanical, and at the same time of the group to the series (that is, to the practico-inert).[8] Or where, as in Chaplin's films, there is patently humanity in humor, Sartre remarks in a note, it is not pure comedy! Moreover, this one-sidedness of comedy can only be corrected, he says later, by the whole apparatus of dialectical reason.[9]

What is wrong with this picture? It is, I find, an excellent analysis of farce—which is what in fact Sartre will need later on in his reconstruction for the interpretation of Flaubert's "Garçon"—but it misses humor, and misses indeed something essential to the nature of laughter as such: the *ambiguity* of the human situation from which it springs. (I am relying heavily here on Helmuth Plessner's *Laughing and Crying;* if I do not give chapter and verse it is not for want of recognizing my indebtedness to his work.) [10] Sartre does, in connection with the young Flaubert's relation to the comic, mention "ambiguity," but what he is referring to is the ambiguity of what he calls the "tourniquet": the back and forth of a turnstile from which there is no exit. Both sides, the vital and the mechanical, the rational and the absurd, *praxis* and its failure, are undeniable and inescapable; there is "ambiguity" in so far as one swings, in comedy, from one aspect to the other. But in the comic as Sartre sees it they never reverberate together. The ambiguity of two-in-one, which is precisely the duplicity of the eccentric position of man—I *am* the body I take a stand to—this organic ambiguity eludes altogether the scope of Sartre's analysis. But it is just this kind of ambiguity—an ambiguous ambiguity—that characterizes the comic. In puns, for example, other than the crudest word plays, one does not *just* swing back and forth from one meaning to another. One has them both together; as in "a little more than kin and less than kind." What sustains comedy, moreover, as distinct from farce, is not the unequivocal casting down of dignity into indignity, but an ambiguity that casts its spell on both sides, on action *and* its failure, and holds them both together. Even comedies as lighthearted as Shaw's *Arms and the Man* or *You Never Can Tell* illustrate this difference.

The sociality of humor, further, is not, or is not solely, what Sartre declares it to be. It is true, of course, that laughter breaks out when action breaks down, and breaks down in relatively harmless circumstances. But what laughter releases is not merely the contagion of the practico-inert. On the contrary, laughing *together* is one of the most characteristic forms of bona-fide reciprocity. The necessary indirectness of language breaks down in laughter, sometimes indeed because communication fails, but sometimes also because it is too powerful for speech. The laughter of two people in love excludes the rest of the world, but it very much unites the lovers. Or again, the laughter of children—whose verbal competence is still inadequate effectively to support their sociability—is not, I should think, as such separative and serializing. Finally, it seems to me, the clown as a person is not necessarily sub-human: he is lovable and indeed loved, just because he is funny and we see ourselves as funny with him. For *contra* Sartre, it is sometimes, and in some ways always, funny to be human.

Sartre's analysis of the comic, in other words, has just the kind of abstraction, of literalness, of strict rationality, that we might have expected from the author of his two major philosophical works. It "totalizes" too soon and too drastically and thus misses the half-lights that make comedy at its best both so elusive for theory and so satisfying a representation of the ultimate ambiguity of the human state.

Yet there are passages in *The Idiot of the Family* which seem to pre-figure a different Sartre. He uses, as I have already pointed out, his old vocabularies, and indeed fuses them effectively into one vocabulary: Nothing and *praxis,* Being and seriality, here live happily together. And in one place at least he presents, with surprising condensation for so rambling a text, a statement in little of his whole philosophic position—but (and here is the surprise) with overtones, or undertones, that seem to be new. Doubtless there are other passages too in these more than two thousand pages that might convey a similar message; but let me take this one as especially telling, since it happened to strike this particular reader so.

Sartre is again discussing the comic in connection with the emergence of the schoolboy Flaubert's grotesque creation "Le Garçon"; he introduces the topic of *"farces attrapes,"* the paraphernalia of the crude practical joke. These work, he says, on a simple principle: a small collective selects a dupe whom it proceeds to mystify "for a laugh." By so doing it "wishes to conjure away the anguish of being-in-the-world." [11] This anguish, he tells us, "specification of a fundamental anguish which is nothing else but freedom, is born of an inescapable contradiction of our *praxis.*" [12] No one, he thinks, in fact lacks the knowledge that "appearances are deceptive," yet, however vigilant we may be in remembering this truth, "the necessities of action—for instance lack of time —oblige us to consider the 'appearances' as manifestations of being." [13]

This is all straight Sartrean doctrine—although it should perhaps be noted in passing: if time is part of scarcity, as indeed it is for any living being, the hope of transcending scarcity and the *practico-inert,* of stabilizing freedom and the "active passivity" of shared action, is exposed as the utopian dream, which, on Sartre's original premises, it is. We are back with the purely negational revolution of the earlier Sartre. That is by the way. Meantime, he tell us here, we do for convenience, and because it conforms to "an original relation of adhesion to the world," and especially if, preoccupied with our pursuits, "we have no time to spare," take the appearances for the reality. But, he continues, "this adhesion, always contestable and silently contested, is not lived without anguish, if not in the particular case, at least as a global feeling of our insertion in the world. It is not a question here of a doubt —explicit and methodic doubt is reassuring at least to a degree—but of a more or less actualized " 'estrangement.' " [14] Usually, he tells us further, we mask this fundamental anguish "by remaining at the surface of ourselves and attaching ourselves to security-inducing constants displayed in external sequences." Thus the basic estrangement which is always there is "hidden by habits or purely and simply *beaten back.*" Moreover, he goes on, it should also be considered that "I come to myself 'from horizons,' the world is what separates me from myself and announces me to myself, so that there is in every 'worldly' (*'mondaine'*) appearance a disquieting menace and a still more suspect promise which address themselves to me in the depths of my existence." [15] And now comes the theme of the *Critique:* daily labor through the mediation of the material we use and through our tools reveals to us "the coefficient of adversity" in things. This, Sartre reminds us, varies with the mode of production which defines it, and so with the society, "whose type of integration is extrapolated and projected in view of objective unification on the entire aggregate of facts in the world." Thus with Marxist loyalty, he assures us: "nature" is defined in every case as "the material and the limit of current techniques." And finally, in this situation, "the environment announces me as coming to myself *also* through others, that is, as alienation and destiny." [16]

Vintage Sartre, it seems, except that as against the *Critique* destiny is equivalent to alienation: it does not appear here as a destiny *of* freedom, but of its loss. But now Sartre moves on to his present theme, the theme of *one* individual's development:

> In particular the relation-to-the-world has been lived from birth starting from our relation to our surroundings: *the text of the world* is the sense of the familial setting, itself conditioned by institutions; we are not *at ease* in the world except to the degree to which we are *at ease* in our own family—and that "ease", in truth, is nothing but a lesser uneasiness. For that reason, every being which reveals itself as appearance and every appearance which confesses its non-being are in danger of denouncing us as *pure seeming* or of revealing our "abysmal being" as ignominious or terrifying.[17]

And so to the interpretation of the practical joke:

Thus when an object in the world appears to us awry, it is the whole world, ourselves and our relation to the world which become suspect: what formerly went without saying no longer holds of itself; compromised to the secret depths of existence, we glimpse a monstrous *otherness of being* which would be the truth of the cosmos and of our person.[18]

Here, it seems to me, is the heart of Sartre's philosophy in a paragraph. He goes on then to describe at length how this fall into uncanniness takes place when he puts into his coffee a seeming lump of sugar that is in fact marble (and sinks) or celluloid (and floats). This particular analysis need not concern us; nor need we linger over the phenomenon of so prolix a writer's putting so pithily what he has taken volumes, and years, to say. What is suggestive about this passage in view of our present question is something rather slight, a shadow, somehow, of a different sense of being-in-the-world, a more rooted sense of existence than had been typical of Sartre's thinking in the past. True, my "ease" in the world must be "only a lesser uneasiness"; true, the abyss is always there. But some phrases are new. "From horizons," which he puts in quotes, is not, I believe, a usual Sartrean concept. Taken the other way, *to* a horizon, it is characteristic of Merleau-Ponty's adaptation of Husserl in the theory of perception. Admittedly, Sartre uses it here to show that I come to myself "from elsewhere"; he refers in a note to "the menacing promise" of discovering to myself at a distance what I am, since every object "can put in question the world as a totality and in consequence myself insofar as I come to myself from horizons." [19] Yet, I submit, the "horizonal" relation to things is less absolute, less uncompromising, than the utter negation of the in-itself by the for-itself and of the for-itself by the in-itself characteristic of *Being and*

Nothingness. True, the for-itself is said to be, as to content, wholly out there; but the relation is one of emptiness to fullness, not of center to horizon: a very different relation. Indeed, it was precisely the sense of being in a landscape, at the center of a perspective, that was missing from the earlier account. The for-itself was over against the world rather than in it. Being in the world as a relation to horizons from which we come suggests, at least to the reader of Merleau-Ponty, a more promising direction for the description of human rootedness in being, which is as ineradicable a part of our condition as is the "estrangement" Sartre has so far preferred to see. More striking, perhaps, further, is the expression "text of the world," reminiscent of the title of Merleau-Ponty's unpublished fragment "The Prose of the World." (This will soon become, in relation to Flaubert and the Garçon, "the farce of the world," but that is another story.) If the world is a text to be read, then, again, the explicit Otherness of reader and read, of consciousness and matter, may yet be overcome. In short, if we put this together with Sartre's very Merleau-Pontyian account of "being in language" earlier in this work, we may hope at least that he is moving to something like a theory of interpretation as the model for being-in-the-world, a theory in which the *implicit* grasp of sense underlying all *explicit* reading is necessarily included. Such a theory, in other words, in which not "negation of being" but "understanding of being" is fundamental, would alter the self-directedness of the non-thetic consciousness (of) self and admit that our way of "living" the world—and ourselves—is directed primarily *from* clues within ourselves, in our inescapably bodily-and-mental being, *to* processes in the world, of which, through these clues, we are constantly striving to make sense. To ignore this vector in non-thetic consciousness, we noticed much earlier, was Sartre's first misstep at the very start of *Being and Nothingness.* But there are, I would suggest, hints in *The Idiot of the Family* that he may yet set his course in a different direction and so evade after all the catastrophic issue of his earlier premises. I may be making too much, in connection with the passage just quoted, of very slight shadows indeed; but there is something about his way of putting things that has changed. For one who is habituated to the analysis of arguments rather than of style the difference is hard to specify; if the reader fails to feel it, especially in paraphrase and translation, I can only say: Sorry; I do. And through these two long volumes there are recurrent places where despite the constancy of the main conceptual framework the same impression of novelty comes through.

Sometimes, indeed, though rarely, the change is very explicit. One case is the passage on language already referred to. I have also referred already to what appears to be Sartre's altered view of love, which seems in turn to be related to a (possibly) altered concept of the person—or rather to *a* concept of the person. Previously, in common with other modern philosophers, that is just what he lacked.

Sometimes, indeed, it still appears that there are only "personnages," not persons. This was in effect the theme of *The Transcendence of the Ego,* and of the doctrine of "the circuit of selfness" in *Being and Nothingness.* It is still with us, conspicuously in the case of Flaubert himself, the very fabric of whose being, Sartre argues, is insincerity. The gap between authentic action, if it were possible (as for Flaubert it is not), and the construct of himself that he presents to others as well as to himself: this gap is forever unbridgeable. But is the doom of Flaubert the doom of Everyman? Is bad faith after all *the* human condition? In the *Critique,* we noticed, one seeks uneasily for information about the *immediate* reciprocity which Sartre obscurely hints at as the alternative to those mediated relations of men to one another on which society is built. In *The Idiot of the Family,* similarly, the philosophical reader is bound to wonder about the hints occurring here and there which suggest that not every man need be a mask. The two problems, of reciprocity and of personal authenticity, of course, are intimately related, since bodily being with others in a social world is the necessary condition of becoming myself. It was this dimension of human existence, we found in *Being and Nothingness,* that Sartre had most grievously misread. What does he make of it here? What does he make, in particular, of the two cases of bodily being together that most conspicuously characterize the development of a human person: maternity (or its reciprocal: infancy) and sex? As to the first, his interpretation is ambiguous. In constructing his legend of Mme. Flaubert and little Gustave, Sartre suggests at least a happier alternative. Flaubert's dislike of himself, he holds, issues from his mother's loveless care of an unwanted infant. Some few babies, he says, *are* wanted by their mothers, and they will be able to *act.* So existence as a free agent seems to be constituted, or enabled, by maternal affection. But sometimes he characterizes this enviable state in other terms: he speaks of the inordinate *vanity* of the wanted child, who is unquestioningly the center of the universe, as for example Flaubert's elder brother doubtless was: a mediocre nonentity made Somebody by the position his father gave him, the very quintessence of the stuffed man, the hollow man. So the situation may be still in Sartre's view as hopeless as ever; the upshot is not clear. There is, however, at least one passage on sexual love that quite unambiguously contradicts the sado-masochistic thesis of *Being and Nothingness.* Sartre is talking about Flaubert's talk with Louise Colet before she seduced him (*sic;* Sartre emphasizes the way in which Flaubert's passivity demanded that women possess him rather than he them). He writes:

> The absurdity of Chamfort is to use the word "contact," which applies to caresses—and not even to all of them —when the essential of love is that a man, *enters, wholly complete* (*tout entier*), a woman who receives him, herself *wholly complete* (*tout entière*), which supposes that, in receiving him, she closes herself on him, contains him and penetrates him in her turn with what Doña Prouhèze calls "the taste I have." Love is not mute, especially when it is silent: through the flesh, its "taste," its smells, its elasticity, its colors and its forms, through the grain of a skin, the distribution of hair, the total but ineffable sense of the person is transmitted to the other person; from one side and the other, this sense becomes a material and silent condensation of all language, of all the phrases said and to be said, of all the actions done and to be done. The two naked bodies, in the present instant, are the equivalent of an infinite discourse which they promise, transcend and instantly make useless.[20]

Is this the man for whom language was a form of seduction, for whom the Other was doomed to be either torturer or victim? Sartre himself has said that he has changed, chiefly, by his own account, because he found politics. It was the Spanish Civil War, then Hitler, that took him out of his preoccupation with the single for-itself, that made him loathe *Nausea* and *The Flies* with their self-centered heroes. And it is Algeria and Vietnam that have kept him there. But, alas, the Sartre of political philosophy, the Marxist Sartre, remains an abstraction, and he remains an abstraction because, believing in the rootedness of all social life in individual *praxis,* he has nevertheless no theory of such *praxis* that can found society on any concrete immediacy of human beings existing with one another, in fellowship rather than in mutual isolation. Not that such fellowship is frequent or permanent; I am not suggesting some rosy idealism as the corrective of Sartrean gloom. We *do* live mostly and most of the time in alienation from ourselves and others; we *are* swept along by the dialectic of the *practico-inert*. Yet if there were no other possibility, no moments, however rare, of a true and more immediate communion, there would be no humanity, not even an unattainable ideal from which we might inevitably fall. In shame and fear, we saw, the Other looms up immediately, demoting me from maker of the world to object in his world. These are the passions which confirm loneliness, which underline the truth that each man is fated both to try to make himself and to fail to do so. But there are also passions which grow out of mutuality: out of a space in which two persons exist together, and in which each becomes himself out of and in that coexistence. The love of mother and infant, when it exists—not always, indeed, but not perhaps as rarely as Sartre suggests—is one such passion, the one which founds, or ought to found, the lived spatiality of each of us. Another is the mature coming together of two individuals in sexual love. Even hatred, the contrary of love, acknowledges, as shame and fear do not, the existence together, if in mutual rejection, of two persons: true enemies can respect one another as true lovers do. (I noted earlier that Sartre himself acknowledges the latter point in a passing remark in the *Critique*.) [21] What is essential in all such cases is the social space—the *Mitwelt*—which I and Thou together have cleared for each of us. Only in such a space is human temporality, and therefore history, personal or social, possible. If Sartre has come to see this, and if he is yet to give philosophical expression to this insight, then the Cartesian Sartre will have been indeed transcended, and the man of words will have become something he was not, or did not earlier know he was to be. He will have conquered his own rationalism, he will have discovered in earnest, and expressed philosophically, the *active passivity* mentioned, indeed, but scarcely used, in the *Critique*.[22] The place of Sartre in the history of philosophy is at least that of the last great Cartesian; for that alone his philosophical work is worth reading, again and again. What his place in intellectual history will finally be, however, is a question still to be answered. On first reading *The Idiot of the Family* one is moved to puzzlement and to patience: we must wait and see.

BIBLIOGRAPHY

Recent works on Sartre have provided detailed bibliographies which I could not hope to match, and which in any case would be out of place at the conclusion of this introductory volume. I am therefore listing only (1) philosophical works of Sartre available in English; (2) a few nonphilosophical works, also translated, on which I have drawn fairly heavily; (3) untranslated works that I have been dealing with in some detail; and (4) a very small selection of the many English titles on Sartre, some to which (as indicated in the text) I am myself indebted, and some that I think might help the English-speaking reader in search of some other introductory approach to supplement or correct my own. For those in search of more, and more exact, information, the definitive bibliography to 1970 is:

Contat, Michel, and Rybalka, Michel. *Les Ecrits de Sartre*. Paris: Gallimard, 1970. In English there is a very careful list of books and articles by and on Sartre at the close of Joseph H. MacMahon's *Humans Being,* which, despite the scandalous title, is a very useful work.

Philosophical Works of Sartre Available in English (as of August 1971)

Being and Nothingness. Translated by Hazel Barnes. New York: Philosophical Library, 1956.

The Emotions: Outline of a Theory. Translated by Bernard Frechtman. New York: Philosophical Library, 1948. (A very unreliable translation; there was a better one by P. Mairet, which is out of print.)

Imagination. Translated by Forrest Williams. Ann Arbor: University of Michigan Press, 1962. (This is the historical portion of Sartre's work on imagination; for his own view see *The Psychology of Imagination,* below.)

Literary and Philosophical Essays. Translated by Annette Michelson. New York: Criterion Books, 1955.

The Philosophy of Jean-Paul Sartre. Edited by R. D. Cumming. New York: Random House, 1965. (Contains passages from the *Critique* not yet available in English elsewhere.)

The Psychology of Imagination. Translated by Bernard Frechtman. London: Rider, 1950.

Search for a Method. Translated by Hazel Barnes. New York: Knopf, 1963. (Translation of *Question de méthode*.)

The Transcendence of the Ego. Translated by Forrest Williams and Robert Kirkpatrick. New York: Farrar, Straus, and Giroux, 1957.

Some Other Works (in Translation)

The Flies. Translated by Stuart Gilbert. New York: Knopf, 1947.

Nausea. Translated by Lloyd Alexander. Norfolk, Conn.: New Directions, 1950.

Saint Genet, Actor and Martyr. Translated by Bernard Frechtman. New York: Braziller, 1963.

What is Literature? Translated by Bernard Frechtman. New York: Philosophical Library, 1949.

The Words. Translated by Bernard Frechtman. New York: Braziller, 1964.

Works Discussed in Some Detail, Available in English

Critique de la raison dialectique. Paris: Gallimard, 1960.

L'Idiot de la Famille. Volumes I and II. Paris: Gallimard, 1971. Volume III, 1972.

"L'Ecrivain et sa Langue," *Revue d'Esthétique,* XVIII (1965), 306–334.

Selected Works on the Philosophy of Sartre

Aron, Raymond. "Sartre's Marxism," in *Marxism and the Existentialists.* New York: Harper & Row, 1969, pp. 164–176.

Cranston, Maurice. *Jean-Paul Sartre.* New York: Grove Press, 1962.

Cumming, R. D. Introduction to *The Philosophy of Jean-Paul Sartre.* (See above.)

Desan, Wilfrid. *The Tragic Finale: An Essay on the Philosophy of Jean-Paul Sartre.* Cambridge, Mass.: Harvard University Press, 1954.

Desan, Wilfrid. *The Marxism of Jean-Paul Sartre.* Garden City, N.Y.: Doubleday, 1965.

Laing, R. D., and Cooper, D. G. *Reason and Violence: A Decade of Sartre's Philosophy, 1950–60.* New York: Humanities Press, 1964. (Summaries of Sartre's work: little exegesis.)

MacMahon, Joseph H. *Humans Being, The World of Jean-Paul Sartre.* Chicago: University of Chicago Press, 1971. (Chiefly literary, but also dealing with the philosophy.)

Murdoch, Iris. *Sartre, Romantic Rationalist.* New Haven: Yale University Press, 1953.

Thody, Philip. *Sartre.* London: Studio Vista, 1971. (A biographical introduction.)

NOTES

Chapter One

[1] J. P. Sartre, *The Words*, trans. Bernard Frechtman (Greenwich, Conn., 1964), p. 25 (paperback edition). The title should have been rendered *Words*, but the translation of the text is nevertheless reliable—though no English could adequately render the style of the original.

[2] *Loc. cit.*

[3] *Ibid.*, p. 30.

[4] *Ibid.*, p. 38.

[5] *Ibid.*, p. 30.

[6] *Ibid.*, p. 114.

[7] *Loc. cit.*

[8] *Loc. cit.*

[9] J. P. Sartre, *What is Literature?*, trans. Bernard Frechtman (London, 1950), p. 5.

[10] J. P. Sartre, *What is Literature?*, trans. Bernard Frechtman (London, 1950), p. 5.

[11] *Ibid.*, p. 6.

[12] *Loc. cit.*

[13] *Loc. cit.*

[14] *Loc. cit.*

[15] *The Words*, p. 31.

[16] *What is Literature?*, p. 6.

[17] *The Words*, p. 159.

[18] *Ibid.*, p. 21.

[19] Simone de Beauvoir, *The Prime of Life*, trans. Peter Green (London, 1962), p. 16.

[20] *The Words*, p. 38.

[21] J. P. Sartre, "L'Ecrivain et sa Langue," *Revue d'Esthétique*, XVIII (1965), 306–334.

[22] *Ibid.*, 333.

[23] J. P. Sartre, *The Transcendence of the Ego*, trans. Forrest Williams and Robert Kirkpatrick (New York, 1957).

[24] J. P. Sartre, *The Psychology of Imagination* (New York, 1948).

[25] J. P. Sartre, Introduction to Jean Genet, *Our Lady of the Flowers* (London, 1964), p. 53.

[26] J. P. Sartre, *Situations*, trans. Benita Eisler (Greenwich, Conn., 1965), p. 125.

[27] J. P. Sartre, *Sketch of a Theory of the Emotions*, trans. P. Mairet (London, 1962), p. 125.

[28] *Ibid.*, pp. 61–62.

[29] *Ibid.*, pp. 62–63.

[30] *Ibid.*, p. 83.

[31] *The Words*, p. 38. *"Ludion,"* "bottle imp," is synonymous with *"litote,"* which can be rendered "Cartesian diver"! The following chapters should make clear the rich implications of this epithet for Sartrean philosophy.

Chapter Two

[1] Cf. J. P. Sartre, "Cartesian Freedom," in *Literary and Philosophical Essays,* trans. Annette Michelson (New York, 1955), pp. 180–197.

[2] J. P. Sartre, *Being and Nothingness*, trans. Hazel Barnes (New York, 1956), p. 254.

[3] *Loc. cit.*

[4] *Loc. cit.*
[5] *Loc. cit.*
[6] *Ibid.*, pp. 110 ff.

Chapter Three

[1] G. W. F. Hegel, *Die Phänomenologie des Geistes*, Philosophische Bibliothek (Leipzig, 1928), p. 50.
[2] J. P. Sartre, *Being and Nothingness*, p. 239.
[3] Louis Mackay, "The Poetry of Inwardness," in G. A. Schrader, Jr. (ed.), *Existential Philosophers: Kierkegaard to Merleau-Ponty* (New York, 1967), pp. 45–107.
[4] Søren Kierkegaard, "The Sickness unto Death," in *Fear and Trembling; The Sickness unto Death*, trans. Walter Lowrie (Garden City, N.Y., 1954), p. 146.
[5] J. P. Sartre, *Being and Nothingness*, p. 78.
[6] Søren Kierkegaard, *Loc. cit.*
[7] J. P. Sartre, *Being and Nothingness*, p. 89.
[8] Søren Kierkegaard, *Sickness unto Death*, p. 147.
[9] J. P. Sartre, *Being and Nothingness*, p. 87.
[10] *Ibid.*, p. 597.
[11] J. P. Sartre, *Critique de la Raison Dialectique* (Paris, 1960), p. 22.
[12] *Ibid.*, p. 23.
[13] *Loc. cit.*
[14] *Loc. cit.*

Chapter Four

[1] J. P. Sartre, *Being and Nothingness*, p. lvii.
[2] *Ibid.*, p. xlvii.
[3] *Ibid.*
[4] *Ibid.*
[5] *Loc. cit.*
[6] *Loc. cit.*
[7] *Loc. cit.*
[8] *Ibid.*, p. xlix.
[9] *Loc. cit.*
[10] *Loc. cit.* My italics.
[11] *Ibid.*, p. 1.
[12] *Loc. cit.*
[13] *Ibid.*, p. li.

[14] J. P. Sartre, *Being and Nothingness*, p. lii. My italics.
[15] *Loc. cit.*
[16] *Ibid.*, p. liii.
[17] *Ibid.*, p. lv.
[18] *Ibid.*, p. lvi.
[19] *Ibid.*, p. lxvii.
[20] *Ibid.*, p. 38.
[21] *Ibid.*, p. 45.
[22] *Ibid.*, p. 77. My italics.
[23] *Ibid.*, p. 90.
[24] *Ibid.*, p. 129.
[25] *Ibid.*, p. 93.
[26] *Ibid.*, p. 102.
[27] *Ibid.*, p. 149.
[28] *Ibid.*, p. 142.
[29] *Ibid.*, p. 218.
[30] *Ibid.*, p. 194.

Chapter Five
[1] J. P. Sartre, *Being and Nothingness*, trans. Hazel Barnes (New York, 1956), p. 221.
[2] *Ibid.*, p. 223.
[3] *Ibid.*, p. 273.
[4] *Ibid.*, p. 282.
[5] *Ibid.*, p. 277.
[6] *Loc. cit.*
[7] *Ibid.*, p. 359.
[8] *Ibid.*, p. 324.
[9] *Loc. cit.*
[10] *Ibid.*, p. 325.
[11] *Ibid.*, p. 346.
[12] *Loc. cit.*
[13] M. Merleau-Ponty, *The Phenomenology of Perception*, Part One, Ch. Six.
[14] J. P. Sartre, *Being and Nothingness*, trans. Hazel Barnes (New York, 1956), p. 446.
[15] *Ibid.*, p. 447.
[16] *Loc. cit.*
[17] *Ibid.*, pp. 447–448.
[18] *Ibid.*, p. 449.

[19] *Loc. cit.*

[20] *Loc. cit.*

Chapter Six

[1] Raymond Aron, "Sartre's Marxism," in *Marxism and the Existentialists* (New York: Harper & Row, 1969), Dialogue Three.

[2] J. P. Sartre, *Critique de la Raison Dialectique*, p. 339. My italics.

[3] Cf. (at a different level) Sartre's comparison of his own method with Kant's in *L'Idiot de la Famille* (Paris, 1971), Vol. I, pp. 653–654.

[4] J. P. Sartre, *Critique*, p. 107.

[5] E.g., *ibid.*, p. 509, and then pp. 658–659.

[6] *Ibid.*, pp. 525–526 (My italics); cf., e.g., pp. 281, 411.

[7] *Ibid.*, p. 635.

[8] *Ibid.*, p. 634.

[9] *Loc. cit.* My italics.

[10] *Ibid.*, p. 688.

[11] *Loc. cit.*

[12] *Ibid.*, pp. 200–225.

[13] *Ibid.*, pp. 225–279.

[14] *Ibid.*, pp. 286–305.

[15] *Ibid.*, pp. 306–377.

[16] *Ibid.*, pp. 279–280.

[17] *Ibid.*, p. 285.

[18] *Ibid.*, p. 420.

[19] Cf. *ibid.*, pp. 487–488; earlier also, Sartre's treatment of the dyad turning triad (see below, Ch. VII) is taken explicitly from Lévy-Strauss.

[20] *Ibid.*, p. 494.

[21] *Ibid.*, p. 462.

[22] C. Audry, *Sartre et la réalité humaine* (Paris, 1966).

[23] J. P. Sartre, *Critique*, p. 533.

[24] *Ibid.*, p. 560.

[25] In S. Kierkegaard, *Philosophical Fragments*, trans. David F. Swenson, revised by Howard V. Hong (Princeton, 1962).

Chapter Seven

[1] "Sartre: An Interview," *New York Review of Books*, XIV (6), March 26, 1970.

[2] Iris Murdoch, "Of God and Good," in *The Anatomy of Knowledge* (Amherst, Mass.: University of Massachusetts Press, 1969), p. 239.

[3] See e.g., J. P. Sartre, *Critique de la Raison Dialectique,* pp. 166, 174.

[4] *Ibid.,* p. 535.

[5] *Ibid.,* p. 168.

[6] *Ibid.,* p. 248.

[7] *Ibid.,* p. 175.

[8] *Ibid.,* p. 166. My italics.

[9] *Ibid.,* p. 435.

[10] *Ibid.,* p. 130n.

[11] *Loc. cit.*

[12] *Ibid.,* p. 277. My italics.

[13] *Ibid.,* p. 206.

[14] J. P. Sartre, *L'Idiot de la Famille* (Paris, 1971), Vol. I, p. 141.

[15] See my account of Portmann's work in M. Grene, *Approaches to a Philosophical Biology* (New York, 1969), Chapter One.

[16] See *ibid.,* Chapter Two.

[17] J. P. Sartre, *Critique,* p. 249.

[18] *Ibid.,* p. 248.

[19] *Loc. cit.*

[20] *Loc. cit.*

[21] *Ibid.,* p. 250.

[22] See e.g., *ibid.,* pp. 261, 361, 369, 435, 507, 535.

[23] *Ibid.,* p. 281.

[24] *Ibid.,* pp. 231–232, 250.

[25] *Ibid.,* p. 431.

[26] *Ibid.,* p. 433.

[27] *Ibid.,* p. 431.

[28] *Ibid.,* p. 142.

[29] *Loc. cit.*

[30] *Ibid.,* p. 141.

[31] *Ibid.,* p. 286n.

[32] *Loc. cit.*

[33] *Loc. cit.* My italics.

[34] *Loc. cit.*

[35] R. Aron, "Sartre's Marxism."

[36] J. P. Sartre, *Critique,* p. 585.

[37] *Ibid.,* p. 47.

[38] J. P. Sartre, *L'Idiot de la Famille,* Vol. I, p. 142n.

[39] J. P. Sartre, *Critique,* p. 321.

[40] *Loc. cit.*

[41] *Ibid.,* p. 323.

[42] *Ibid.,* p. 181.

[43] *Ibid.,* p. 180.

[44] *Ibid.,* p. 182.

[45] *Ibid.,* p. 688.

[46] *Ibid.,* p. 192.

[47] *Ibid.,* p. 193.

[48] *Loc. cit.*

[49] *Ibid.,* p. 192.

[50] *Ibid.,* p. 688.

Chapter Eight

[1] J. P. Sartre, *L'Idiot de la Famille,* Vol. II, p. 1372.

[2] *Ibid.,* p. 1692.

[3] *Ibid.,* p. 1591.

[4] *Ibid.,* p. 1376.

[5] *Ibid.,* pp. 1645 ff.

[6] Cf. M. Grene, "The Aesthetic Dialogue of Sartre and Merleau-Ponty," *Journal of the British Society for Phenomenology,* I (2), May 1970.

[7] J. P. Sartre, "Merleau-Ponty vivant," *Les Temps Modernes,* 1961, 17n, 184–185, 304–376.

[8] J. P. Sartre, *L'Idiot,* Vol. I, pp. 811–824.

[9] *Ibid.,* Vol. II, p. 1440.

[10] H. Plessner, *Laughing and Crying,* trans. J. Churchill and M. Grene, Evanston, III., 1970.

[11] J. P. Sartre, *L'Idiot,* Vol. II, pp. 1311–1312.

[12] *Ibid.,* p. 1312.

[13] *Loc. cit.*

[14] *Loc. cit.*

[15] *Loc. cit.*

[16] *Loc. cit.*

[17] Loc. cit., "the text of the world." My italics.

[18] *Ibid.,* p. 1313.

[19] *Ibid.,* p. 1312n.

[20] J. P. Sartre, *L'Idiot,* Vol. II, pp. 1274.

[21] I am grateful to Professor Donald Lowe of San Francisco State College for a conversation on this matter.

[22] The phrase in fact recurs in *The Idiot of the Family* in connection with Flaubert's own assimilation of his own neurosis (1742 ff). We are promised further interpretation of this event in a future volume.